The

New

Religions

JEREMY P. TARCHER/PENGUIN

a member of Penguin Group (USA) Inc.

New York

The
New
Religions

❖

Jacob Needleman

JEREMY P. TARCHER/PENGUIN
Published by the Penguin Group
Penguin Group (USA) Inc., 375 Hudson Street, New York, New York 10014, USA • Penguin Group (Canada),
90 Eglinton Avenue East, Suite 700, Toronto, Ontario M4P 2Y3, Canada (a division of Pearson Canada Inc.) •
Penguin Books Ltd, 80 Strand, London WC2R 0RL, England • Penguin Ireland,
25 St Stephen's Green, Dublin 2, Ireland (a division of Penguin Books Ltd) • Penguin Group (Australia),
250 Camberwell Road, Camberwell, Victoria 3124, Australia (a division of Pearson Australia Group Pty Ltd) •
Penguin Books India Pvt Ltd, 11 Community Centre, Panchsheel Park, New Delhi—110 017,
India • Penguin Group (NZ), 67 Apollo Drive, Rosedale, North Shore 0632,
New Zealand (a division of Pearson New Zealand Ltd) • Penguin Books (South Africa) (Pty) Ltd,
24 Sturdee Avenue, Rosebank, Johannesburg 2196, South Africa

Penguin Books Ltd, Registered Offices: 80 Strand, London WC2R 0RL, England

Most Tarcher/Penguin books are available at special quantity discounts for bulk purchase
for sales promotions, premiums, fund-raising, and educational needs. Special books or book
excerpts also can be created to fit specific needs. For details, write Penguin Group (USA) Inc.
Special Markets, 375 Hudson Street, New York, NY 10014.

Library of Congress Cataloging-in-Publication Data

Needleman, Jacob.
The new religions / Jacob Needleman.
p.   cm.
Originally published: Garden City, N.Y.: Doubleday, 1970. With new introd.
Includes bibliographical references and index.
ISBN 978-1-58542-744-4
1. Sects—United States.   2. Religions.   I. Title.
BL2525.N43   2009   2009025854
209.0973—dc22

Printed in the United States of America
1 3 5 7 9 10 8 6 4 2

BOOK DESIGN BY NICOLE LAROCHE

While the author has made every effort to provide accurate telephone numbers and Internet addresses at the
time of publication, neither the publisher nor the author assumes any responsibility for errors, or for changes
that occur after publication. Further, the publisher does not have any control over and does not assume any
responsibility for author or third-party websites or their content.

In the writing of this book, I have been greatly assisted by the generous support of the Ella Lyman Cabot Trust at Harvard University and by the Marsden Foundation of New York. I wish to express my thanks to them.

I am especially grateful to Mrs. Laura DeWitt James for her criticisms and suggestions, and to Judy Barkan for her tireless help in preparing the manuscript.

Contents

Preface to the Cornerstone Edition

In the tumult and ferment of the late 1960s, a new understanding of the meaning of religion was brought to the attention of America and, soon after, to the modern world. In an era convulsed by the Vietnam war and galvanized by a revolutionary struggle for civil rights, large numbers of young Americans began turning toward an aspect of religion that had long since been marginalized and mostly forgotten in the West: religion not as a belief system, not as a moral code, not as a political force or as a source of ethnic and cultural identity—none of these. What was being rediscovered, however awkwardly—and however mixed it sometimes was with the incalculable influence of psychedelic drugs and emotional agitation—was the idea of religion as a practical method of deep inner change, nothing less than the transformation of our being.

From India, Tibet, Japan, Central Asia and the Middle East, there appeared, at first mainly in California and mostly among young Americans, religious teachings and practices bearing exotic names and using alien religious language: there was Zen and Tibetan Buddhism; Hinduism, including yoga in its bewilderingly varied forms; Sufism; Taoism; Tantrism; and much else. There were strange-sounding words and ideas; there was *karma* and there was *om*; there were *gurus, roshis, bodhisattvas,* and *avatars*; there was *samsara, satori, kundalini.* There was something called "meditation" that bore little resemblance to the mental activity commonly denoted by the word. And there was ritual chanting in the streets, and prayers to *Krishna* and *Rama.*

Thousands and then hundreds of thousands of young men and women began turning away from the religions of their parents and grandparents, not in defiant atheism or materialism but from a spiritual hunger that was not being met in the churches or synagogues of our modern world. In these "new" religions they were finding ideas about man, God, and the universal order that seemed to soar beyond the consensus worldview of both scientific materialism and conventional Judaeo-Christian theology. They were looking to ideals of sacred self-knowledge and inner liberation that were perceived as far more humanly relevant and psychologically profound than the conventionally understood goals of psychotherapy or religious devotion.

Moreover, and this is of chief importance, these ideas and these ideals were being presented not only by academicians, journalists, novelists, or philosophical adventurers, but often by individual teachers coming from deep within these Eastern cultures and traditions. And these teachers, living and moving in the life of California, offered what was understood to be practical guidance leading to the actual experience of what these new ideals represented. In the followers of these new religions, the conviction took root that the dangers, the crimes, and the chaos of the world and our personal lives were not ultimately due to external causes such as political or economic policies, repressive moralistic dogmas, or the greed and heartlessness of those in positions of power. The idea—ancient, but passionately rediscovered—was that such elements are not causes, but results; that the world is what it is because we human beings are what we are in the depths and totality of our being. What was most needed, therefore, was the transformation of our inner world. Without that inner transformation, no amount of social, political or institutional change could amount to more than an unstable rearrangement of social conditions that would all-too-soon spawn the same forces of violence, injustice, and heartlessness that these external changes were intended to overcome.

Of course, notions about the causal primacy of psychological factors in the processes of individual and collective human life had long since been the underpinning of the modern disciplines of psychotherapy and psychiatry. But the attraction of these "new religions" had to do with some human possibility that was said to be both higher and deeper than what modern psychology, in its broadest sense, conceived of as normal, emotional health.

And not only that. This human possibility was also understood to be higher and deeper than anything conceived of—or at least spoken about—in the dominant religious institutions of the West. Which brings us to the central question: *What is religion?* And this immediately raises the even more fundamental question: *What is a human being?* Have we entirely forgotten who we are? And what we are meant to be?

Our world has greatly changed in the decades that have passed since these new religious movements began to appear in California. Although some of the teachings described in this book no longer attract public attention, it is safe to say that this whole phenomenon has significantly altered the spiritual landscape of America and the Western world. Buddhism, especially some of what were once considered its more "esoteric" doctrines and practices, is now a major, broadly accepted intellectual and spiritual influence in our culture. Yoga, in one form or another and for one purpose or another, can be found in almost every American city or town. And a dynamic new appreciation of the mystical and contemplative heart of our own Western religious traditions has emerged partly as an aspect of this renewed spiritual hunger and the challenge it has offered to institutionalized Christianity and Judaism. At the same time, the movements grouped under the catchphrase "New Age"—so often caught between superficiality and a genuine expression of human longing—are also the off-spring, however unwelcome in many of their aspects, of the new religions. In addition, the scholarly study of the new religions in America—including the worrisome question of harmful cults—now comprises an important area of research within the field of the social sciences in many universities here and abroad.

Of course, America has always been fertile ground for bold and sometimes reckless experimentation and innovation in religion, spirituality and communal living. But as we now look back on this specific phenomenon of the new religions that began in the late 1960s, we, too, may have come to recognize that the immense, unprecedented threats to our whole planet and civilization are not only economic or political in the usual sense but also, and perhaps at root, philosophical and spiritual. Our world is under siege in relation to the most fundamental questions of the meaning and purpose of our very existence.

Yet, after all we have lived through in the last hundred years of massive war, genocide, and moral disillusionment, we see that this question of what a human being is cannot be answered simply by intellectual philosophy or theology or by scientific investigations alone, no more than the question of the real nature of religion can be answered only by reading books, headlines, histories, or by ideological reactions to the chaos and violence of human life—a chaos and violence that often takes its energy from both misappropriated religious ideas and scientific discoveries. Human beings, it seems, stubbornly remain what they are no matter what they believe or do not believe.

Therefore, the question insists itself: What kind of change is necessary and possible for us? From whence will come the help we need in order to become fully human? It is the entry into our society of this kind of questioning that may constitute the greatest influence and the greatest source of hope that these new religions may bring to our lives and our global world.

The aim of this book is to show that what is genuinely *new* about the phenomenon of the "new religions" are the questions it enables us to ask about ourselves and about our relationship to what is called God, whether that relation takes the form of the struggles of faith or the honorable defiance of honest skepticism. We are saying that the help our society desperately needs is neither an imaginary miracle from God, nor a resurgence of a new or old political ideology, nor naïve faith in modern science and technology. What we are searching for in these pages are new and deeper questions about ourselves and our world. These questions may be the fundamental legacy of these new religions for our present era. And if we follow this indication, follow it deeply, down to our bones—if we stop inside ourselves and with each other, and work to allow the process of self-questioning to accompany the new ideas and ideals these teachings present to us—then something extraordinary can occur in ourselves and in our world.

—JACOB NEEDLEMAN

2009

The

New

Religions

Introduction

Suspicions

I came to San Francisco in 1962, quite sure that I understood the place of religion in the history and psychology of man. Having been trained as a philosopher at the best New England universities, I was able to speak sympathetically about the depths of man's "religious imagination" while retaining what I felt was a "cold and critical eye" toward his need to deny his mortal nature as a creature of the earth. At the same time, some practical experience as a clinical psychologist had confirmed my belief that contemporary psychology in all its forms addressed itself only to a very small portion of the human psyche and that even there its "successes" were much smaller than it pretended them to be.

I had cast my lot with the existentialists. Man's real burden was an unlimited psychological freedom bound in some mysterious and ironic way to the limitations of the body, death and the Other. Religion, at its deepest level—as in the Old Testament and the Gospels—was a demonstration of this freedom shared by all men, the freedom to choose oneself with passionate intensity against a universe that reason showed was indifferent and blind. As for modern religious forms, they had degenerated into an effort to take away all responsibility from man, to separate him from the truths of the body, to comfort him with fables and to rob him of his ultimate possibility: action in the world.

My courses in philosophy and in the history of Western religion were explorations into these themes. I agreed with Bultmann and others of the New Theologians that once the mythology was excised from the Western Bible, it could be read as an overpowering emotional statement of the existentialist insight that man is alone and unique, his tragic greatness consisting in the fact that he can make no echo in the universe. Such words as immortality, higher life, faith or righteousness applied to the moment, *now*, and were a call for man to accept his total mortality and in accepting it to find his own destiny *in* himself and *for* himself. In reading these ideas into our Bible, I felt an immense sense of relief. I had never been entirely comfortable thinking of Jesus, Moses, St. Paul and others as irrelevant—or worse.

With the sole exception of Zen Buddhism, the religions of the East were anathema to me, as was what I confidently labeled "mysticism." All this talk about "merging into the All"! destroying the self!—when man's essential task was to affirm and preserve his self and to increase his individuality. And all this talk about ineffable experiences, incomprehensible truths, going beyond the ordinary mind—that rankled. I was very suspicious of anyone who claimed to know something but was unable to express it. In sum, I thought of mysticism as simply bad poetry: the poetry of men too weak to accept the joys and sufferings of our earthly nature.

No one was more ready than I to denounce the natural-scientific view of man as reductionistic. But if science had reduced man to less than he was, the religions of the East inflated man to more than he was. Besides, wasn't there something "unholy" about these so-called holy men of the East? What had religion or spirituality to do with such things as *energy, psychological power, consciousness, astral bodies* and God knows what else? There was something demonic about all that. Life was too short to bother with this spiritual circus of the Hindus or Tibetans. The antidote was a good reading of Ecclesiastes or Isaiah, against which this Eastern lust for extraordinary powers showed itself for what it was: yet another pathetic attempt to escape the human condition.

What Is California?

The person I was then could never have undertaken to write this book, a portrait of the Eastern teachings which are establishing themselves in this country and which, taken together, bid well to change the religious life of the Western world itself. Even apart from my intellectual convictions, there was this whole matter of *California.* As a transplanted easterner, I felt duty-bound not to take anything in California very seriously. I certainly felt no need to *understand* California; I simply allowed myself to record the usual impressions; millions of Americans breaking away from reality, looking for a dream; everything in excess; Forest Lawn Cemetery (which I never visited); the charm of San Francisco, an American island in time; the giant trees, the thunderously rugged coastline, etc. When natives told me this was where it was "happening," when they said California was the future, I was quite ready to believe them simply because I had no real hopes for the future anyway. To me, California was a place desperately lacking in the experience of limitation, a dream factory in every sense of the word. No wonder all these cults and sects were flourishing here.

I still do not claim to understand California, but I am certain that it cannot be taken lightly from any point of view. Sooner or later we are going to have to understand California—and not simply from the motive of predicting the future for the rest of the country. We are going to have to stop thinking about it simply as a phenomenon of people leaving reality behind. Something is struggling to be born here amid all the obvious absurdity and grotesquery.

It is, in any case, not reality which Californians have left behind; it is *Europe.* It was not until several years had passed that this came home to me. I began to see that my idea of intelligence was a modern European idea: the mind, unfettered by emotion, disembodied, aristocratically articulate, gathering all before it in the sweep of its categories. Descartes, Newton, Kant; the ideal of explicitness and the publicness of all communication. At the same time, I saw that I judged California on its lack of the European element. It is difficult to put this into words because, in one way or another and at one time or another, Europe has *said* everything, and believed in almost everything. If I claim that many Californians are searching for experience rather than accomplishment, someone will surely cite Rousseau to me or some German poet. If I speak of their iconoclasm and futurism, someone will bring forth a document from modern French literature. As for much of California's attitude toward sex, marriage and the family, there is always modern Scandinavia to match against it. What I call the non-European element of California is not any one or group of these things, for the truth is that the ways of life in California are enormously varied. For every "libertine" there is a "puritan"; for every "hippie" there is a "four-square youth"; and for every radical there is at least one archconservative.

The Loss of the Cosmic

I am no historian, but perhaps my point will come across more clearly if we recall that for the most part what we know as American religion has emanated directly from modern Europe. We are really very far in time, and perhaps in practice as well, from the Christianity of the early fathers and the medieval monastic communities, and from the Judaism of the great rabbinic followings in the Middle East and Islamic Spain. In Europe the scientific revolution destroyed the idea of a sacramental universe, and religion became a matter between man and God; science took care of the cosmos—and very quickly erased all concepts of mind and intelligent purpose from it. Only in the Eastern Orthodox Church does the idea still live that nature and the universe itself is involved in man's religious life and in his quest for self-perfection.

By eliminating the cosmos from man's relationship to God, the European came to emphasize more and more the ethical and even legal aspect of religion. Religious life became a matter of belief or performance; the question of man's *ableness* to believe or act faded into the background because his dependency upon the universe with all its forces and purposes was no longer taken into account. It was taken for granted that man had the *power* to be righteous; the only question was whether he had the goodness. Along with this, the idea of religious *training* receded; man needed only to be told or persuaded and he could then either act well or wait intelligently for the grace of God.

Since it is one of the purposes of this book to show how the new teachings may bring the cosmic element back into the religious thought of the West, I shall not pursue this point further here. Nor is this the place to discuss the sort of relationship to God and the universe that was brought to this continent by many of the founding fathers, themselves intimately involved in certain mystical orders such as the Rosicrucians and Freemasons which cherished the cosmic element of the practical religious life. My intention here is simply to show that my own attitude toward religion was a direct reflection of the popular American concept of man's religious powers, which in turn was derived from the encounter of organized European religion and the scientific revolution.

I wish I could state clearly what it is about California that makes so many of its people—and not just the young—so much more accessible to the cosmic dimension of human life. More on this will emerge as our study proceeds. But the undeniable fact is that by and large the west coast does not exhibit the sort of intellectualism found in our eastern cities, an intellectualism rooted in European acosmism and its accompanying sense of the human mind as autonomous and outside nature. Without wishing to sound darkly mysterious, I would have to say that there broods over this state a strong sense of greater universal forces. Whether this is California romance or not, it is surely one of the factors that accounts for the large following commanded by these new teachings.

A Wider Sense of Psychology

In any event, during my years of teaching philosophy I witnessed at close hand the birth of the hippie movement, the flower children, the drug scene and everything that went with it. I was quite convinced that the drugs led nowhere and I still am convinced of that; but what I underestimated was the sincerity of these young people with regard to the religions of the East. I think this book will rather clearly show the nature of that sincerity. I see now that conventional psychological analysis of this interest is really of secondary importance, especially as the religious systems we shall be dealing with contain their own psychodynamic categories which in many cases strike much deeper, in my opinion, than those formulated by twentieth-century Europeans like Freud, Jung or Heidegger.

I am sure it would make many of us less uncomfortable if we could subject this interest in the new religions to a comprehensive psychological study. It can be done; I myself was doing it for several years. But even apart from the fact that—as will become apparent—our modern idea of psychology is seriously challenged by these new teachings, we should miss the whole point if such analysis were a main concern of ours. These teachings resonate with something in people which is utterly untouched by everything else in our society, something which "makes no sense" from one point of view, but which makes the most essential and urgent sense in the world from another point of view.

The reader who wishes to fit these new teachings into familiar psychological, sociological or literary categories is, I am afraid, in for some bad moments. I recall one winter afternoon several years ago in New York discussing Jewish mystical communities with the great scholar Abraham Heschel at a time when he was working on the translation of a particular Hasidic text. He pounded his finger on a stack of manuscript in front of him and quoted something he had just translated: "God is not nice, He is not an uncle. God is an earthquake." Many of those we shall be quoting, the young as well as the older, the hippies as well as the established members of the community, including some highly articulate and urbane people, have been struck by just such an earthquake. We shall often find, if we have the patience and the sensitivity, that they are speaking from a very particular "place" in themselves. We may even find—as I found to my own surprise—that they are speaking *to* a similar "place" in ourselves.

Not long ago I discussed some of my findings with a very large group of interested psychiatrists and clinicians at the Langley-Porter Neuropsychiatric Institute in San Francisco. I am sure there were many reasons why they came to hear about the new religions. Certainly one of these reasons was that so many of their younger patients are deeply involved in the literature of this "spiritual explosion." But in their questions and in the discussions I had with them afterward, they made it clear to me that their motives were not only professional. They themselves were searching for ways to come in touch with something deeper in themselves, something of which, they felt, modern psychology was largely ignorant. Like many of us, they saw very little for themselves in the Judaism and Christianity of our society; indeed, from their professional perspective they judged much of contemporary religion as psychologically harmful. Was there something in the religions of the East, they asked, which could really call forth those human depths and heights which neither psychology nor Western religion seemed able to reach? If so, how, they wanted to know, could they come in touch with it? The directness and clarity of their questions brought me up short once again. Not only had I underestimated the sincerity of the younger followers of the new teachings, I had seriously underestimated the hunger in these people— trained, intelligent professionals who had staked their careers on the European psychological view of man—for a new sort of psychology and a new way of searching for the purpose and sense of their existence.

I trust that many others whose view of man has been similarly influenced by modern psychology can find in this book a basis for deciding if there is anything in the new religions worth exploring further. But, equally important, the presentations in this book may serve in similar fashion for those who have not turned away from our established religions, but who wish to deepen their understanding of the metaphysical and psychological basis of all religion. For, as will be quite apparent, the new religions pose absolutely no threat to the old—unless the reassessment of man's inward potential and psychological fallibility is understood as a threat.

In as much as the condition of a society, its hopes and aspirations, are reflected in the condition of its religion, it is America and the West as a whole which stand to benefit from this "invasion from the East," and not just our religious forms. When our younger people rebel against our institutions, they are rebelling against our hopes both for ourselves and for them. If we wish to understand their hopes and the nature of the world they seek to live in, we must understand something about these new religions.

As I have said, it is not only the young who are turning to them. But they have certainly been the advance guard and it is still they whose numbers swell the ranks. This has been one of the principle factors determining which of the religions I have chosen to cover in depth. I have been especially interested in those which have a strong and vital appeal for our young people, and which are in a condition of vigorous growth. As a result I have neglected many which, while still forming part of this whole movement, have been with us for some time and have more or less sedately blended into the foliage: for example, Vedanta Society, various Yoga organizations and Buddhist societies, and certain mystical Islamic sects.

Important though this criterion was, it was not my only one, I confess to having guessed about the future significance of some of these teachings, and I have included others because in my opinion they are the most instructive for us, regardless of the size of their following. For example, a considerable space is devoted to Tibetan Buddhism in this country, although at this writing the Lama Tarthang Tulku now residing in Berkeley does not have more than fifty steady pupils. Nevertheless, Tibetan Buddhism, as I shall try to show, is one of the most complete and powerful spiritual systems that has ever been brought to mankind. The migration to the West of these extraordinarily resourceful Tibetan Lamas has, moreover, only just begun, and we can now expect to see a rapid general interest in the religion of Tibet. I daresay that Tibetan Buddhism will be for the West in the coming decade what Zen Buddhism has been in the past decade and that it will enrich our understanding of religion no less than Zen Buddhism has.

The Agonies of Religious "Relevance"

What, then, have they found, these followers of the new religious teachings? It is possible that a serious look at them and at the people involved in them, will change our whole idea of religion.

Who will deny that some such change is necessary? When God was recently pronounced dead it was not because people were no longer asking fundamental questions about life and death, human identity, suffering, and meaninglessness. On the contrary. Never before have men been more desperate about these questions.

True, our established religions are alive to this desperation. They are in agony because of it. We see them twisting and turning, seeking to change form without altering their essence. They wish to become *relevant* to the times, for the times are torturing us all.

But how are they, how is religion, to do this? We are tortured—agreed. The scientific world-view, recently so full of hope, has left men stranded in a flood of forces and events they do not understand, far less control. Psychiatry has lost its messianic aura, and therapists themselves are among the most tormented by the times.

In the social sciences, there exists a brilliant gloom of unconnected theories and shattered predictions. Biology and medicine promise revolutionary discoveries and procedures, but meanwhile we suffer and die as before; and our doctors are as frightened as we.

And we cling violently to forms of life which, perhaps, were not even meaningful to us in quieter times.

So, when religion, in the name of relevance, seeks to adjust itself to the times, the question is bound to arise: Is the leader being led? As church and synagogue turn to psychiatry, the scientific world-view, or social action, are they not turning toward what has failed and is failing? And has not the very failure of these non-religious enterprises shifted the common mind back to a renewed interest in the religious?

Men turn to religion and find, to their ultimate dismay, that religion turns to them, to their sciences, their ideas of action and accomplishment, and their language. This is what is known as secularization: the effort by religion to be "relevant," to "solve" human problems, to make men "*happy*."

How, one asks, could this aim be wrong? Should religion strive to be irrelevant, out of touch? Should it try to make men *un*-happy? And in any case, by rigidly maintaining the purity of its traditional forms does it not simply become spinsterish and, finally, extinct? Who needs the dull sentiment of antique languages and meaningless rituals? Who needs a system of moral behavior which no one can or will follow?

Certainly, such questions require that we keep an open mind toward anything new which could refresh our understanding of the religious process. We want to know: What do these Eastern teachings say about man's existential situation, his place in the universe, his relationship to God? What do they promise? What do they demand? What sorts of people do they attract and what have these people experienced? Who are the leaders, what manner of people are they? We shall try not only to understand their doctrines, but to get a feel of their activity.

The Sense of Asian Teachings

Most of these teachings are sourced in Asia. Therefore, if we wish to know what they have brought to America, we have to begin by understanding something about Eastern religion.

Almost all the religions of Asia have one thing in common: "self-centeredness." Their goal is always release from suffering, *my* suffering as well as the suffering of humanity. Their cosmology and metaphysics, their imperatives to act morally or to serve God, are almost always instrumental toward this goal. What is true or good is what helps me out of my suffering; what is false or evil is what locks me in it. The well-known Buddhist simile expresses this exactly: the human situation is that of a man who has been struck in the chest by a poisoned arrow. He does not waste time trying to discover who shot it or why; he is not interested in learning what the arrow is made of. He wishes only to get it out of his chest so that he will not die.

What is this suffering? And how is this goal any different from the contemporary Western effort to make men happy, which we have just characterized as "secularization"? The answer to this question involves an idea that is markedly alien to our modern minds: *the satisfaction of desire is not happiness.*

Because human desires are so multiform and contradictory, the satisfaction of one is always at the expense of another. And even if it were possible to satisfy all our desires, it would still be a contradictory and chaotic satisfaction corresponding to the contradictory and chaotic condition of the desires themselves. Contradictory satisfaction is what we call inner conflict, and the modern man experiences inner conflict as suffering.

In religious literature the desires—physical as well as emotional and mental, the wishes, hopes, fears, and so forth—are often symbolized by animals. It is as though within man there were a thousand animals each seeking its own food and comfort. Some of these animals are, moreover, the very food that the others seek. *What is called "pleasure" or satisfaction is the feeding of one or another of these animals.*

Thus, in this view, man's suffering is based on the mistake of identifying his whole self with these animals as they appear in him and make their wants known by howling for their food. No sooner is one fed than another appears, hungrier than ever, and sometimes hungry for the very food that has just been given to his predecessor—and is therefore no longer available. By identifying himself with these animals, man forfeits the possibility of inner unity and wholeness, a possibility which represents another level of existence for him.

In these traditions, this level is variously spoken of as "higher" or "deeper" or "inner." It is that level from which consciousness can control and care for the animals in a way that corresponds to their true needs as part of a whole. In its function as master, this level of consciousness is spoken of as a special force; as guardian it is called knowledge; as action in the world it is known as love or service. It is *able*, *conscious*, and *beneficent*: i.e., "divine."

According to Eastern psychology, there is something in man which he squanders by understanding himself to be no more than these animals, a sort of energy or life which he ignorantly gives to them, and which they really do not need or use. To turn that energy to its proper use, to direct it toward the work of integration and awareness is one of the primal functions of religious discipline. But it is much, much harder to do than one thinks, for there is always an animal in man, a kind of monkey, perhaps, which imitates the real work and which wants to *feel* whole rather than *be* whole.

In this perspective, religion becomes "secularized" when its main concern is more to feed than to control the animals—that is, when its concern is primarily with the external conditions of human life. In this sense what we ordinarily call happiness is the exact opposite of what the Eastern traditions understand by release from suffering.

In Eastern thought these animals, these desires, are much more various than we might suspect. Physical desires—for ordinary food and drink, warmth, sexual gratification, etc.—comprise only a small fraction of the total. Some others are: the desire for praise and recognition, the wish to be superior, the fear of pain, the desire for security, the wish to control others, the desire to be desired, the desire to express oneself, the fear of the unknown, etc., etc. The list is very long, and relatively few religions become secularized in the sense of seeking to gratify only the basic physical desires. The difficulty is that certain non-physical desires are identified and officially sanctioned as corresponding to the inner or divine in man, whereas in reality they are merely "animals" on a level with all the others.

When this happens all the other animals go hungry, and when they are hungry enough they go crazy.

Religions have, for example, existed for the sole purpose of allaying man's fear of the unknown. This often takes the form of scholastic or highly rationalistic and doctrinaire systems of belief and explanation. Some anthropologists and religionists have even theorized that this is the fundamental purpose of religion at all times. Of course, from the perspective we are now presenting, this view is superficial.

Closely related to this, religions have existed for the purpose of making man feel secure and "cared for." At present this is a very popular form of religion and a very popular view of the function of all religion. Modern psychology gives this view of religion its blessing because, in our age, it has "officially sanctioned" the desire for recognition and "love" as the real inner spring of the human psyche. This has been done by labeling this desire a "need."

Later in the book we shall explore this general idea at greater length. The main point here is that the central thrust of Eastern religion is toward the *transformation of desire*, not satisfaction of desires. At its purest, it is a radical and constant movement inward, into the "self." Thus, the contemporary idea of "relevance"—which by and large has to do with the satisfaction of certain desires, or the allaying of certain fears—is antagonistic to the sense of Eastern religion. And thus the revolution in religion that is brewing among these new teachings in America is one that may run directly counter to the direction of contemporary religious reform.

No one can say that this "inward turn" is not also central to the Judaeo-Christian tradition, but it is also certainly true that this dimension of Western religion has been overlaid or neglected. Therefore, in looking at these new teachings we will want to know what light they can throw on our own traditions. Perhaps the East has to come West in this way for the West to rediscover the sense of its own religion.

Why Now? Why Here?

It is, in any case, this "inward turn" which has drawn so many Americans to these new religious teachings. What has happened to our culture and to our religions to make this inward turn so necessary? If we can begin to answer this question, we shall see something of the significance of this whole movement.

Here we immediately face an interesting difficulty. It is easy enough to argue that technology, affluence, the routinization of religion, and the like have stifled a deep longing in man, a "dark" side of his nature which is now welling forth to claim its own. From there, it is but one step to our "approving" of these new teachings because they satisfy an "irrational" need in the psyche of all men. We might even go so far as to argue that we must transform our view of reality by liberating our inherent attunement with the magical and by abandoning what has been called the "myth of objective consciousness." This has been done, and brilliantly, by Theodore Roszak in his book, *The Making of a Counter Culture*.

But to take this approach is, in the last analysis, to confess that we really do not wish to be serious about religion. It means that we have relied upon modern psychology or sociology to tell us what our possibilities are and which of them are not being realized in our society. Or, it means relying on our own feelings of frustration to tell us what reality should be like, or upon our responses to literature and art, themselves produced by men like us.

The Inclusion of the Mind

The terribly embarrassing thing about the great religions of the world is that *they* pass judgment on *us,* and that the moment we begin to pass judgment upon them without having submitted to their instruction, there is a real question whether we can understand them at all. Even to put the matter like this is already to have come upon one of the most striking ways in which the new teachings may change our contemporary concept of religion. To put it succinctly: they bring the idea that our mind and the power of thought itself is wretchedly inept without exposure to a spiritual discipline.

The exclusion of the mind from the religious process is one of the central characteristics of our religious forms. It was not always so, but by and large it is so now. We may be willing to grant religion the power to move us and stir us to the "depths" of our emotions, but we reserve the autonomy of our reasoning for ourselves. If we wish to train our minds, we know where to go, and it is not to religion.

Our popular religious forms long ago acquiesced to this. They spoke of human depravity, sin, faithlessness, immorality—but not so much of stupidity, illusion and bad thinking. It is true that Christianity and Judaism are essentially religions of the will, but the intellect was always understood as in the service of the will. Today, however, they, the will and the intellect, are tacitly recognized as separate.

Not so for the Eastern religion. Returning for a moment to our metaphor of the animals as symbols of human desires, the Eastern religions tell us that each animal has its own practical intelligence which operates only to procure its "food," namely the satisfaction of desire. Thus, when we are at the mercy of these animals our intelligence is also at their mercy. And as they are interested in pleasure and not in truth, so our minds inevitably follow the line of pleasure and attraction. Logic is a whore serving anyone who can pay the price.

The "inward turn" of the Eastern religions may thus be understood in part as the effort to include the mind in the process of psychological regeneration. "Who are *they* to train *my* mind!" one might say. Quite a legitimate question, but the problem is how are we to find out *who* "they" are? What in ourselves or in others do we trust to ascertain the truth: do we know? are we sure? That is the question which immediately comes back at us from the Eastern religions, and which used to come back at man from the Judaeo-Christian tradition.

To put the point another way, the established religions of the day tend to emphasize choice and action. But under the Eastern diagnosis of the human condition, choice without intellectual freedom is only impulse, the impulse of the animal. We might agree with that, but not with the added stipulation that we lack intellectual freedom outside of a spiritual discipline. In short, the Eastern religions tell us, as did Plato, that we are chained by our subjectivity. It is therefore quite wrong to see even our most ecstatic bursts of subjective feeling as a step toward spiritual regeneration in the Eastern sense.

Here I must hasten to say that when I speak of "our" religions, I am speaking of church and synagogue, not of what takes place in Western monasteries or convents. At the same time, it is also indicative of our idea of religion that monasticism is by and large considered on the fringe, as secondary to church religion. Of course, this is a complete reversal of the historical relationship between church and monastery, where the latter was the source of life of the former. Today, most of us tend to think of monks and nuns as a bit odd, rather than as holy people.

The Return of the Practical

Which brings us to the second main point about our contemporary religious forms, namely, the absence in them of practical technique, method and discipline. Various rituals, prayers, services and the like no longer function as part of the mechanics of the religious process, but mainly as an emotional "lift," something to help us return to our ordinary life feeling better, psychologically more secure. In this way they help to preserve the quality of the life we lead, rather than transform it.

This general forgetting of the instrumental nature of religious forms is in a way really quite bizarre. It is as though millions of people suffering from a painful disease were to gather together to hear someone read a textbook of medical treatment in which the means necessary to cure their disease were carefully spelled out. It is as though they were all to take great comfort in that book and in what they heard, going through their lives knowing that their disease could be cured, quoting passages to their friends, preaching the wonders of this great book, and returning to their congregation from time to time to hear more of the inspiring diagnosis and treatment read to them. Meanwhile, of course, the disease worsens and they eventually die of it, smiling in grateful hope as on their deathbed someone reads to them yet another passage from the text. Perhaps for some a troubling thought crosses their minds as their eyes close for the last time: "Haven't I forgotten something? Something important? Haven't I forgotten actually to undergo treatment?"

It is impossible to say when this forgetting of the fundamentally instrumental nature of religious forms began in the West. But obviously the general clergy—priests, ministers and rabbis—forgot it quite as much as their congregations. No wonder the young became disillusioned with religion. They heard exhortations, commandments, prescriptions by the basketful, but nobody was telling them *how to be able* to follow them. I do not say they formulated it this way to themselves, but they—and not only they—saw the absurd discrepancy between the ideal preached in their churches and the actual behavior of men, behavior which seemed reinforced rather than seriously challenged by religion.

The Eastern teachings which are attracting so much interest in this country have by and large preserved this instrumental aspect of religion. That is why they come to us with such things as meditation techniques, physical and psychological exercises, and why they tend to emphasize the necessity of a *guru*, or master. It takes no great research to discover that practical psychological methods were always a central part of Christianity and Judaism, and that they still exist in monastic settings or, for example, among certain communities such as the Jewish Hasidim. The point is only that this aspect of religion has been forgotten by almost all other Westerners.

It is only because it was forgotten that Judaism and Christianity were so shaken by psychoanalysis and various other movements in modern psychology. Compared, for example, to the early Christian diagnosis of the inner human condition, Freud's "expose" of the nature of human motivation is a very weak tea indeed. For one thing—and this is the very least of it—he retained his trust in the power of reason, his own, and observation, also his own, to arrive at the truth about human psychology. But for the early Christians, and for several of the most interesting new teachings, the power of thinking and observing clearly is a quality only of a higher state of consciousness, and not something that man is able to rely on without work in a spiritual discipline.

The main point here, however, is that because the instrumental nature of religious forms was forgotten, the science of psychology suddenly appeared as something *new*. Such an absurdity could only arise on the basis of a total misunderstanding or ignorance of the history of Judaeo-Christian thought and practice. One need only glance again at the writings of Augustine, Eckhardt, the Eastern Orthodox Fathers, or the great rabbis to confirm this point.

The Modern Underestimation of Man

Modern psychology did indeed bring one thing that was new, namely an underestimation of human possibility. Which brings us to our third point about the nature of contemporary religion.

There is really a tremendous irony at this point. Because religion forgot the instrumental function of its forms, these forms changed to accommodate the ordinary desires of men—as we pointed out in discussing the idea of "secularization." As a result of this forgetting and this change of form, religion was no longer able to effect the essential improvement of human life. Observing this, various "original thinkers" immediately concluded that religion was a fraud and began to produce, by the dozens, their own methods for improving human life. For they quite accurately saw that what men were getting out of religion (religion which was no longer instrumental) could be gotten faster without all the rituals, "mumbo jumbo," metaphysics, and so forth, all of which originally formed part of the instrumentality of the Judaic and Christian *Way*, but whose essential function nobody seemed really to understand. To return for a moment to a medical metaphor, it was as though patients and doctors began to insist that medicine taste good and make one *feel* rather than *be* well, and as though certain clever benefactors of mankind discovered that this could be done more effectively by removing from the medicines precisely those ingredients which had genuine therapeutic properties.

What modern psychology offered as an improvement of human life was precisely that quality of life which drove men originally to the instrumentalities of religion, the only addition being the conviction that this was the highest quality of life one could realistically expect. Religion was dismissed as an illusion—and indeed the religion which psychologists dismissed was perhaps illusory because it had forgotten its practical function and had lost its instrumental forms. Thus psychology became much more efficient than religion which, pursuing the same goals as this new science, found itself hampered by "outworn" beliefs and rituals. Modern psychology began to lead religion. The destruction of religious forms proceeded at an accelerated pace, and the underestimation of human possibility became fixed in our society.

It is only partially true that this estimation of man was based on a premature acceptance of human limitation, itself based on a mistaken extrapolation from the failure of non-instrumental religion. To be sure, there were some thinkers, not in the majority, who claimed that all man could ever hope for was the illusion of freedom, the partial gratification of instinctual desires and a more or less tolerable, though meaningless, existence between oblivions. The freedom, immortality, higher consciousness and inner unity spoken of by religions was to them a romantic dream. At least they tried to some degree to avoid replacing this so-called romantic dream with a naïve belief in their own innate, fully developed powers.

Not so the majority of psychologists. They coupled their underestimation of man's possibilities with an emphatic over-estimation of man's and their own actual psychological condition. Simply to mention one example, Freud's whole theory of dreams, parapraxes and neurotic symptomology is based on the assumption that there is a basic unity of purpose underlying all human behavior, and that everything man does is an expression, though unconscious, of this instinctual unity. Since it is precisely this unity which many of the Eastern religions call into question, from their perspective it is Freud's assumption which is the romantic dream. He once said, "Man has always known he possessed spirit; I had to show him he was also an animal." Unfortunately, he settled for only *one* animal, whereas the fundamental religious diagnosis of man is that he is an entire menagerie.

Blithely accepting the "tough-minded" scientific view that there are no purposes in the external world, psychoanalysis substituted the rather sentimental belief that there is nothing but purpose and intention in the psychic world. At least the positivists made a clean sweep of all purpose, inner and outer, and after them one could much more clearly see the dust bowl of modern thought for what it was.

Coupled with this assumption that everything in one's psychic life had "meaning," was the psychologists' belief that they were able to ascertain this meaning, to control their own feelings toward the patient, and to communicate the truth to the patient in a way that could be effective—all this being the general sort of thing which a spiritual master does, but toward an aim entirely different than "mental health" and only after he himself has submitted his life (including his mind) to the instrumental rigors of a spiritual path.

One obvious aspect of the modern, Western concept of religion was its picture of a "holy" man. He was nicer, kinder, gentler, more moral, perhaps, than other men—but more intelligent? more perceptive? emotionally stronger? psychologically more balanced? more creative? more unified? Were not these *"secular"* properties of men? Again, it is the Eastern religions with their practical methods involving work with the body, the attention, the intellect and memory, the training of the emotions, which has begun to supplant this simplistic picture of holiness. Till now, it has been entirely possible for many of us to be surprised if not slightly offended by the idea that Jesus Christ had a mind as well as a heart, and to be genuinely astonished that almost all of the enduring art in the world has been produced by men with obvious religious ties.

Summing up, there are three ways in which Western, and particularly American, religions are vulnerable to correction by the religions of the East: exclusion of the mind, the absence of religious techniques and methods, and the underestimation of human possibility. One could cite still more ways in which our religious forms have moved away from their original direction, but these, perhaps, are enough to have exposed as well some of the conditions of our American culture which make it ripe for this invasion from the East.

It may be helpful now briefly to explain some of the main philosophical elements of those Eastern systems which form the background of the new teachings. It must be remembered, however, that this is no more than background, and that what is most interesting and important about the new teachings does not lend itself to abstract philosophical exposition. Just as the Torah has its "fence" and just as Jesus spoke to the multitude in parables, the founders of these movements, each in his own way, attempt to direct their communications to the more intuitive side of man, What we shall later speak of as "the intelligence of the heart."

The new teachings thus present themselves in ways that strongly resist conceptual formulation. One obvious reason for this is their intense emphasis on practice and method, and their mistrust of the isolated intellect. Like Kierkegaard, their founders are strongly aware of the tendency of the mind to believe it has understood and to accept or reject what it has in fact only cognized on the basis of a very limited store of experience.

For this reason, the reader will find no neat summary of each teaching's "doctrine and precepts." My intention is to allow the "doctrine" to emerge within a description of the teaching's existential impact. For similar reasons, criticism and evaluation of this general movement is reserved for the end of the book.

We need not be quite so careful about approaching the Eastern religions which lie behind the new teachings and which have long been in existence. They each have their own well-developed philosophical side which was acquired as the teaching spread beyond its initial following to the world at large. We can trace this process quite clearly in the growth of Christianity and Judaism, and it is equally apparent in the history of Hinduism, Buddhism and Sufism. There are many who take this sort of development as a sign of degeneration and mere intellectualization, and perhaps it often is such in the hands of those who have not gone far in the discipline. But it is much more reasonable to understand it generally as a process of opening the gates to the multitudes and of directing the life-impulse of the original teaching to the needs of various types of men in later times. We shall have more to say about this in our discussion of the concept of transmission in the Tibetan tradition. For now, the main thing we need to remember is that the doctrines that follow have always been meant to serve as a help in the practical work of self-transformation.

Hinduism, Buddhism and Sufism

Like all the great religious traditions of the world, each of these three is unimaginably vast in its inner variety and gradations. Here, however, we shall focus only on elements that are most directly germane to understanding the sense of the new teachings in America. For purposes of clarity, we shall contrast these systems with the teachings of popular Judaism and Christianity, bearing in mind that what today is generally accepted as Judaeo-Christian doctrine may bear little or no resemblance to the mystical, practical core of our traditions wherein they often exhibit an astonishing similarity to the religions of the East.

HINDUISM

There are three aspects of Hindu philosophy which generally jar the average Western investigator into realizing he is on quite a different terrain. They are (1) the impersonality of the divine being; (2) the designation of this divinity as the Self which is fully present within each individual human being; and (3) the doctrine of *Maya* or the unreality of the world.

(1) In Hinduism the highest reality is just that: pure reality with no admixture of limitation or definition. Unlike the Judaeo-Christian God who cares for man and acts in history on his behalf, this pure reality is eternal and unchanging, and what appears to be its activity in creating, preserving and destroying the world is fundamentally a reflection only of man's imperfect understanding. As pure reality, it is even incorrect to speak of the Hindu God as the highest Being. Divinity is Being itself. At the same time, it is pure consciousness and pure energy, not localizable in any space and independent of the determinations of

time. It is spoken of as *Brahman* or *Sot-Chit-Ananda* (Being-Consciousness-Bliss).

To speak of this pure consciousness as impersonal is only one of many ways in which we may think of it by the method of negating familiar determinations without at the same time affirming anything of it. For, obviously, such pure being and pure consciousness are beyond the grasp of the ordinary human mind. In contemplating this pure and total reality we, as human beings, are brought immediately to the question: what of me? my cares, my needs, my life? Of what use is this divinity to me, how can I turn to it if it is everywhere and everything? Who *am* I?

(2) Hinduism relates this supreme reality to the reality of individual human life by designating it as the Self. I, too, am this Self and all my cares and suffering arise because I do not understand this. In the popular Judaeo-Christian view, man is separated from God by an infinite abyss. The greatest of sins is to equate myself with God; He is Creator and I am but the creature. But, for the Hindu this separation obtains only so long as I believe it, only so long as I take myself to be the cares, fears and desires which prompt me to supplicate an alien reality as God. I do not know my own nature; this is the source of all human ill. *Atman*, the individual self, is in reality *Brahman*, the pure Subject and all-encompassing reality. Therefore, the only sensible aim which a man may have in his lifetime is fully to realize this identity and to reunite himself with his own divine essence. This work of reuniting is called *Yoga*.

The doctrine of the identity of Atman and Brahman is commonly misunderstood in two ways by Westerners. It is often taken in the vague, sentimental sense that characterizes the popular Western notion that "we are all children of God." But the doctrine is infinitely more penetrating than that; it states in effect that it is man's bizarre and confused love of his present misery which accounts for its perpetuation, and that right under the surface of everything we think, feel or do is precisely that power and consciousness which, were we to move toward it, would transform our lives into a condition of godliness.

The other misunderstanding is closely related to this, being the idea that all men, as they are, are God. The Hindu teaching, however, is that the ordinary mind, meaning yours and mine, is as far from God as any table or chair taken by itself. We do not, in fact, actually live in the consciousness which lies within ourselves and which is the supreme reality. Without the work of a genuine *Yoga* it is destined to remain, for us, the *un*conscious. The Hindu concept of the unconscious is in this sense the direct opposite of the psychoanalytic concept, being the difference between a level of consciousness above the ordinary and a level of consciousness below the ordinary.

(3) The popular Judaic and Christian conception of the world is that it was created by God and, though dependent upon God, has a reality of its own and a goodness of its own. To say that the world is unreal is, in this view, to derogate the work of the Creator. The doctrine of Maya, which states that the whole of the world is a grand illusion, does not really contradict this idea, but, generally speaking, it emphasizes the contingency of the world upon the mind of God. And since God is the *Atman* in each man, then as man attains to the realization of his own divinity, he sees all about him the dependency, relativity and contingency of all that he had previously taken to be real—including his own body, feelings and thoughts. That is, he comes to see the world as God "sees" it, a dream which has reality only for those in the dream.

There is one crucial aspect of the doctrine of Maya which is left out of many accounts. That is that the illusoriness of the world in which man lives is an expression of the fact that he values the world in a wrong way, taking that to be important which is not important and vice versa. Man perceives wrongly because he desires wrongly. The importance of this aspect is that it roots the cognitive side of Maya in the volitional, and renders it more a religious doctrine than an abstract philosophical hypothesis. When seen in this way, it overlaps with much traditional Western religious thought, for example, Augustine's concept of the illusoriness of evil.

In addition to these three basic elements of Hindu thought, it is important to mention what is a general characteristic of the Indian mind and tradition: their absorptiveness. For the Indian, there is no such thing as a false religion; and there is a place in his teachings for all ways to God, the way of love, of knowledge, of action, and many others. Since the supreme reality is unlimited and inconceivable by the ordinary mind, all ways that start from the ordinary mind must have both their truth and their falsehood. In this, Hinduism contrasts strongly with the sharper missionary strain of Christianity which insists that its way is the only way and that all others lead to perdition. The Indian mind is thus imbued with the sense of the relativity of all things and enterprises in the world, and vigorously resists the yes-or-no, black-or-white tendency of much modern Western thought.

BUDDHISM

The Hindu religion can be likened to an Olympian armed campaign with great generals dispersed abroad, their huge armies and infinitely variegated weaponry converging upon the "enemy" under some divinely conceived master strategy. Compared to this, Buddhism appears upon the Indian scene as a direct hand-to-hand attack with no holds barred, striking instantly and mercilessly at the "enemy's" weakest point. By and large, Buddhism has retained this quality of one-pointed practicality even amid the later flowering of a metaphysics and mythology which, in all of its aspects, quite easily rivals the entirety of Hinduism.

Put quite succinctly, the Buddha, who is understood to have lived and taught in the sixth century B.C., taught that the principal cause of all human suffering and desolation is the deeply ingrained belief that there is such a thing as a self, or ego, that persists through time and change. Everything else in Buddhism, its art, philosophy, rituals and techniques originated as tools for the destruction of man's illusion that he is a self. This doctrine of no-self or non-*Atman* is, as it is said, the *diamond* which cuts through all errors and confusions of humanity.

According to this teaching, everything in human nature is in flux, and a man is nothing but a serial bundle of sensations, thoughts and feelings, one proceeding from another with nothing to hold them together either in life or death. And not only man, but all things in the universe are without self, without a fixed nature that abides from moment to moment. In the endless and rigorously determined chain of cause and effect that constitutes the universe, man fixes his interest or desire upon one or another phenomenal aggregate, either within "himself" or external to "himself," and therein is the root of all our sorrow. What liberates man is the deep and thorough understanding of all things, including the personality, as a causally determined process of becoming.

Consciousness—meaning the totality of thought, feeling, perception, sensation, pleasure and pain—is not a being, but a passion, not an activity but only a sequence of reactions in which "we," who have no power to be either as or when we will, are fatally involved; individuality is motivated by and perpetuated by wanting; and the cause of all wanting is "ignorance"—for we "ignore" that the objects of our desire can never be possessed in any real sense of the word, ignore that even when we have got what we want, we still "want" to keep it and are still in the state of desire. The ignorance meant is of things as they really are, and the consequent attribution of substantiality to what is merely phenomenal; the seeing of self in what is not-self.

At first glance, this doctrine of no-self seems in direct opposition to the Hindu view. Actually, Eastern scholars have debated this important point at great length, and we shall return to it in a moment. But if there is any general view with which the Buddhist doctrine conflicts, it is surely our own Western world-view as embodied not only in the popular understanding of Judaeo-Christian doctrine, but in the goals our whole civilization has set for itself.

The religions of the West have inbued us with idea of an individual, eternal soul created by God (also, in His way, an "individual"), infinitely precious, and irreducibly real. As our modern society drew away from religious doctrine, it substituted for the soul the idea of individual personality, not immortal perhaps but for that very reason all the more our own and precious. The establishment of our "identity," our "role" has been the banner cry not only of scientific psychology, but of all the major intellectual movements of modern times, including existentialism and humanism. We measure a person's strength by what we take to be the distinctness and vividness of his "individuality," and we all seek to "make our mark," either as artists, scientists or businessmen. To the Buddhist, all this striving is the pursuit of a phantom. The "identity" we seek to establish is nothing more than a thought, a picture in the mind of what we are or can be; it is in nowise based on fact. Our sense of persistence and sameness through change is a trick played upon us by the automatic functions of memory and buttressed by the fact that we are given a name and treated by others as though we were a self. Indeed, our whole society is but a vast collection of sleepwalkers each addressing the other and conceiving of himself within his own dream of selfhood. All our ideas of morality and obligation, blame and praise, are based on this dream and serve only to strengthen the illusion of its reality.

Putting the Buddhist doctrine of no-self in the above way, its congruence with Hindu thought becomes clearer. We might say that for the Hindu or Brahmanic religion, human ignorance is the ignorance of who we are, where for Buddhism, it is ignorance of what we are not. It is in fact a cardinal trait of Buddhism that its teachings are in negative terms. Break down the illusion, the error, and the truth will appear by itself, for it is always there; it is only obscured and hidden by our ignorant beliefs about ourselves and the desires attached thereto.

Of all the great religious teachers of the world, none has incarnated and lived the idea that ultimate reality is beyond the grasp of the ordinary mind with such purity and concentration as the Buddha. This, in part, explains why the Buddha's discourses say nothing about the existence of a Supreme Being, for example, or about immortality. Such questions "tend not to edification" since they are put by the deluded mind which is quite content to speculate endlessly about these matters while clinging to the very beliefs which perpetuate its suffering. It is especially this negative aspect of the Buddha's method of teaching which must be kept in mind when we come to discuss the work of Zen Center in San Francisco.

Its "strategy" of negation, has misled many Westerners into thinking Buddhism is pessimistic and anti-life. Some have even thought of *Nirvana*, the ultimate goal of Buddhist discipline, as a sort of spiritual "suicide." Nothing could be further from the truth and, in fact, there is no religion which has a higher estimation of human possibility. It is only that it is not spoken of directly and positively. The exalted level of Nirvana can be seen indirectly by attending to everything which the Buddhists say it is *not*. It is not love, consciousness, peace, freedom, happiness or immortality in any sense that we understand. We are given no words for it because we have no experience of it; and in the absence of a corresponding experience, names merely purchase further illusion. The Gospels, we may recall, also speak of the "peace that passeth understanding."

We come to the conclusion that just as the great mystics and saints of out own traditions could describe the Supreme Reality only by negation and analogy, so the Buddhist tells us of Nirvana. Since, however, Nirvana also designates the *whole* of reality, then we see why Buddhism also refuses to admit that our ordinary thinking and language can accurately be applied to *anything* that is real. Thus, reality is also named the Void or emptiness (*Sunya*).

A final note—especially important when we come to inquire if a genuine Buddhist way can take root on our own soil: Buddhist moral rules are never ends in themselves. In the light of what has already been said about instrumental religion, this should not surprise us. But it is essential to realize that these ethical "commandments" (not to kill, steal, lie, lust, covet, and so forth) are understood as *necessary* preliminaries to any greater spiritual development. How, then, will the Buddhist spiritual disciplines find a solid place here in the West where the meaning and even the desirability of a life in accordance with ethical rules is seriously in question?

SUFISM

The towering religious system of the Middle East founded by the prophet Muhammed seven hundred years after Christ is so perplexing to the West that many of us are not even sure of its proper name. It is *Islam*, an Arabic word that means "surrender." Its holy book is the Koran (or Quran) revealed by God (Allah) through The Prophet. In depth and intelligence, in its rules of conduct, its explanation of the human condition, and in the many-layered profundity of its form, the Koran is an ocean quite as deep and alive as our own Western Bible. Like Judaism and Christianity, which of course were also born in the Middle East, Islam declares the total majesty and reality of the One God, the God of Abraham, Moses, Jesus and Muhammad, the last of the prophets. The universe, with its worlds within worlds, is a reality created and sustained by the One God and is an expression of His mercy and wisdom. Man, His highest creation, is a theomorphic being containing within himself both the power of God and the qualities which generate the entire order of creation from the highest to the lowest. Man sins by ignoring or forgetting his divine nature and by following that in himself which is lower in the cosmic order. Because of the complexity and imperfections that are an essential part of man's nature on earth, and because of his overpowering tendency to forget his divinity, the Divine Law was revealed. Like the Judaic Law, the Islamic Divine Law is a network of injunctions and attitudes which governs all of human life and which functions to bring every aspect of man's life into relationship with his central spiritual nature. Without the Divine Law, man in his multiplicity of actions and impulses becomes dispersed and fragmented.

Of Islam in general, these few broad strokes are all that we have place for here. It is Sufism, understood as *esoteric* Islam, which is of direct interest to us in this book. Indeed, there is very much about the new teachings which cannot be understood until the customary Western associations connected with the word "esoteric" are set aside.

For most Westerners, the word calls to mind the worst aspects of secrecy, obscurantism and mystagogy. At best, it is taken to apply to things which are of real interest only to a peripheral few, and which need not or ought not concern anyone else. There is a tremendous horror in the West concerning secrecy in general, but particularly in matters of religion. All truth should be open to everyone, for all men are equal under God, and all men are in need of truth.

Even more than horror, we in the West tend to feel contemptuous and derisive toward such secrecy. Such is our trust in the soundness of our own interests that if we have not heard of something, we are almost sure it is not very important. Certainly nothing *central* could be hidden, not in this day and age and certainly not from *me*. And, as a matter of fact, the so-called "secrets" we have stumbled upon have turned out to be generally preposterous. We have come to see those who revel in secrecy as neurotically in need of something to make themselves feel important.

Yet none of this has much to do with the sense of the idea of esotericism. The term means "inner" and refers to that part of any spiritual teaching which embodies in concentrated form the *discipline*, the *methods*—psychological and physical—by means of which the teaching in all its metaphysical and moral aspects can be fully assimilated into the lives of certain individuals who wish for this assimilation. *Exoteric* religion may be understood as a way of life in which, as we have said, men's and society's daily activities may become centered around the question of the relationship to God. Esoteric religion, or the *path*, exists only for men to whom this question has become so intense and troubling that it begins to take precedence over every satisfaction in their way of life.

A contemporary Islamic scholar has described it this way:

The *Ṭarīqah* or Spiritual Path which is usually known as *Taṣawwuf* or Sufism is the inner and esoteric dimension of Islam . . . Being the heart of the Islamic message it, like the physical heart, is hidden from external view, although again like the heart it is the inner source of life and the center which co-ordinates inwardly the whole religious organism of Islam. Although Islam in its totality has been able to preserve throughout its history a balance between the two dimensions of the Law and the Way, there have been occasionally those who have emphasized one at the expense of the other . . . They are the superficial . . . who would break the balance and equilibrium between the exoteric and the esoteric dimensions . . . According to the well-known Sufi symbol, Islam is like a walnut of which the shell is like the *Sharīah* (The Divine Law), and the kernel like the *Ṭarīqah* (The Path) . . . A walnut without a shell could not grow in the world of nature and without a kernel would have no end or purpose . . . Today many want to transcend the world of forms without possessing the forms. They want to burn the scrolls, to use a Buddhist term, without having the scrolls. But man cannot throw away that which he does not possess. The Sufis who were inviting men to throw away the external forms were addressing persons who already possessed these forms.[1]

This last poses for us the identical problem that arose in connection with Buddhist ethics as the precondition for the spiritual path. What relationship can obtain between the new teachings with their predominantly "internal" dimension and a society which is losing its hold on all of its external forms? We shall have to ask this question in earnest in our concluding evaluation at the end of the book.

Meanwhile, it is clear that the secrecy which often characterizes esoteric thought bears no resemblance to the common Western idea of secrecy. The latter refers to ordinary (if that) knowledge which is withheld from view. The former refers to knowledge which is not useful, understandable or even visible to one who is not on the path, or under the discipline. If I see a man floating in dangerous waters and throw a life preserver to him, everything depends on whether he takes notice of it—and even then he may so trust his own assessment of the situation that he uses it only to swim even further out to sea. Of such a man we would have to say that even though he makes use of what is offered to him, he does not value it correctly, and hence it does him harm instead of good. My first step should have been to be sure he understood his situation, and until then I should have withheld the life preserver. Such is the "secrecy" of the esoteric.

This said, it remains to be added that unlike the Hindu tradition, Sufism tends to synthesize rather than sharply differentiate the various ways to self-perfection, such as the ways of love, action and knowledge. The Sufi thus stresses the idea of *equilibrium* both in the universe and in the perfected man. With its dominant idea of an organic, many-leveled universe, Sufism relates equilibrium to wholeness or unity. The revelation of God is understood to be the revelation of this unity and of the path which the individual must take if he is to experience this unity as himself. Man is thus potentially a microcosm, a "scale model," as it were, of the divine unity. The "intelligence of the heart" is that faculty in man which when awakened understands the place and the good of everything that is, both within himself and within God's universe. Thus the highest goal of Sufism is called "divine knowledge" or *gnosis* which may be thought of as both knowledge about God and God's own knowledge acting through the medium of a finite man.

To move toward this exalted plane, Sufism constantly stresses the need for individual men to be aware of their own ignorance apart from the revelation of God. Indeed, the term "Sufi" is, strictly speaking, reserved only for those who have attained to the divine knowledge. The proper term for one upon the path is *faquīr*, meaning "poor" in the sense of spiritual poverty. Though Sufism ends with the attainment of divine unity, the practical essence of the path and its instrumentalities is the realization by men that they are as nothing and that Allah is the one and only Being. If the Sufic background of several of the new teachings is to be of any help to us in placing them, this dual aspect of esoteric Islam must be borne in mind: man can participate in divine consciousness only to the extent that he is conscious of his own nothingness. The arousal of this dual consciousness is the specific purpose of the extraordinary variety of labors that make up the forms of Sufi discipline.

The Occult

A word now about *occultism*. Almost everyone has strong associations connected with this word: the acquisition of mysterious powers, spiritualism, conversing with the dead, astral projection, turbaned swamis with piercing eyes, levitation, mind reading, reincarnation; talk of vibrations, emanations, auras, secret languages, cosmic forces, elderly gentlemen and ladies in chintz-curtained apartments complacently treasuring The Hidden Knowledge, weird rites in weird places at weird times, Atlantis, Lemuria, and so forth, and so on.

The educated Westerner laughs at all this—perhaps not quite as heartily as he used to, but still he sees it as little more than escapism and charlatanry. For one thing, he cannot see anything remarkable in the quality of life that these occultists lead. Like him, they are vain, nervous, inept, neurotic and fearful, perhaps even more so. Like him, they can be bought, seduced, overwhelmed, perhaps even more easily than he. Perhaps some of them can do something remarkable on the order of telepathy or such; he is willing to grant a few of them psychic powers. But what of it? *He* is a neurotic businessman, *they* are neurotic mind readers. That is, he senses in these occultists an even sharper lack than in himself of what might be called understanding or wisdom.

In short, the occultist leads a life no better—often even worse—than the rest of us. What characterizes him is not so much the extravagant plumage of his ideas, but the absence in him of self-questioning and the search for a new inwardness. Seen this way, the traditions which the new teachings are based upon are very far from being occultistic.

For, as we have said, the center of gravity of these traditions is the movement inward and the hard questioning of man's passive reliance upon his desires.

But this does not mean that these traditions approach the cosmos in a way that is comfortable and familiar to the average Westerner. Quite the contrary is true. Eastern cosmology presents us with a nature and a universe saturated with purposes and a consciousness which we do not understand. The conventional Western idea of a blind mechanical universe in which life and mind are at best a puzzling anomaly is to the Eastern mind an absurd delusion.

Therefore, that interest in metaphysical ideas and psychological possibilities which we often associate with the "occult" finds a very congenial soil within these traditions. But in coming to know the followers of these new teachings I found that, with many of them, their questions as to the nature of the cosmos were a natural part of the search for their own identity. Later in the book their own words may bring this out more clearly, but even theoretically it is not hard to see how this must be so. Since I am a part of reality, then what I am or can become is dependent on the nature of reality. If, for example, the universe is unalive and indifferent, I will hope and work for something in myself quite different from what I will seek if the universe is laden with mind and life. I cannot with sanity search for radically new possibilities in my inner life unless there is a real place in the universe for them.

Surely, this is a primal meaning of the emotion of wonder. In sensing the vast order of the cosmos, I sense in myself and for myself possibilities beyond my imagining; for I am part of this order and I see that I do not understand it or myself. At that moment I need knowledge that corresponds to this emotion. And if the only knowledge that is available is such that it denies the validity of this emotion, or judges it as "merely" subjective, and vague, then the emotion may eventually be either lost or corrupted into mere fantasy without hope of my finding the appropriate labor of my life. I shall then, perhaps, become an occultist who dreams of the miraculous without the search for his individual task, or, on the other hand, a mere technician who labors in dead alienation from the question as to his purpose on earth.

So, we must not pass hasty judgments on the interest in "occult" questions. Though most of us cannot presume to estimate another's inward effort—certainly not from reading any book—we can at least keep the thought of it alive as we listen to these people, leaders and followers, older and younger, who are immersed in these new teachings.

The real danger of occultism lies not in its ideas, however extravagant, but in its organization. Very many occult societies exist, it seems, for the sole purpose of fattening the ego. Easy hierarchies are set up, grand titles are dealt out, spiritual authority is assumed, initiations and "tests" are passed. People become "teachers" before they even know what it means to be pupils. All in all, the result is an armored complacency that one has found the way, or the truth. There is a certain aura about such organizations, a certain "smell" that characterizes the institutionalized absence of questioning.

We shall, therefore, be very interested in the organizational structure of these new religious teachings.

The Place of California

As we have said, California plays a unique role in the gestation and nurture of what is unusual, and often downright weird, in American life. The variety of psychological flora and fauna here is amazing. Cults and sects grow like weeds. "Gurus" abound.

This aspect of California is not, of course, limited to the religious. It is true of politics, food habits, sexual behavior, clothing, education, medical practice—probably every *outré* or extreme aspect of human behavior is well housed here. Even a passing, superficial glance at the list boggles the mind: nude psychotherapy, astral projection societies, private armies, grape sugar mysticism, "Yoga" youth cults, moon worshipers, etc.

In all this, one naturally thinks first of southern California: Los Angeles, Hollywood, movie people, but it is true more or less throughout the whole state. At the same time there exists here a vast, solid middle class and working class typical of the rest of America.

In short, California is a place where, by and large, a man can find what he wants. If what he wants is only a whim, a fantasy, or even a perversion—it is here and, probably, there is even an organization devoted to it.

It has been said that every time and place has its own despair. The despair of California is the despair of people relentlessly getting what they want. In this it is certainly an especially clear mirror of contemporary America. Most of us, for quite some time now, have been getting what we want. So many of our "animals" are being fed—in ways, and to an extent undreamed of in previous centuries. This is so not only for what are called biological needs. We travel where we want to, read what we want, have such things as cars, boats, television, experience such things as flying, sexual extravagance, Xerox machines, televised assassinations, etc.

One of the things which makes California unique is the degree to which all this is taking place. In all the world there is probably no other place where the "attainment" of satisfaction occurs on such a scale.

The thousand strange cults, sects and fads that flourish here may be seen as part of this fever of satisfying the desires and allaying fears. But among these organizations there may be some that are reaching out for something more fundamental than gratification. Of this handful of groups, some may perhaps be channels through which timeless traditions are speaking anew to modern man.

No mere book can say for sure which of these groups speak in this way and which do not. All that we can do, as interested observers, is to try to understand their thought on the basis of what we ourselves grasp of our own tradition.

So whether or not we are drawn to these new teachings, we shall have learned from them.

2

Zen Center

The Embrace of Zen Buddhism

When it first became known in America, Zen Buddhism brought with it a picture of the fierce teacher with his strange laughter and incomprehensible responses, the explosive moment of enlightenment called *satori,* the breath-taking irreverence and contempt for what was tradition-bound and intellectual. There were the stories of blows and shoutings. There were the koans, super-riddles designed to break through the tyranny of thought. From the East had come an approach that turned askew all our concepts of religion. No talk of morality, God, immortality, love, duty, faith, sacrifice or sin. No prescriptions, no commandments, no judgments. Only the constant and unfathomable call for man to see into his own nature.

In trying to understand such an approach, our minds were assaulted by one negation after another and we swam in an ocean of the unsaid. We simply could not figure out what Zen was. We never accepted it; yet we never really rejected it.

Not even when others seemed to grasp it so quickly and easily—too quickly and too easily! Even when the koans and haiku poems were flying thick and fast, when the Beat generation was flinging Zen in our faces and drumming our heads with it and when so many others were using it as a whip to beat every dog, real and imaginary, that existed in our culture and traditions— even then, Zen itself (whatever it was) commanded a corner of our respect.

Instinctively, we felt there was a difference between Zen and those who were shouting about it.

At the very least, the Zen stories were excellent theater. The monk striving and straining for illumination, the countless obstacles, the false successes, the despair, the hopelessness, and yet the persistence, and then, finally, the climax, *satori!* All of this in flesh and blood, with spontaneity, and a certain light touch, rescued the idea of a spiritual search from the doldrums. Masters and monks were not what we pictured as the gaunt, somewhat inhuman Christian mystics, and their struggle was for a life and vitality that we ourselves could recognize and wish for. Zen was showing us that the life of the spirit, and its reality, was not less but perhaps more interesting and dramatic than our own lives and the reality we lived in.

Quietly and persistently, the writings of D. T. Suzuki and a few others survived their long flash of popularity to take a solid place in the important thought of our time. Zen became the paradigm of practical, tough-minded religion. It outstripped even the existentialist writers in its impatience with thought that had no bearing on the everyday realities and crises of life. It went even further than psychoanalysis in emphasizing the emotional, experiential basis of insight. About nature it was more unsentimental than even the most positivistic scientist, yet, in some extraordinary way, as sensitive and alive to nature as any artist or poet among us.

It was unprecedented that people whose orientations toward life seemed mutually antagonistic all drew inspiration from the same source: humanists as well as psychoanalysts, scientists as well as artists. Amid all of its innumerable negations, Zen rejected nothing. Consequently, no one among us felt compelled to reject it. Zen made no enemies.

True, the place of Zen was only in our minds. Very few of us practiced it, or even dreamed of practicing it. From what we had read and heard, that would have meant renouncing everything to go off to Japan to search, we knew not where or how, for some monastery and teacher who might either reject our suit or demand intolerable demonstrations of sincerity. We had been very impressed by stories such as that of the monk who was made to stand in the snow for months before being admitted.

We thus felt no need to chase Zen from our minds when we saw that we could not put it into practice. We could accept it without expecting ourselves to live it or even understand it. Within the individual psyche, too, Zen made no enemies.

Some would complain about this, that it was *only* in our minds, but the extraordinary thing, reflecting the particular genius of Zen, was that it *stayed* in bur minds without prompting us to do much of anything about it. It was a kind of miracle that the Zen approach, which undercut everything the Western world lived by, faced it so little as a challenge, provoked so little in the way of resistance and interpretation.

The way Zen appeared in the West is an intimation of the way it seems to act upon the individuals who now do practice it in America. Perhaps we could call it the method of intra-psychic non-violence. In order to understand something about this, it is best to look first at what is termed Soto Zen, that sort of Zen which has now taken root as practice in the city of San Francisco and in a monastic setting in the midst of a California wilderness.

"Just Sitting"

There are two main sects of Zen: Rinzai and Soto. Both present themselves as methods by means of which the individual may directly experience the truth about his own nature: that it is, at any instant, the completely real. Without this experience, human life is at every moment generated by the sense that something necessary is lacking. This is the state of desire. What we call the par-

ticular desires, fears, feelings and the thinking associated with
them, result from this basic state. According to Buddhism, the
only thing really lacking in man is the experience that nothing is
lacking.

Unenlightened man is characterized as lacking the experience
of what is. His experience of what is, of the real, is mixed with
thought that is in the service of desire. This thought, or judging,
is not an experience, but is itself an aspect of the real. It, too, is
something to be experienced. But unenlightened man rarely, if
ever, turns simply to experience his thought or his feelings as such.
Thus, he desires instead of experiencing his desires. Now desire
(and hence the thought which serves it) is part of the effort to
change what exists, make it better, more pleasing, and so forth.
Unenlightened man, therefore, never experiences reality.

According to the Buddhist tradition, there is that in a man
which is able, quietly and directly, to experience rather than desire. This is called the Buddha-nature. Life submerged in desire
and its thought can itself be experienced. The awakening of this
experience is thus an important element in what is called the realization of the Buddha-nature. Zen Buddhism is a means to help
an individual come to this awakening of experience.

Soto Zen differs from the Rinzai in that it does not emphasize
use of the koan* to bring about this awakenings. In fact, almost
the entire picture which we Westerners have of Zen is based on
reports about Rinzai practice and not Soto.

My first investigations of Zen Center, which practices the Soto
way, were therefore something of a shock. The same is true for
many of the Americans who later become practicing members.
They come geared for the koans, the "anti-rationality," the "de-
mandingness" and existential warfare that is part of their picture
of Zen practice. Instead of this they receive some simple instructions in posture and are told to "just sit." For this sitting, or *zazen*,

---

* Such as the now famous "What is the sound of one hand clapping?"

they are invited to join the other students at Zen Center early each morning and in the evening.

"Just sit": hardly a gauntlet thrown at the feet of the aspirant! But, in its way, this is the great koan of Soto Zen: "Just sit." Only it does not manifest immediately as a challenge, nor does it correspond to the student's preconceived idea of a test: some external difficulty which he must overcome to obtain what is desirable. Such "tests," which face all men throughout their lives, leave the individual basically unchanged. One passes or fails, one gets what one wants or one does not. But the wanting, the desiring, itself remains: unexperienced, unknown except as the object of a kind of thinking which is itself in the service of another desire in the "ego."

The students come before sunrise to an old synagogue in the center of San Francisco's Japanese section. Inside the building little has been changed. It is extraordinarily clean and quiet. In the main auditorium, some figures of the Buddha have replaced the ark of the covenant, and upstairs the large meeting room now serves as a *zendo,* the main room for the sitting. *Zafus,* the small, nearly spherical black sitting cushions, are lined against the wall in fresh precision, tatami mats cover the floor and at the head of the room is an altar holding figures of the Buddha and Bodhisattvas. Small black cushions are also arranged outside the zendo in the balcony of the auditorium. In Orthodox synagogues, the balcony is the place reserved for women, but now this one is used for the newer students practicing their zazen.

This is, then, very much a Western building,* but one touched by a Far Eastern light. In the history of the spread of Buddhism, it has always been so: as Buddhism moved out of India to China,

---

* As this book was going to press, the students moved to a large new building where they are all housed together, and where the Master now also resides with them. Strange to say, the Star of David also decorates this building, which was a residence club for young Jewish women. The reader is free to draw his own conclusions about the interlocking karma of Judaism and Buddhism in America.

Tibet, Japan, and throughout the rest of Asia, it was not its way to replace the traditional forms and structures of the culture it was entering. It seems never to have arrived as a substitute for anything, never as a new religion. In this, of course, it is unlike the well-known aspects of Western religious-missionary activity. Nor does Buddhism seem to come as a synthesis, or bringing-together of the various traditions in a culture.

It is true that there are many rigorous forms of practice connected with Zen Center, most of which are obviously rooted deep in the traditions of Japanese-Zen practice. The picture before our eyes will, therefore, be this: American men and women, many of them young; their faces are our faces and the faces of our children; their manner, their dress, their walk—far from the self-indulgence of an escapist. Except for a lack of extremeness in their behavior and talk, they seem quite ordinary and varied.

Yet there they are in California, seated in the lotus posture, monotonously chanting—in Japanese—"Form is emptiness, emptiness is form," words and concepts we simply cannot understand. Then there is the extraordinarily detailed "ritual" of taking meals together, the unwrapping and wrapping of the bowls, the bowing as each portion is served. Is this not the process of institutionalizing a new structure of ritual forms? In a way, the answer must be *yes*. But, in a much more interesting sense, it is really not so. For the center, the axis around which all the forms revolve, and for which all the forms are instrumental, is just: *sitting*.

All the ritual forms are means to an end; one might very well call them practical aids toward the awakening of experience. Such a goal is strange to the average man because he usually seeks a certain *kind* of experience, whereas the goal of Zen practice is the experiencing itself, no matter what it is experience of.

Our well-known Western religious rituals, for example, provide a certain kind of experience, and most of us participate in them in order to have such experiences: the experience of God, of repentance, of consolation, of being understood or accepted, of harmony, of awe. But the Zen teaching is that we err in expecting these future experiences to make us complete and whole. In fact, when we are "having" these experiences, we are not really having them at all. Even in the midst of these rituals, we are still seeking the experience that awaits us in the next minute or hour. We are always seeking for the completing experience, and when certain pleasant feelings finally arise in us, our minds merely label them as the experience we looked for. In a word, something makes us unable to have the experiences we seek, because something makes us unable to have experience itself. We are always seeking, expecting.

This is the basis of what appears to be the anti-religious nature of much Zen writing. If religion strengthens, instead of dissolves, the mental habit of expecting, it ceases to operate as a means of realization or "salvation."

When such ideas first appeared in contemporary America, many people—especially the young—took them as sanctioning a sort of libertinism. But they obviously provide no such sanction, since libertinism under any name is equally the seeking for certain kinds of experience.

Drugs and "Extraordinary" Experience

This misconception naturally brings up the question of drugs and "the drug experience." Regarded in this way, it is already clear why the taking of drugs forms no part of the practice at Zen Center. To take drugs is to crave a certain experience. And to crave a certain experience is to deny, now and here, the Buddha nature in oneself; it is to believe that, now and here, one is incomplete. In this belief, one denies the present possibility of experiencing oneself, and one lives in and for the future no less than does someone craving a "life beyond the grave." In Zen this is called deluded thinking.

Nonetheless, almost all of the American students I interviewed spoke with respect of drugs such as LSD. Some said that without the drug experience they would never have been opened up to the possibilities in themselves which are being realized in their Zen

practice. Drugs gave them, so to say, a "taste" or "glimpse" of enlightenment. Yet those who continue to take drugs almost never
persist beyond the beginning stages of practice at Zen Center.
Conversely, those who persist gradually reduce and, eventually,
stop the use of drugs.

This state of affairs throws some interesting light on the nature
of the drug experience itself and how it differs from "enlightenment." Over a period of time, the regular practice of zazen seems
to weaken the motives that lead so many young people to drugs.
One young woman said that after a year at Zen Center she was
more able to accept other people as they really are, without expecting things of them in advance. Even more important: she was
more willing and able to accept herself for what she was, whatever
she was.

Something of this attitude of alert acceptance was communicated in one way or another by all of the older students (older in
terms of length of time at Zen Center). By "alert acceptance" I
mean the simultaneous acceptance of both what appears in one's
mind and what appears in the external world, particularly the behavior of others. Even an instant of such simultaneous acceptance
is probably a glimpse of what Zen means by, enlightenment. It is
this quality of acceptance (so different from the "long-suffering"
passivity which acceptance usually implies) that, I think, weakens
the need for drugs.

Indirectly, and over a long period of time, the desire itself for
the drug experience comes to be experienced. As the desire is experienced, it is placed—not in so many words, perhaps—as merely
one among all other desires and aspects of the personality.

We might speculate here that ordinarily, without such a discipline as Zen offers, the desire for the drug experience is itself ele-
vated by other aspects of the personality. The desire itself is desired,
or defended, or—on the other hand—hated and feared. My own
impression of many drug users, even the most intelligent and so-
phisticated, and even those who write so brilliantly about it, is
that they lack this remarkable quality of acceptance. Rather, they

defend and adore their desire. Consequently—because the personality is freighted with so many varied and contradictory impulses and aspects—portions of the personality come to be denied or rejected. Such rejection is, again, what Zen calls the deluded mind.

It is a well-known theory that what are called the mind-expanding drugs act, really, as inhibitors of certain mental or emotional functions, thus "releasing" others. Whether, this is physiologically true or not, those who take drugs consistently report that the ordinary categorizing and logical function of the mind disappears in the drug experience. In the absence of this functioning, the world takes on an incredible beauty and power, things come alive in their exquisite variety; the universe changes each moment, colors, sounds, tastes become ends in themselves.

But all of this, remarkable as it may be in one sense, has no relationship to the Buddhist idea of enlightenment. For, the drug experience is still based on the idea of exclusion and on the judgment that the "ordinary" state of what is called "being uptight" needs to be destroyed or suppressed. But enlightenment involves, rather, the experience of this "uptightness," this ordinary mind. Moreover, this experience can be awakened now, at this instant. There is nothing to wait for, to expect; nothing to do, or to take.

If the effort to awaken this experience is not made now, at this instant, then one has totally misunderstood the idea of Buddha-nature, and one is still submerged in the state of delusion and desire—delusion all the darker if what is desired is given the name enlightenment.

No one will deny that the drug experience is extraordinary. But what does that mean: "extraordinary"? It means, among other things, that certain standards are fulfilled, certain personal criteria are met or even surpassed. But where do these standards and requirements come from? From oneself, obviously; they are yet another expression or form of desire. And so, it is the direct experiencing of these requirements or desires, rather than the satisfaction of them, that constitutes a moment of enlightenment. It is a question of the experience of the ordinary, rather than the search for extraordinary experience.

The Zen term for enlightenment is, of course, satori, and one finds much discussion of satori in the literature of the Rinzai sect. Soto Zen brings the reminder that this satori is not an "extraordinary experience." Thus there is very little talk of satori at Zen Center.

> People who practice Zen aren't so interested in enlightenment. People who want to practice Zen are interested in enlightenment because they think Zen people have it.

The speaker is a man in his thirties. He was asked about the aim of his Zen practice:

> The trouble with an idea like "aim" is that if you have an aim, it suggests that you're not satisfied with what you have. And if you're not satisfied with what you have, you can never practice Zen . .

Difficulties

Yet, there is no question that these students of Zen are engaged in a struggle; there is a labor in their practice. Zen is not easy.

> The kind of situation we have here is where people really include themselves in or out. At some point, you really have to be serious to stay. It's hard to do it.

"In what way is it hard?" I asked.

> I really don't understand the practice well enough to answer that question the way it should be answered, but, my own experience has been that practicing zazen, sitting meditation, has made me much more aware of myself and of what's

going on. And I find myself repeatedly wanting to run away from that process. There's some very old patterns and very old habits of running away from certain things in yourself.

Also, it's hard to be living in the city, with the kind of distractions there are in the city. There's a kind of pace in living in the city and it's very easy to stay up late and talk to people. And so, a practice which demands that you regulate your life to go sit at five or five-thirty in the morning with some kind of rhythm which becomes your life rhythm—that's hard.

Responding to this same question, another student said, "It's the sitting that sifts people out." He continued:

Some people are just too active in body or mind. Sitting doesn't appeal to them. Sitting is really very boring. And if you're still interested in grooving or having a good time, or in some ecstatic religious experience, then sitting is not what you want. There's no ecstasy involved in it. There is a joy and there is a bliss, but it's not what we usually think of as joy and bliss.

What he then said I found especially interesting:

I've been sitting zazen for years and I still don't like it particularly. It makes me mad. I shake, sometimes very violently.

The difficulties and rewards of Zen practice are, of course, greatly accentuated during the intensive practice period known as *sesshin*. Sesshin lasts anywhere from a day to a week. During that time the student sits from morning to evening with short breaks every forty minutes and with a few pauses for taking a silent meal or, in the evening, listening to a lecture. Even more demanding is *tangaryo*, a period of days in which the student also sits from four in the morning to ten at night with pauses only for the communal meals.

In their publication, *The Wind Bell,* the students write about their past experience with tangaryo at the mountain retreat at Tassajara.[*]

> The students were not told what to expect from tangaryo . . . All Roshi (the Master) said was, "Be prepared to sit." And that we did, for three days straight from four in the morning until ten at night with no breaks except for eating.
>
> . . . It tested us to our utmost in a way most of us had never experienced before. And yet we knew the test was an encounter with ourselves in a way and in a situation which could only help us. Many experiences come out of a practice like this. After tangaryo there was a kind of alert joyful feeling at Tassajara that lasted throughout the practice period.[1]

Like everything else about Zen Center, the "testing" is all self-administered:

> The advice to just "be prepared to sit" means that the student should be inwardly prepared to have an experience that . . . there are no guidelines for . . . The student must decide for himself how long he is going to sit in one position, how long he will change his position, with what dignity and composure can he live during the time of tangaryo.
>
> . . . It is a kind of time/space experiment which the student freely enters into by himself, in which his own functionings become the unavoidable subject of his attention. It

* The name of the Zen Mountain Center, located some 150 miles south of San Francisco. See page 67.

is here that he decides whether this practice which throws his self and being into such relief is what he can and wants to do.[2]

The intensive practice periods, sesshin and tangaryo, are approached by the students with "anticipation and dread,"even though there is not an atom of psychological compulsion about them. Any idea of success or failure exists solely in the mind of the student and does not come from the Master.

One such "failure" was a young man who left Zen Center to enter the Christian ministry. He had no difficulty adapting to the daily rhythm of morning and evening zazen in San Francisco, but his experience of intensive practice and the extended communal work at Tassajara was, in, his words, "a disaster."

I had felt for a long time that I couldn't do sesshin. But in Zen Center in San Francisco it didn't matter. My home was my base. Zen was the most important thing to me, but I could always walk in and walk out. But at the monastery I lived there all the time, day and night, and there wasn't any escape from the fact that I couldn't do it.

This young man is now attending a theological seminary in the San Francisco area. I asked him if he felt his four years with Zen Center had changed him:

Yes. I'm less interested in being calm. I'm more willing to live in a way that makes me tired and agitated. I used to be interested in a kind of serenity. But now I'm more willing to hassle things . . . I'm less moody, I'm more able to go through things, including being angry . . .

I wanted to know why these students came to Zen, rather than to psychotherapy. One man answered me this way:

I had some feeling that everyday life as most people are living it is not enough—it's not fulfilling. Desires that we have and satisfy—that's not enough. That isn't what I really want. All the things that I wanted, they weren't what I wanted. Something more basic, something deeper—it wasn't a woman, a family, a car, or education, or money, or anything like that. And . . . when I had those things, that wasn't it. And it wasn't just a matter of getting rid of anxieties—so that I could work better so that I could have money, or something like that.

I think most psychiatry has to do with what we call small mind and straightening out the small mind. It's still not as deep . . . doesn't extend to big mind. Doesn't go beyond samsara (the ceaseless, repetitive flux in which the unenlightened are imprisoned). Psychotherapy tends to enable you to get along more smoothly and in a certain sense more fulfillingly, in the samsaric world.

Suzuki Roshi

WHAT IS A MASTER?

Shunryu Suzuki is the man through whom the work at Zen Center is sustained and guided. He is called *Roshi,* meaning "master" or "teacher." Short and slight, he appears to be in his early sixties; his head is shaved, and he wears the robes of a priest. One's overwhelming first impression is of openness and warmth. He laughs often, noiselessly—and when I was with him, trying to discuss "profound questions," I found myself laughing with him throughout the interview. Beneath the lightness and the gentleness, however, one feels as well his tremendous rigor; more than one student has called him "awesome."

But apart from describing him further, the question naturally arises: *what* does a Zen Master teach?

In order to approach that question, one must, I think, ask another question first: *whom* does a Zen Master teach?

When, for example, Roshi first came to the United States in 1959, it was as a priest of the Japanese Zen Buddhist congregation in San Francisco. Only when he was sought out by some young Americans did he respond with Zen instruction geared to their minds and backgrounds. The development of Zen Center, from its very slight beginnings with a handful of students to its present scale of activity, can only be understood as Suzuki Roshi's *response* to the sincerity of his American pupils. The fact that he now devotes so much of his time and energies to the Americans—more so, now, than to the Japanese—is a measure of that sincerity.[*]

Said one student:

I came because I was desperate. People come and stay because they're desperate. Not in an insane way. Desperate, not disturbed. Roshi says that if you're disturbed, you can't sit.

There's a piece of wood at Tassajara with a Japanese inscription on it, and, roughly translated, it says "Pardon me, but Zen is a matter of life and death."

Another young man, comparing the American pupils with some of the San Francisco Japanese community, said the Japanese are where the Americans were twenty-five years ago: "hung-up on cars, success, material things."

It's amazing who Roshi takes under his wing. Some of his closest disciples are people who if you looked at them you wouldn't believe it. People you'd think were pathetic, or inept. And he gives them some responsible position or something. It's wonderful what he's able to see in people; he sees their potential, he sees something in them that the rest of us don't see.

---

[*] Recently, Roshi separated himself completely from the Japanese congregation to devote full time to his American pupils.

Whatever it is which a master like Suzuki teaches, it can only exist as a response to this quality of sincerity or desperation. If the desperation is deep and persistent, then the process of teaching is deep and persistent. When some of the older students say that Roshi is "always teaching," it means that he is always responding to their sincerity. Of course, this responding can be rather subtle and is certainly invisible to an outsider or even to a student whose need is not quite so intense. Such a student will receive a response appropriate to the degree of his sincerity.

Now, the remarkable thing is that this sincerity is not necessarily manifested in the intellect, or consciousness, what Suzuki calls "the thinking mind." Suzuki has said that man has more than one mind, and that the thinking mind in the head (which we usually identify as *the* mind and even the "self") is, as it were, only a "branch office" of the more fundamental mind known as the *hara* centered in the abdomen. Thus, a man may be in despair without "thinking" or "knowing" it in any simple or clear way. Conversely, a man may believe he is seeking Zen practice and instruction, but this search may be only an idea in the thinking mind.

The process of teaching is not directed primarily to the thinking mind. One might say it is directed to the unconscious mind, but nowadays such an expression is associated with certain psychoanalytic concepts which are themselves products of the thinking mind. In any event, the teaching is not done mainly with words. Thus, to the degree that a man is identified with verbal or conceptual formulations, the process of teaching is either incomprehensible or invisible. For those without sincerity or desperation, it is even unreceivable.

"Roshi is a teacher because he lives what he says."

"In his presence everything is different. Whatever he does or says to you, in passing or just very lightly, it gets you right in the gut." Saying this, the student, a man in his forties, pounded his fist against his belly. "Like a sword," he said. In *The Wind Bell,* the students wrote:

> One of the most helpful experiences for the students was to work with him or just watch him working . . . But it was not just his skill in moving huge stones to direct the course of the stream, or in shaping stones to rebuild the large supporting wall under the bridge that affected the students so directly. It was the energy and attention with which he did his work. He seemed able to work without rest all day long, even when moving bigger stones than anyone else, and by midday to completely tire out the strapping students who were working with him. One student who was helping him finally observed that Roshi was always at rest, unless he was directly pushing on a stone, and that even when he fell he was relaxed and found his balance naturally. Suzuki Roshi is very modest, even embarrassed about this and says that he is too attached to hard work; but to the students he is what they hoped a Zen Master would be like.[3]

Equally instructive—perhaps more so—for the students is Roshi's ability to live the instantaneous self-acceptance of the enlightened, whether he is coughing, sneezing, or even dozing during zazen. In this sense, he teaches by example, by what he is—not so much by what he says. This, plus the quality of immediate and appropriate response to sincere need, plus no doubt many other things of which I am not aware, helps the student to practice zazen right there on the spot. It is as though his presence is, for the sincere student, a continuous and varied reminder that he, the student, is the Buddha.

Such a reminder is no balm for the ego. Quite the contrary. Since most emotional crises of our daily life manifest as the desire for something external—be it words of praise, or a material thing—this reminder is a call to discover within oneself the strength and freedom to experience the crises, rather than to re-solve them. Thus the famous Zen saying: "I owe everything to my teacher because he taught me nothing."

It is not an easeful thing to live in the presence of such a teacher.

THE USES OF RITUAL

The ritual forms at Zen Center and at Tassajara are also such re-minders. One obvious example is the frequent bowing, with the hands pressed together under the chin. In the meal ceremony, known as *oriyaki,* the one serving the food or bringing the wash-ing bucket bows to each student he serves, and each student bows in return. In such cases, one is not bowing to this Smith or that Jones, but to the Buddha-nature in Smith and in Jones.

For Americans, educated in ideals of independence and human equality, such bowing to another is difficult. Probably for that very reason it can be an especially effective reminder that one's usual sense of self does not correspond to the latent Buddha-nature. Even more uncomfortable is the experience of being bowed to, especially by the Master himself!

Another function of the ritual forms which Suzuki Roshi has brought is the training of attention or "mindfulness." I was told that the eating ceremony was itself a form of zazen in which the forms were so complicated that a certain sort of mindfulness was absolutely essential. This work on attention is related to the task of engaging the whole of oneself in any activity. It is thus an im-portant tool in the gradual discovery of one's original unity.

This discovery, however, is not associated with any particular successful performance of the ritual. In one of his lectures, Suzuki likened these forms to a handle by means of which one lifts a cup. "We try not to make mistakes," he said, "but only as a help to-ward engaging ourself. Not making mistakes is not the main thing."

Another of his lectures began this way:

I want to explain shikan taza, what it means just to sit. Some monk said to a Zen Master, "It is very hot. How is it possible to sit somewhere, where there is no hot or no cold weather?" The Master answered, "When it is hot you should be hot Buddha. When it is cold you should be cold Buddha."

Even though we say *just to sit,* to understand this is rather difficult and that may be why Dogen Zenji (the thirteenth-century Master who brought Soto to Japan) left us so many teachings . . . When you sit you know what he means without thinking or expecting anything; When you accept yourself as a Buddha, or understand everything as an unfolding of the absolute teaching, the truth, the first principle, or as a part of the great being, when you reach this understanding, whatever you think or see is the actual practice of Buddha. Problems arise because you are trying to do something or because you think that nothing will result from doing something or because you feel that you rely on something.[4]

THE PLACE OF THE INTELLECT

Americans accustomed to the available literature about Rinzai Zen are often surprised by the fact that at Zen Center there is a great deal of intellectual study and frequent lectures by Roshi. After one lecture that dealt with the excessive influence of the thinking mind and the lack of contact with the more fundamental mind called hara, one student asked the Roshi: "With which mind should we try to listen to your lectures?" Suzuki paused for a moment and then, with his usual gentle laugh, answered, "With the thinking mind. These lectures are *sword,*" he said, with a short sweep of his *kyosaku* (the flat stick used to whack the faltering sitter). "They are sword to kill thinking mind. But when we say kill thinking mind, we mean become free from it, its authority."

At Zen Center, there is no attempt at suppression of thought. The teaching, said to be more profound than the thinking mind can reach, nevertheless must manifest in a form that reaches the thinking mind—another example of the appropriateness of response that characterizes the way of Zen. Similarly, a teacher who presumably is communicating from and to the more fundamental mind recognizes that, man being what he is, communication through the thinking mind is also necessary. The tendency of all valid zazen experience to drift into the rigid forms of thinking mind must be met by a quality and structure of thought that itself is rooted in the fundamental mind of the Master and his teaching. Only in this way can the student be helped to experience rather than reject his thinking mind—for that too is the Buddha!

I personally witnessed several striking examples of the way Suzuki communicates to his students on the level of thought and ideas. At one lecture in San Francisco a student raised the question of being natural. To appreciate Suzuki's response, one must remember that his audience of students is made up almost entirely of men and women under thirty-five, most under thirty. Many of them are barefooted or wear sandals (said one student to me: "everyone here is an ex-hippie"). Most of them live in a communal setting in the adjacent block of old Victorian houses rented by Zen Center. And although most of them have given up the use of drugs, earn their own living and, in general, participate effectively in society, they do not really believe in this society and are strongly and seriously drawn to the ideals of "naturalness."

Suzuki answered, addressing all who were present:

"You like naturalness so much. I think you cling to it, it is not natural anymore . . . " Even as he said this I felt the audience register the shock of recognition of the teaching and its special perspective.

"Natural means to do something without any idea of what result will come. We are very unnatural beings. Before we discuss 'natural' we should know how unnatural our life is.

"To go to extremes is natural for you. Your naturalness is to eat as much as you want. But that is not the naturalness we mean. Natural mind means more flexible mind, without sticking to something. When our mind is perfectly free and open to everything—like a mirror—it is natural mind."

This was all said very lightly, with smiles and quiet laughter echoed by the students. At the same time, as he spoke, they all seemed to sit up straighter. Suzuki was utterly turning around their beloved ideal of naturalness and through their own special language was, to some degree, reaching the part of them which sincerely wished to struggle for inner change.

"Your naturalness is just superstition. It is not so natural. May be only the 'naturalness' that comes out of thinking mind."

From the way he interacts with his audience, it is clear that these public lectures are manifestations of the master's presence and therefore part of his way and his means of pointing to something beyond words.

One student asked the following:

It seems that sometimes you emphasize the idea of non-attainment, that there is nothing to do except simply give up and sit and be whatever you are at each instant. Yet at other times it seems that you speak of exerting your best effort, and when I think of exerting my best effort it is in order to attain something. Why bother speaking about effort at all? Why not stay to the teaching of not trying to do anything?

To this, Suzuki replied:

That is a very good question. Even though I say 'do whatever you want' you are doing something with some effort. Can you do it without any effort? No, you cannot . . . If you weren't making an effort, didn't sit, hadn't come to Tassajara, I don't know what you would be doing right now.

But for you to know what you are doing moment after moment is very important.

If your purpose for doing zazen is *just to sit*, then it is possible for you to improve yourself, to find out what direction you are going in. But before you realize who you are, it is not possible for you to go your own direction. Because you are bound by some idea, you cannot find your way for yourself. Only when you can *just sit* can you find your way.

I am explaining this as if it were some good teaching, as if I knew some secret. It is not so, I am speaking about everyone's own way. Why we put emphasis on *just to sit* is because everyone does have his own way. There are myriads of ways . . . and moment after moment you will find your own way when you are exactly you yourself.[5]

Another student then asked if it were possible to be *just* angry and nothing else. Suzuki's reply to this was extremely interesting, especially as contrasted with certain modern psychological teachings and methods which encourage the "honest expression" of such things as anger. Suzuki said:

"If you could forget all about anger after you were angry, that would be good. But usually anger lasts for a long time because ideas like 'he made me angry' or 'I am no good' afterwards make you even more angry. Then you are not *just* you. That is why we say you cannot *just* sit when you are angry . . . Anger, greed and delusion appear when you are not *just* you."

"But," said the student, "is it possible to forget about everything, just become so foolish, greedy, or angry that you don't think of anything else?"

"I don't think so. Animals may be able to but not human beings."

"What about *just* loving?"

"Love is usually a very egocentric idea. We know that, but we make some excuse for it. We know pretty well why we love; there are many becauses. You don't *just* love anyone. Love is a very mysterious thing. Don't laugh."

Then, he concluded:

"We don't say that anger is not good, anger that is *just* anger, that is. But if you find or have some excuse for being angry . . . that is not *just* anger. And unless you practice our way . . . it is rather difficult to be *just* angry—like a thunderstorm. Kiiihh! Next moment nothing. That is beautiful. Raaa! That's all. I wish I could do that."[6]

THE QUESTION OF DISCIPLINE

I spoke to one pupil who at the age of twenty had entered a Japanese Rinzai Zen monastery, remained there a year and a half and then left in a state of great discouragement:

> I got sort of overwhelmed by this business of enlightenment . . . and this "true self" and these kind of terms—I got a heavy trip laid on me there . . . you gotta find this and you gotta find that. But I wasn't especially looking for it, though I dug the way the monks did zazen, but as far as those abstract terms—I wasn't into that and consequently, I suppose, I couldn't get into koan study. I sort of came in not knowing what I was looking for and I couldn't get with what I was supposed to be looking for . . . I mean, satori, that wasn't what interested me . . . it just wasn't my problem—it may be my problem yet to come, but dammit, I don't want that problem if it's not my problem. I was really worried about it, and okay, I'll do it, I'll try. It got harder and harder and I got all tight, and they say, keep trying, and it gets tighter and tighter and then . . . bleeagh! I was a— well, a wreck, to put it bluntly. I felt: well, I can't make it at Zen. They said you haven't got enough faith, so I say okay, faith, so I'll work on that. But where can you drum up faith? Or not enough energy or concentration—okay, so

what to concentrate on . . . ? Anyway, I sort of flipped out,
came home to my parents and sort of went through a scene
with them—let them have it . . . and that didn't help, upset
my mom. I went back to school and everything was very
difficult after that monastery. In the meantime I'd taken
acid a couple of times—and it was a means of opening some
things up. I had been away from Zen for three years. The
acid kind of turned over the ground, it really socked it home
to me what I'd been through. It opened up the ground of
the idea of the need to practice . . . maybe for the first time
feeling the need to practice. Instead of saying like I want to
do zazen because like it's groovy or something . . . But here
at Tassajara it's the kind of work that really involves me,
carpentry, keeping up the place—it's just enough more than
I can handle; every day it's a problem, it really involves you.
In Japan they don't even work in their own garden, just a
little sweeping, not the kind of thing I could get
into . . . . I had been looking for a Zen gardener or Zen
painter and I couldn't find them there. In a sense I found
them here—I mean Roshi's pretty much a gardener and I
really dig the way he feels for rocks—like there's only one
way they go in the ground. I just wasn't interested in the
way they did it in Japan. The way Roshi is here . . . I mean
some people may put him down for being "soft," but God-
dammit, he speaks right to us. The difference was that there
Rinzai was push, push, push, but I couldn't care where I was
going, you know—and *here* with Roshi it's kind of like right
in front of us. It's not a question of reflecting back on myself whether I'm good enough, no more so than anything in
the world where you gotta get yourself together. But like
hearing him talk, and the way he puts it all together—I just
want to do it, I want to do it, it's something for us, there's
no question about it. And it isn't that pressure that you
gotta do it now and you gotta do it here . . . I don't know,
in so many ways he tied so many things together and yet in

such a beautiful way, you know, a little bit at a time, or in an indirect kind of way . . . that it, it just dawns on you . . . Well, so, it didn't come to me right away here, but after a few months listening to him and then after that first sesshin, well, I went out and told him that that was it, that I wanted to be considered his disciple . . . Like I don't talk with him very much on a formal master-disciple level, but all the stuff is clean in my head, I mean, hell, I don't know if it's even Zen, and I don't care. I mean with the kids that come here—like with my background with drugs and so on—they feel their own personal problem so much that you don't have to lay *that* on them, I mean like the problem I had in Japan. People that come here need a problem that's big enough for them to work on but not too big for them to handle, and . . . in an infinite number of ways that's what happens down here . . . and yet you can't say what it is, it's not based on enlightenment, on gaining anything or attaining anything. I mean Roshi makes that pretty clear that there's nothing to gain. I'd be pretty hard-pressed if someone were to lay it on me and ask me . . . I don't know, but there's no question about wanting to do it.

The point at issue is not the severity of external discipline, but of how the idea of discipline is communicated to these young Americans. In one of the earlier sesshins, Suzuki presented it this way:

When you practice zazen, you will of course have physical pain in your legs and mentally you will have some difficulty. You will find it difficult to be concentrated on your breathing . . . I have many difficulties in my practice, so I think you, too, will find it very difficult to sit in good zazen. The difficulties you have in zazen should not all take place outside your mind. Your efforts should be kept within your mind. You have to accept the difficulty as not being other than what you are.

You should not try to make some tentative particular effort based on small mind like: "my practice should be better." *My* practice, you say, but zazen is not your practice, it is Buddha's practice . . . Your effort is based on Big-Mind which you cannot get out of. If your small self begins to act without the care of Big-Mind, that is not Zen . . . Our practice should be based on *Mind,* our original way-seeking mind which works on and on continuously.

(This) secret of practice is also true in observation of Buddhist precepts. The dualistic idea of whether or not to observe the precepts takes place within your *mind* when you practice Zen.[7]

In this way, Suzuki brings home the remarkable orientation of Zen discipline: that there are no external precepts to break and no one who is breaking them. Yet precepts are given and effort must be made to adhere to them. The effort is to be made, but the failure is also part of oneself and is to be experienced. Thus does Zen widen the stage of the self.

To make up your mind to make the very best effort to observe the precepts constantly, forever, whether your effort is complete or not, is Buddha's, Buddha-Mind's effort. If your activity is involved in Buddha's activity, whatever you do is Buddha's effort. Then even if it is not perfect, you are manifesting Buddha's mercy and activity.

Some form is necessary because it is not possible to be concentrated on an uncertain way. There must be strict rules to observe. Because of the rules, of the ways of sitting, of the way of practice, it is possible to be concentrated.

. . . My master Kishzawa Roshi used to say that we had to have a vow or aim to accomplish. The aim we have may not be perfect in its strict sense, but even so it is necessary for us to have it. It is like the precepts. Even though it is almost impossible to observe them, we must have them.

Without an aim in our life and the precepts we cannot . . . actualize our way.

. . . Strictly speaking we must have more precepts in
America. You think 250 precepts for men and 500 for
women is awful and that it should be made simpler. But I
think you have to add some more to the precepts we have in
Japan. Actually, I think you will have more difficulty in
practicing zazen in America than we do in Japan. This kind
of difficulty should be continued forever or we will not have
peace in our world.

By reflecting on our human life and by respecting the
precepts and rules of humanity, we will know the direction
in which to make an effort and we will have the right orientation in our life.[8]

In another lecture, he told of conducting a service for numerous American Buddhists at a large church in San Francisco. He
decided to have everyone bow (meaning, in this case, full prostration with head touching floor) "in the way we usually do at Zen
Center":

But someone said if we bow in that way, people may be
discouraged. It is true, very true. I know people will be discouraged. I know we are causing a lot of discouragement for
American people when we bow nine times, when they bow
only three times in Japan. I know that very well. So I bow
nine times here in America. Buddhism needs our continual
effort eternally. Until you are interested in this point you
cannot understand Buddhism.[9]

And, finally,

Eternity is in mortality. When you become a mortal being through and through you will acquire immortality.
When you are absorbed in sheer ignorant practice, you have

enlightenment. So in order to be a true Buddhist, you must find the meaning of life in your limited activity. There is no need you to be a great man. In your limited activity you should find out the true meaning of yourself. If you pick up even a small stone you have the whole universe. But if you try to pick up the tail of a comet you will be crazy. For this limited activity, we need . . . precepts . . . [10]

How Suzuki interprets these precepts (such as do not kill, do not steal, do not commit adultery, etc.) is quite another story. His interpretation of these precepts is such as to help the student resist externalizing them, setting himself over against them and thereby narrowing the stage of his practice by excluding or rejecting "failure." "Do not kill means to realize our true nature. It does not mean just to have mercy. It is deeper than that." Or: "Do not sell liquor means not to boast or emphasize the advantages of things. . . . If you boast about the profundity of Buddhist teaching, you are selling a kind of liquor to the people. Any spiritual teaching by which we are intoxicated is a kind of liquor. Do not sell liquor means absolute freedom from all teachings. We should keep our precepts and yet not be bound by them. That is our way."

Toward Suzuki, every student feels the same thing: love, respect and the willingness to obey. Among these students, young and old, are many of the sort which we would ordinarily call "fiercely independent spirits." From all that has been said, it is perhaps understandable that this sense of independence is increased, rather than decreased, by obedience to the teaching and its forms as they are exemplified in the presence of the teacher.

I asked many of the younger ones what their future plans were. One said, "It's up to Rqshi"; another: "I feel that my life is in Roshi's hands." My initial reaction to this was that there was a great deal of sentimentality in their attitude. Perhaps this is true, but it is now a bit clearer to me that this "It's up to Roshi" means also: "It's up to that in myself which can be sensitive to the Master and his teaching, the master in myself, the Buddha-nature."

Tassajara

AN AMERICAN ZEN MONASTERY

Zen Mountain Center—*Zenshinji,* meaning Zen mind/heart temple in Japanese—is now the center of gravity of Zen practice in America, and, perhaps, the whole Western world. It is situated within some five hundred acres of rugged mountain land about one hundred and fifty miles south of San Francisco. By car it can be reached only by driving over twenty miles of precipitious, winding dirt road that is impassable to ordinary traffic eight months out of the year. The only other access is by foot over the mountain trails of Los Padres National Forest which surrounds it. For American Zen students, it is a dream come true.

Before its purchase by Zen Center in 1966, it was known as Tassajara Hot Springs and was the site of a secluded resort hotel which catered to a clientele seeking the refreshment of woods and stream, and intense starry nights. The owner of the hotel, seeking to preserve its natural beauty, held back from selling until he found a buyer who shared his feeling for the area. Zen Center was that buyer.

The students immediately set to work raising a large sum of money in the form of benefit performances by dozens of artists and entertainers and by donations from well-wishers throughout the country. When the money appeared, a huge amount, it was a concrete indication of how the ground had already been prepared in America. America was very much "Zen conscious."

At the same time, other students began the task of putting Tassajara into physical order. They rebuilt the large stone-and-stucco house, redesigned the porches to fit the natural, curves of the clear, winding creek. Partitions were removed, hardwood floors put in, door openings walled up, windows replaced, redwood lamps in-

stalled, and the interior furnished anew with furniture carved
from old fence posts.

Another building, an old slatestone dining room dating from
the late 1890s, was converted into a zendo (meditation and dining hall) by removing the bar and constructing an altar over the
open hearth. The many cabins on the premises were painted and
reshingled. The cold springs and hot springs reservoirs and the
springs themselves were reroofed and an old bathhouse by the
pool was torn down. The area around all the buildings was cleared
of fire-hazardous brush, a vegetable garden was planted, landscap-
ing started, and root-infested pipes were replaced.

Quoting again from *The Wind Bell:*

> (The) beginner's spirit pervades the practice and activity in
> San Francisco and Tassajara. Everything is done by the Stu-
> dents and there is little distinction between leaders and
> workers. We grow as much of our food as is possible, cook
> for and serve ourselves, repair, maintain and build the fa-
> cilities, raise the money to purchase them, administer the
> monastery, and develop the practice there. We had learned
> how to find our own way by having experienced eight years
> of taking care of Zen Center in San Francisco. By not hav-
> ing many explanations from Suzuki Roshi on how many
> sesshins there should be, how often we should meditate
> each day, or as to why we bowed, chanted or meditated in a
> certain way, we developed over the years an independence
> and an understanding of our own practice and how to take
> care of group practice. Thus we knew something of how to
> approach the development of Tassajara, and to come to our
> own determination about the need for strictness and free-
> dom in Zen practice.[11]

The need for intensive group practice and prolonged periods
of exposure to the master was, of course, the central and closest
reason for the development of Zen Mountain Center. To see it in

operation and to observe its effects on the students raises some interesting general questions about the nature and function of monastic life in all religions.

WHAT IS A MONK?

In modern times, most Westerners have come to accept this rather grim picture of a monk: not quite strong enough for the pressures of ordinary society, he retreats to a secluded and protected place where he and others like him may devote their lives to God. It is a picture of a man starving himself existentially, cutting himself off from the vital forces of life, a man "holier" than we, but less human as well. Granting him his slightly questionable mystical communion, he is envied by us only in those moments when the press of life seems unendurable. In such moments we ourselves dream of "going off to a monastery or something." It is one step short of wishing ourselves dead; at best it is very much like the need for rest and respite. One recognizes that the life of a monk is not easy; he rises early, the labors hard at some physical or mental task, he eats little, etc. But, in our moments of stress or disillusionment—and only in such moments—this seems a small price to pay for the luxury of being told what to do.

At Tassajara, however, one comes to see monasticism not as a flight from society, but to society. The principle difference between the monastic society and ours is surely not that ours is more real, but that in this monastery everyone has a common aim. Moreover, this aim is for themselves: each to awaken to his true nature, each to "find his own way."

In such a community, there exists the constant danger that in the name of charity and kindness someone will find my way for me, will directly or indirectly tell me what to do, what is good and what bad. As a result, I may find a way, but not my own way; I will discover a nature, but not necessarily my own nature.

This "danger" is rooted in an overwhelming force inherent in human nature: to put it in Buddhist terms it is the deep-rooted belief that inwardly we are incomplete and can reach completeness and actualization only by acquiring something external to ourselves: be it material things, "love," "knowledge," "respect," etc. The hardness and unsentimentality of the Zen community, called the *sangha,* is based on a precise awareness of this tendency in man and on the axioms that man is both essentially alone and essentially complete.

But what is complete is the Buddha-nature—not what we may now call the human-nature. This distinction is crucial, at least for a long time along the way. The experiencing of our human nature, of our faults and weaknesses, our wavering and anxiety, our desires and fears, is in itself a complete experience, a complete actualization of the Buddha-mind. The Buddhist way is lost when what is wished for is completion and perfection of the human-nature. This explains, to some degree, why the hardness of the Zen community also manifests itself in the teacher's acceptance of whatever the monk does, so long as he knows the monk is maintaining the aim of finding his own way. But this acceptance can be the hardest thing to bear to our human nature which constantly seeks external support.

The sense of how Buddhism should exist in America was in sharp focus during the first practice period when we (the students) were faced over and over again with details like: Do we wear robes or not, and what kind of robes? Shall this ceremony be simplified? How? Shall it be in English? Should we chant in English or Japanese? Japanese has more resonance but English we can understand. Should there be three, five or seven days of tangaryo? How much zazen, study time, work time should there be? Should the organization and spirit of the practice be along the lines of original Buddhism, or present-day Buddhism in Japan, or what combination of these? How strict should the practice be made? Should we follow the Soto way completely, or should we apply the approaches of various schools according to the needs of the students? To what extent should the experiences of zazen, koans, mantras and the other techniques of Buddhism be used? These questions . . . suggested guidelines that pervaded our whole practice, and perhaps prepared some of the ground for Buddhism in America.[12]

A MONASTERY IN THE MIDST OF LIFE

Time and again, Suzuki Roshi has emphasized that Zen practice is for everyday life, in all circumstances. Consequently, Tassajara is not a place where students may expect to live permanently. They come there for periods of time, short and long, and thereafter return to their lives, their professions and jobs. They may return to Tassajara again and again, but only those few who are to become priests will for a few years make it their home—and even they will have to go out into the world to insure that their way is not based on the support of such favorable conditions.

Unlike most monasteries, Tassajara has both men and women. Each married couple has a small cabin. The single men live together in the dormitory or two to a room in four-room cabins; the women likewise live together in their own four-room cabins.

There are also extended periods when visitors may come and live at Tassajara as outright tourists. The effort to run a complete summer resort while maintaining the forms of Zen practice provides an unusually interesting set of conditions under which everyday life, both "inner" and "outer," may be experienced. "We really don't have to return to the world," said one student. "The world comes to us in the summer." One result, incidentally, is that this task of opening up to the public and caring for them has created a resort hotel that must be unlike any other in the world: the pleasures of swimming, sulphur springs, good food, comfortable lodgings, interesting fellow guests, breath-taking mountain scenery—all within the silent ambiance of the work of Zen. But of this later.

Twice each year for several months Tassajara is closed to visitors and guests. These are the practice or training periods. "Through the practice period," writes Suzuki

Buddha's way will be known in America. The practice period originated with Buddha's sangha (community of disciples) during the rainy season in India when the monks
could not go wandering from village to village begging and
teaching. In Japan only certain Zen temples are given the
privilege of being able to hold practice periods. Now this
indispensable practice has begun in America and must not
be discontinued. Each year we must have at least one practice period; it is indispensable for the students at Zenshinji
and for the existence of Zenshinji itself. Strict observation
of the practice period with qualified teachers and qualified
students is one of the foundations of Zen Buddhism and is
the most important reason why we started Tassajara.[13]

The students rise each day in darkness to the wake-up bell carried past their quarters at 4 A.M. Shortly thereafter the *han* is
sounded, a foot-square piece of ash planking struck sharply in di-
minuendo with a wooden mallet. This is the signal for zazen and
fifteen minutes after awakening the students must be in the zendo.
It can be very cold, for there is no heating.

We're not encouraged to bundle up to the extreme, but
we're also not encouraged to go to the other extreme—like
some people did, with only a T-shirt. People go through
great trials with that: how they should adapt to that, how
severe with themselves they should be, how rigorous. It was
a big subject for discussions—asceticism—how far we
should go with that.

After zazen comes work—construction, kitchen, cleaning or
maintenance—for several hours, followed by zazen again, then
lunch, rest period, study period, more work, baths in the sulphur
spring, supper, lecture and more zazen before bedtime at 9:45.
    That is the daily round, with but a few hours "off" every fifth
day, during the entire period of two or three months. The practice

period begins with the five days of tangaryo and ends with ses-shin, the two highly intense periods of zazen. Said one student: "You're all there together, committed to that period of time. There are no people coming and going—there's the sense of a community, a group, the sangha, for two months, everyone with the same goal." I asked him about sleep. He answered, "If you're sitting at all well, you don't need much."

When the guest season comes, the schedule is slightly relaxed. There is still the early morning zazen, the black-robed men and women moving quietly along the gravel past the flickering path-lamps. Next to the zendo, in the fresh morning darkness, a shaven-headed young man's face is caught in a globe of firelight as he stands motionless before the han, mallet poised, his free hand held vertically before his chin.

We go into the zendo (the guests may participate in all the student practice except the meals). Each student bows twice in two directions before sitting on his round black cushion. The positions are taken, the eyes lowered and the last blunt round of han is heard outside. The Roshi and his priests enter and take their seats on the altar stage. The meditation period begins with the sounding of the deep ceramic bell. For the first ten minutes, ceramic bells are struck in regular succession, followed by the great drum—more than three feet in diameter—which echoes through one's entire organism. (Said one of the priests to me: "When I instruct the students in the drum and the bells I tell them 'You are not hitting the drum, you are hitting the students.' From the sound of the drum, I can tell from a mile how many years the student has been in Zen practice.")

Then silence. Every now and then one hears the smart slap of the *kyosaku* against a student's shoulders. And with eyes lowered toward the wall, one sees the prowling shadow of the Roshi or a priest holding the upright kyosaku like an unsheathed sword as he moves past looking for the bow of the head which indicates a drowsy student's wish to be struck. After the hit, the Roshi bows again, as does the reawakened student who then resumes his position.

After some twenty-five minutes, the bells begin again and, finally, the deep bell sounds, indicating the end of the sitting period. The students turn round, bow, and for ten minutes may engage in *kinhin,* known as walking meditation, a slow, measured and mindful walk round the zendo.

After this there is a service beginning with the nine prostrations and the chanting, in Japanese, of the Heart or Prajna-Paramita Sutra. The following is Roshi's word-for-word English translation of this fundamental sutra:

GREAT PRAJNA-PARAMITA SUTRA

A valokitesvara bodhisattva practice deep prajna paramita when perceive five skandas all empty, relieve every suffering.

Sariputra,[*] form not different (from) emptiness. Emptiness not different (from) form. Form is the emptiness. Emptiness is the form. Sensation, thought, active substance, consciousness, also like this. Sariputra, this everything, original character; not born, not annihilated, not tainted, not pure, (does) not increase, (does) not decrease. Therefore in emptiness no form, no sensation, thought, active substance, consciousness. No eye, ear, nose, tongue, body, mind; no color, sound, smell, taste, touch, object; no eye, world of eyes until we come to also no world of consciousness; no ignorance, also no ignorance annihilation, until we come to no old age, death, also no old age, death, annihilation of no suffering, cause of suffering, Nirvana, path; no wisdom, also no attainment because of no attainment. Bodhisattva depends on prajna paramita because mind no obstacle. Because of no obstacle no exist fear; go beyond all

---

[*] The name of the historical person being addressed in this sutra.

(topsy-turvy views) attain Nirvana. Past, present and future every Buddha depend on prajna paramita therefore attain supreme enlightenment.

Therefore I know prajna paramita is the great holy mantram, the great untainted mantram. Is capable of assuaging all suffering. True not false.

Therefore he proclaimed prajna paramita mantram and proclaimed mantram says gone, gone, to the other shore gone, reach (go) enlightenment accomplish.*

It is now 6 A.M. The students go to study and the guests are on their own. During the summer, morning and afternoon work periods find the students engaged mainly in running the resort—manning the office, helping the kitchen prepare the three hefty meals for the guests as well as the vegetarian meals for the students, cleaning the cabins, making beds, etc. All this is done with a great sensitivity to the desires of the guests.

---

* A somewhat more grammatical rendering of Suzuki Roshi's translation: The noble bodhisattva Avalokitesvara, practicing the great crossing-over wisdom, perceived the five skandas all to be empty, and therein the release from all suffering.

Sariputra, form is not different from emptiness. Emptiness is not different from form. Form is emptiness. Emptiness is form. So it is as well for sensation, thought, active substance, and consciousness. Sariputra, this is the original character of all things. Thus all things are neither born nor destroyed, neither tainted nor pure, neither do they increase nor decrease. Therefore, in emptiness there is no form, no sensation, no thought, no active substance, no consciousness. There is no eye, ear, nose, tongue, body, mind; no color, sound, smell, taste, touch, or object. There is no eye, no world of eyes until we come to: no world of consciousness. There is no ignorance and no annihilation of ignorance until we come to: no old age and death. There is no suffering, no cause of suffering, no Nirvana, no path. There is no attainment of wisdom and no non-attainment.

Sariputra, the bodhisattva depends upon the great crossing-over wisdom because the mind is no obstacle. Because it is no obstacle there is no fear and he goes beyond all topsy-turvy views and attains Nirvana. All past, present and future Buddhas depend upon the great crossing-over wisdom and therein attain supreme enlightenment.

I know, therefore, prajna paramita is the great holy mantram, the great untainted mantram, the supreme mantram. It can assuage all suffering. It is true, not false. Therefore, he proclaimed the prajna paramita mantram which says "gone, gone to the other shore gone; gone to and reached enlightenment, enlightenment complete."

THE MONASTERY AS A LABORATORY

Mingling with the guests at mealtime, or swimming in the creek, or at the baths, the students are in a way like children when school is out. Though to us they still are quieter and calmer than most people we meet in the city, they take the summer as the time to let go a little. There is much chatter among them and the guests about metaphysics, astrology, drugs, war, politics, problems of life and death, movies, psychiatry. Tassajara in the summer is a microcosm of the spiritual and intellectual ferment of California and America. The students thus have the chance to experience their "interests," and no doubt to sense in some ineffable way the weight of their practice over against these "interests." The guests, for their part, may begin to sense a certain quality of response and life in the students. Thus are outsiders exposed to Zen at Tassajara.

One comes to the conclusion that Tassajara is as much a *laboratory* as it is a monastery in the ordinary and contemporary sense of that word.

No one in his right mind would think a scientist was an escapist who used a laboratory for his experiments. In a laboratory, conditions are arranged which make certain observations possible that are impossible in the everyday mixture of life conditions. Furthermore, in a laboratory certain results can be obtained much more easily and with less waste of time because all the materials are provided and on hand, and because everyone there has a certain preparation and a definite common aim. At the same time, results obtained in a laboratory must also be applicable to conditions outside the laboratory. But this application cannot be attempted prematurely, otherwise even more confusion will be produced.

Suzuki writes:

There are not many teachers in this world, and there are many students. Of course teachers and students are not different, but we must begin with a teacher. The teacher works and practices under the same conditions as the students. But there is some difference. The student perceiving this difference is shown the way to the Buddha in himself and the Buddha in his teacher. . . . It is possible to practice by yourself, but when we practice in a group we can help each other; and by practicing with people under the same conditions we can eliminate self-centered practice.[14]

In a sesshin lecture he said:

The more you reflect on yourself . . . the more conscientious you become . . . (and) you feel as if you are doing 99 per cent bad things. That is actually human nature. It is not a matter of what is good and bad. It is a matter of our human nature. When you realize this fact in your everyday life, you have to wonder what we should do. If you realize this fact, you will not be fooled by anyone. You may take some pleasure in entertainments, but you cannot fool yourself completely. You cannot deceive yourself when you realize the true state of our human nature.

Some people say, "If we have a perfect social construction, we will not have these difficulties." But as long as there is human nature, nothing will help us. On the contrary, the more human culture advances, the more difficulties we will have in our life. The advancement of civilization will accelerate this contradiction in our nature. When we realize the absolute presence of our contradictory nature, the way-seeking mind arises, and we begin to work on ourselves instead of the material world. Most people who are interested in Buddhism are more or less critical of our social condition, expecting a better social framework. Some people become disgusted with our human life. We cannot approve of these criticisms fully, however, because they do not rest on the full understanding of our human nature . . .

It is necessary to know actually what is our human world, or what is our human nature. This is a very important point. If you fail to observe our human nature fully, even though you study Buddhism, what you acquire is not what Buddha meant.[15]

This study, undertaken through the awakening of the way-seeking mind, or Buddha nature, by means of zazen and group practice in the presence of the teacher, is, for the students, the primary meaning and purpose of laboratory called Tassajara. In this the mind and the heart of each student is the stage upon which the study is made and the process begun of discovering the instantaneous completeness of the Buddha-mind. Thus, at Tassajara and at Zen Center, each man is his own monastery.

3

Meher Baba

The Age of the Avatar

How is one to place a man who says he is God, the Christ of this era, the avatar? This, and nothing short of it, is the claim made by Meher Baba and by thousands of men and women throughout the world who are his followers. "I am the Highest of the High," says Baba, "the Divine Beloved who loves you more than you love yourself."

> There is no doubt of my being God personified . . . I am the Christ . . . I assert unequivocally that I am infinite consciousness; and I can make this assertion because I AM infinite consciousness. I am everything and I am beyond everything . . . Before me was Zoroaster, Krishna, Rama, Buddha, Jesus and Mohammed. . . . My present Avataric Form is the last Incarnation of this cycle of time, hence my Manifestation will be the greatest.[1]

His followers are not madmen. Among them are scientists, professors, psychologists, industrialists, businessmen, actors and even the very young.

"This is an avataric age," said one, "just look at the world." It is not only the Baba-lovers, as they call themselves, who hold to this thought. Almost everyone who is drawn to the new teachings accepts the Eastern idea of cosmic cycles of time in which the whole of creation progresses further and further away from divine unity until the last cycle, the darkest age, will see a complete dissolution and destruction of civilization and the immediate birth of another grand cycle, introducing a new golden age.

This idea is not unfamiliar to one who has read the apocalyptic chapters of our Western Bible. Though written in highly enciphered language, the books of Ezekiel and The Revelation of St. John both agree with the Indian idea of an ultimate spiritual regeneration signaled by upheavals on a universal scale. Indeed, Eastern Orthodox Christianity still emphasizes the cosmic dimension of the human situation and its redemption through the suffering, death and resurrection of Jesus Christ.

Generally speaking, Western religion has lost this cosmic dimension. Both Christianity and Judaism have for long concerned themselves almost exclusively with man's moral and "legal" relationship to God. No doubt this abandonment of the cosmic dimension was to some extent based on the idea that God, if He is to be found at all is to be found within each individual's mind and heart. But, we fail to realize what has been lost by turning over to science questions as to the nature of the universe, the structure of matter and the definition of life.

PSYCHE AND COSMOS

The idea that God can be found within man was originally inseparable from the idea that the universe itself was in some way mirrored in man. Thus the discovery of God-in-man was impossible without the corresponding discovery and experience of cosmic law as well. As the cosmos became secularized under the banner of "scientific fact," the thought was fostered that one need only turn "directly" to God, while the study of the practical and experiential *laws* governing this turning were relegated to men with "a taste for the mystical."

The whole idea of the psychological effort of turning to God was set in terms of morality rather than cosmically determined psychodynamics. Man inappropriately estimated his resistance to this turning in terms of blameworthiness because he did not see this resistance as rooted in the laws governing the great scheme of nature.

In the religious disciplines of the East, this cosmic dimension of the human predicament and potential remains essential. And as new scientific developments such as the exploration of the moon, the discoveries of radio astronomy and microphysics, etc., once again bring Western man to a more emotional relationship to cosmic questions, it is that much more understandable that our young people have turned to the religions of the East.

The concept of the avatar is deeply rooted in this traditional Eastern sense of the universe. Within man is a finer quality of life which becomes obscured by the attractions of the isolated intellect and the concomitant force of individual desires. Relative to the ordinary "fallen-away" condition of the human being, this finer quality is divine. It is closer to, if not identical with, the quality of life by which creation itself is governed. Since it is finer than our ordinary mind, it may be said to be more intelligent, more conscious, as well as more loving and more powerful.

Moreover —and this is crucial—the universe *requires* that man in some measure come in touch with this finer quality of life. In so doing, of course, man himself profits in the coin of understanding, consciousness and life. But this is a fact which he can accept only when he actually does experience a moment of connection with this inner life.

In India the word "avatar" is often applied to any man who has realized this connection in a deep and persistent way. Understood in the above context, an avatar is quite literally God, or the highest quality of life, in the form and organism of man. All men are thus potential avatars, but the task of an actual avatar, in conformity with laws and requirements of the cosmos, is to help the rest of mankind toward the realization of its potential. "God needs man" is the way it is sometimes expressed in Western religious thought. The avatar is the Eastern embodiment of this need and, for man, of this opportunity. The appearance of the avatar is therefore a cosmic necessity when man has become lost to his own potential for intelligence, consciousness and power.

In the West, people who say they are God are almost by definition crazy. Probably, most of them are. And most of the rest are no doubt charlatans. But if we examine our own minds in this respect, it becomes clear that the standards we would apply to establish if someone is the God-man have to do mainly with his ability to satisfy our desires—by changing external conditions and providing us with various pleasures or allaying our fears. In other words, miracles.

The Instrumentality of Love

But the question arises: Is the performance of miracles a help toward awakening in man a need for inward freedom and an awareness of the illusions which govern his life? Are miracles a help in the work of obtaining that freedom?

This question in its relationship to the concept of the avatar may well be kept in mind when we attempt to understand something about Meher Baba and his followers. Otherwise, we shall find many reasons to be put off by the surfaces of this movement—unless, of course, we are one of those whose feelings immediately respond to what has been called "the immense and overpowering love that radiates from Baba and through his disciples."

If we are not one of these, we may well recoil at the "grandiose" statements of Meher Baba, some of which were quoted at the beginning of this chapter. He is God, he created the universe, his message supersedes all others, he is the Highest of the High, *the* avatar, the Master of Masters. Or we may shake our heads at the countless photographs which his followers tack to their walls, wear on their breasts, make into rings, etc.

Some of these photographs show an avuncular older man with warm, soft eyes, a wide and startlingly beaked nose descending over an enormous moustache, that spreads out in an all-engulfing grin. Others are of a garlanded young "mystic" with flowing hair and an intense gaze. Still others are of a face in great concentration and suffering. The variety is endless, but they have one thing in common: the immediacy of the emotional.

We may smile indulgently at the sentimentality of the Baba-lovers who speak unabashedly of adoring their Master, whose prayers may say, "Oh, God, most Beloved Baba, may we show our gratitude for Your Supreme Gift of Yourself by receiving Your Love and giving Your Love and living Your message of Love in our lives." At their meetings they embrace each other, prop up each other's cushions as they sit on the floor, and warmly hold your arm as they shake your hand.

And we will search in vain for any firm lines of organization among his American followers. In Baba's own words:

> Your love for me should have free expression in the mode or form best suited to you. It should shine through you to others, awakening their hearts to receive this divine gift. Gatherings and meetings in my name should be a channel for the expression of my love, and to give them any other importance is to misunderstand my cause.
>
> Organizations may be necessary for carrying out work of a routine nature, but if I am the avatar I need no such things for my own work. Although I would not be worth loving if I were not aware of someone's unexpressed love for me, why should anyone who wishes to express it be compelled to do so through some office or organization?
>
> My office should be the heart of everyone who loves me. The heart of each should be my shrine, and my lover the priest of that temple of love . . . Love, and the heart which

has love, are of greater importance than questions of the
position or prestige of those who choose to take up my
work.[2]

It is said that the avatar of the Kali Yuga, the dark or iron age
which embraces our present span of history, shall reach mankind
only by virtue of charity, the free giving of love, because man in
the Kali Yuga is so far in delusion that nothing of his own efforts
can be demanded of him save the effort to return God's love. One
who has studied the history of Christianity will, however, acknowledge the mysterious fact that nothing is harder to give to
man than love. And if the surface impressions of the Meher Baba
movement lead us to think that Baba was nothing but "sweetness
and light," a closer look will soon show how sharp is his demand
upon his followers and how much they must struggle to come
closer to him. The teaching of Meher Baba brings us directly in
front of the problem of the laws of love, considered not only as a
human feeling, but as a spiritual tool and a law of the universe.

The Life and Work of Meher Baba

What follows is a sketch of the life of Meher Baba gathered from
his own statements and those of his disciples.

He was born February 25, 1894, in Poona, India, of Persian
parents and reared against the background of Sufism and the Zo-
roastrian religion. At the age of nineteen, after attending a Christian high school and while still in college, he sought out a certain
Hazrat Babajan, an ancient Mohammedan woman, one of the
five Perfect Masters of the age. (According to Meher Baba, five
Perfect Masters or God-realized souls exist at all times for the
spiritual governance of the world.) Upon seeing him, Babajan instantly kissed his forehead and, in so doing, "ripped away the veil
which separated him from his consciousness as the avatar of the
present era."

With just a kiss on the forehead, between, the eyebrows, Babajan made me experience thrills of indescribable bliss which continued for about nine months. Then one night she made me realize in a flash the infinite bliss of self-realization (God-realization).[3]

For three days he lay like a dead man with wide vacant eyes.

(My mother) believed that I had gone mad. In her anguish she could not refrain from going once to Babajan and demanding to know what she had done to me. Babajan indicated to my mother that I was intended to shake the world into wakefulness, but that meant nothing to Shirinmai in her distress.[4]

There then followed a long, agonizing process of returning to normal consciousness while still retaining the ecstasy of being one with God, and the awareness of all levels of reality in the universe. In describing this process, Baba distinguishes the consciousness of the God-man from all other exalted states of mind in that it, and it alone, participates fully in the highest reality as well as in the world of illusion which is the object of ordinary consciousness. The Incarnation of God suffers to the last detail everything that ordinary man suffers, even as he continuously experiences the bliss of God. The reason that is given for this is that He comes to show the lowliest and poorest that they can live divinely without supernatural powers or magic.

Although the infinite bliss I experienced in my superconscious state remained continuous, as it is now, I suffered agonies in returning towards normal consciousness of illusion. Occasionally, to gain some sort of relief, I used to knock my head so furiously against walls and windows that some of them showed cracks. In reality there is no suffering as such—only infinite bliss. Although suffering is illusory, still, within the realm of illusion, it is suffering. In the midst of illusion, Babajan established my reality. My reality, although untouched by illusion, remained connected with illusion. That was why I suffered incalculable spiritual agonies.[5]

The disciples of Meher Baba assert that his entire life on earth involved this simultaneous participation in the highest and lowest states of human existence. Baba often reminded his followers of his dual nature, sometimes in small unexpected ways. For example, at a *sahvas* (a fixed period of, time in which a number of disciples live in close physical proximity with the Master) Baba reproached a man who was suffering from a cold and who came up to be embraced: "While you are like this you would embrace Baba and give him a cold too?" In large and small, Baba's life is understood by his followers to have been a form of constant crucifixion.

The process of "coming down" continued for some nine months, during which time he sat, talked, walked purely by instinct, with no awareness of himself and his surroundings. He relates that for this entire period he neither ate nor slept. Finally, after he had regained some measure of normal awareness, he consulted another Perfect Master, Sai Baba.

I intuitively prostrated myself before him on the road. When I arose, Sai Baba looked straight at me and exclaimed, "Parvardigar" (God-Almighty-Sustainer).[6]

He then tells of how he was immediately impelled to walk to a certain nearby temple where a highly advanced disciple of this Sai Baba, a Hindu Perfect Master named Upasni Maharaj, had been staying for three years.

At that time Maharaj was reduced almost to a skeleton due to his fast on water. He was also naked and surrounded by filth.

When I came near enough to him, Maharaj greeted me, so to speak, with a stone which he threw at me with great force. It struck me on my forehead exactly where Babajan had kissed me, hitting with such force that it drew blood. The mark of that injury is still on my forehead.[7]

With that stroke, Maharaj had begun the task of returning Meher Baba to full consciousness of the world of illusion, the world in which all men live. This final "descent" was not completed until seven years had passed under the guidance of this teacher.

At the end of this period Maharaj made me *know* fully what I am, just as Babajan made me *feel* in a flash what I am.[8]

Finally, on one occasion his teacher folded his hands before Baba and said "you are the avatar and I salute you."

At this point, one might well ask: What is going on here? What are these so-called Perfect Masters who are said to be nothing less than the pinnacle of a world-wide spiritual hierarchy and who were very conveniently located within a close geographical radius of Meher Baba? And while it is understandable that certain people, particularly the young, may be attracted to this rather Dostoyevskyan tale, how is any reasonable person supposed to take it seriously as a representation of fact? Furthermore, there are hundreds of these Eastern gurus who make the same enormous claim for themselves: they are "the world's guru," or "the Master of Masters." All this while apparently oblivious to the reach of the great religious traditions and teachers in the rest of the world, in Tibet, Japan, Mount Athos, Rome or the Middle East, or even here in America among the Hasidic Jews and in Christian monastic communities.

The more one studies the Meher Baba movement, the more this sort of questioning may increase. One may hear wondrous stories involving not only Baba, but, his followers—how they

came to him, what he knew of them, what happened in their lives
as a result of acceptance of him. But all these "wonders," including even the wondrous tales of Baba about himself, always occur
or are related by Baba *in the framework of a teaching situation* and
are always directed to the feelings of the personally involved aspirant. They do not compel surrender to Baba—hence they are not
"miracles" in the objective sense. Rather, they seem mainly to *reward* surrender.

In 1921 he drew together his first close disciples (called *mandali*) and soon established an ashram near Bombay. It was these
disciples who gave him the name Meher Baba, which means
"Compassionate Father."

After years of intensive training of his disciples, he organized a
colony at Meherazad near Ahmednagar, some seventy miles northeast of Poona. It still exists today and remains the geographical
and spiritual center of the world-wide movement. Externally, his
work involved the caring for the sick, the establishment of various
free hospitals and schools, and the organization of shelters for the
poor. No distinction was ever made with respect to caste.

He moved from one thing to another, alternating long periods
of seclusion with intense periods of physical service to the needy
of India, including thousands of lepers.

> Often my external activities and commitments are only the
> external expression of the internal work I am doing. In ei-
> ther case, my external activities and commitments may be
> continued indefinitely or I may end them promptly at the
> end of the inner work, depending upon the prevailing cir-
> cumstances.[9]

A continuing element of his mission was his work with the
deranged. Like Plato, Baba distinguished between two fundamental types of madmen: those who were insane in the ordinary sense
in that their mental functioning is impaired, and those who in
transcending the limitations of the intellect are so God-intoxicated

that they are unconscious of their bodies and surroundings. He cared for hundreds of the former by providing for their physical needs and indulging their innocent idiosyncrasies at what was called the Mad Ashram. As for the others, called *masts,* he spent a great period of his life and traveled thousands of miles throughout India and Ceylon searching them out in order to care for them and work with them. "The masts alone know how they love me and I alone know how I love them. I work for the masts, and knowingly or unknowingly they work for me."

Apparently, from what he has said about the masts, Meher Baba considered it possible for man to be spiritually advanced while lacking certain aspects of consciousness that even ordinary men possess. One of Baba's oldest American disciples told me there were often times when she just "blanked out." "In fact," she said, "all of us who have been with Baba do this from time to time. We couldn't tell you our own names sometimes—we don't know where we are, you see, so we're just *non compos mentis* for a few seconds."

The Silence

The most well-known aspect of Baba's life was "the Silence." In 1925 he voluntarily ceased to speak. For the rest of his life he communicated by the use of an alphabet board with which he also dictated the many messages and discourses that have appeared under his name. Later, in 1956, he abandoned even the use of the board and reduced all communication to a uniquely expressive system of hand gestures.

What it must have involved to be Baba's interpreter and, as it were, his voice, we can only guess. Those who met Baba were astonished at the speed and fluidity with which his interpreters relayed their Master's words. In this respect these men surely served as a sort of paradigm of attention and surrender to the mind of their teacher. People very soon lost the sense of translation and felt they were being addressed directly by the Master.

Then, why the Silence? Was it that words are too tied to the intellect? Was this part of the Master's way of reaching directly toward the feelings? For there is very little about Meher Baba's way that is beamed to the mind alone. Was he silent in order to raise in the pupil the question "Who is speaking these words?"

In fact, the followers of Baba do not claim to know the reason for the Silence. "I don't think it was so much for its effect on people," said one.

No, the Silence is much more important than that. It's the biggest mystery about Baba, and the mystery of it will be the main issue that will challenge everyone in the future, probably the main thing that will bug Baba-lovers and start all sorts of trouble.

He was very explicit: he kept Silence—yes, because they had had enough words and now it was time for action; and yes, because he wanted to encourage non-dependency on externals. But mainly, he kept the Silence so that he could break it. That's what he said once: I knew I had to break my Silence, so I had to start keeping it. He said that the only miracle he would perform was when he broke his Silence, that this would be the most significant event in the history of humanity. He never said when it would be . . . he'd kid people about it, give dates, and they would just go by. Some people even thought he was going to break the Silence in the Hollywood Bowl. And then Baba split for China and he laughed and laughed: Did they really think I was going to do it in the Hollywood Bowl?

Baba's own message on the subject is contained in the following statement:

I have come not to teach but to awaken. Understand therefore that I lay down no precepts. Throughout eternity I have laid down principles and precepts, but mankind has ignored them. Man's inability to live God's words makes the avatar's teaching a mockery . . .

Because man has been deaf to the principles and precepts laid down by God in the past, in this present Avataric Form, I observe Silence. You have asked for and been given enough words—it is now time to live them. To get nearer and nearer to God you have to get further and further away from "I," "my," "me" and "mine." You have not to renounce anything but your own self. It is as simple as that, though found to be almost impossible. It is possible for you to renounce your limited self by my Grace. I have come to release that Grace. I repeat, I lay down no precepts. When I release the tide of Truth which I have come to give, men's daily lives will be the living precept. The words I have not spoken will come to life in them. I veil myself from man by his own curtain of ignorance, and manifest my Glory to few. My present Avataric Form is the last Incarnation of this cycle of time, hence my manifestation will be the greatest. When I break my Silence, the impact of my Love will be universal and all life in creation will know, feel and receive of it. It will help every individual to break free from his own bondage in his own way. I am the Divine Beloved who loves you more than you can ever love yourself. The breaking of my Silence will help you to help yourself in knowing your real Self.[10]

Meher Baba "dropped the body" (the term Baba-lovers use instead of "death") January 31, 1969, at the age of seventy-four, after months of prolonged suffering from a variety of diseases which affected almost every system of his body, and which physicians were unable to diagnose. The predicted breaking of the Silence had not taken place, at least not in any obvious way.

"The controversy is already beginning about whether or not he broke the Silence," said one young man, a psychology professor in his late twenties. "There's already a school of thought that thinks he has." Another follower, a lively, articulate woman of perhaps seventy, said, "Some of the lovers say he broke his Silence and no one is able to hear it, but I don't think so. The breaking of the Silence will come, and when it does it will be very interesting and very wonderful for everyone. There'll be no mistaking it."

Shortly before his death, his health long since failing, he broke a three-year period of tight seclusion to announce that he would receive his followers at a *darshan* starting in April of 1969. He allayed the anxiety of his close disciples, who feared for his health, by adding that he would give the darshan (a traditional Indian occasion for followers to enjoy the presence of their Master) "while reclining." After his death, the mandali cabled those in the West and told them they could still come to India and that darshan would still be given. Thus, for his last darshan, the body of Meher Baba was reclining in its tomb.

Thousands came, among them a great many young Americans who had never seen Baba. All claimed to have felt the overpowering, loving presence of the Master.

The Baba-Lovers

For several years I had been planning to go to India. I had made a pact with myself that I wouldn't go until I had fulfilled certain obligations, like finishing college—which filled an obligation to my parents. That was a very strong thing I got from studying Gurdjieff—paying back one's parents. So, when I did fulfill these obligations I left for India—about four or five months before then I had come across Baba.

Here was a slight, dark-eyed young man of twenty-six, with a full, neatly trimmed moustache. He spoke slowly and thoughtfully, smoking dark Indian cigarettes called *Bedes*.

I knew why I wanted to go to India. I figured that if there was one chance in a billion that Baba could be what he says he is, how can I not afford to give some of my precious time to find out. Every level that I came to Baba on, he was always there—he still is. I had been in so many different things for so many years—I was able to recognize that thread of truth which is unmistakable in certain teachings—Ramakrishna, Maharishi—I mean it was just there, you can't miss it. And in Baba I found a completely cohesive synthesis of all the various teachings I had read, the same one truth was so obviously the place from which Baba communicated. And with such undeniable authority behind what he said that—he couldn't be anyone else except Baba!

So, anyway, I said to myself, if this cat knows, I gotta go to him and like find out. Because everybody I had met in my life like had ideas and opinions—and nobody *knew*. Like on acid, you know, you try to delineate the moment, delineate the perception of reality: it's so totally absurd. But with Baba, like he doesn't *talk!* He doesn't *talk*—no words! Fantastic. He didn't speak for forty-three years. So, I had heard there was supposed to be a sahvas, you know, a gathering to share the presence of the master. So I said: "Far out."

Some people were supposed to fly out there from the States, but I decided to go overland. So I left the country about September first, got to London and took off and hitchhiked from there. I got to India about the middle of November. The closer I got to India it became incredibly obvious to me that it was a pilgrimage, an inner pilgrimage, to myself. And, for that reason, nowhere on the trip—about 8000 miles—did I use any public transportation, buses, trains—just my thumb and God's will.

I was very tired when I got there and I felt God, if *Maya* is everywhere then this is just Indian Maya and, like who needs it? So, I felt there was just nothing left for me to do but go to see Baba. So, I hitched to Poona. I got a ride on a truck full of furniture that was all lashed down and covered with tarps, except for this one armchair. So I made the whole journey to Poona through the mountains sitting on the back of this open truck sitting in an armchair.

Got to Poona, dropped off my knapsack at the railway station and I thought I'd go out and check out the town. So, I was sitting in a restaurant having dinner and an Indian came over to me and said, "What is the purpose of your visit?"—they're always asking questions like that. I said, "Oh, I've come to see someone." "A philosopher, perhaps," he said. I laughed. "No, I wouldn't call him that." He said, "Who is he?" I said, "Meher Baba." Ha said, "Oh tcha! Meher Baba, yes, you know there is large center here in Poona." I said, "Far out. I didn't know that."

After dinner, he took me over there, and I was sitting in the office and they said, "What is the purpose of your visit?" I said, "I've come for the sahvas." I got there a month early and I figured that in that month I could help in some way to set things up. He looked at me. "Surely you must be joking." I said, "No, I'm not joking." He said, "Oh! Didn't you know? Baba's canceled the sahvas."

I said: "What?" I mean, it floored me, like I've come twelve thousand miles and you tell me that he canceled it? "Oh, yes, Baba's canceled it." He took out a little pamphlet and showed me. It had been canceled September fourth. I had left September first and since I was on the road, no one was able to get in touch with me to tell me. "Well," I said, "here I am."

So, I said, "Where's Baba?" "Oh, he's in Meherazad," which is about eighty miles northeast of Poona. "But Baba's in very strict seclusion. He's not seeing anyone." I said, "Well, man, I mean I'm this close, I gotta go try." So he said, "Oh, well, you go in the morning to Ahmednagar," which is about seventy miles northeast of Poona. "There lives Adi Irani, who is Baba's secretary and who is a very close disciple of Baba. And, go talk to Adi."

So, I went up to Ahmednagar and after a series of strange events I found his office. And it was the same thing like "What are you doing here?" And, well, I laid my trip on him and he said, "Well, wash up, take some tea." In the meantime he had sent someone up to Meherazad where Baba lives with just a few close disciples. So, after I washed up, he told me that he had sent a note up to Meherazad and that "you should come up there. Eruch—Baba's spokesman—will talk to you." So I went up there and when I got there Eruch met me at the gate and said, "Sit down in this bench in the shade." So I took off my knapsack and sat down.

Eruch says, "What is the purpose"—you know. So I told him. I think I should mention that when I went there I expected absolutely nothing. I mean like if he saw me, wonderful, but if not, I mean such is the way of the world. And after we talked a while, Eruch I guess went in to see Baba and he came out a few minutes later and said, "Baba will see you in the morning." I said, "Cheuooo! Incredible!" "He says you're to rest, have dinner, get a good night's sleep and be here at nine o'clock in the morning."

I went to my cabin and then Eruch came over again. "Baba wants to know if you want to see him now."

So, he led me to the building where Baba was living.

Baba was sitting on his bed. Naked from the waist up. I think there were two other men in the room. And Baba just—*beamed* at me, man. I always have difficulty talking about Baba. I mean, I'm not given to having visions or hallucinations. For me, it was just this incredible, extraordinary *light,* like his head was the center of it, like emanating in all directions. It filled everything. To the extent that tears started forcibly coming out of my eyes like as a reaction to all this incredible light.

And Baba was just *beaming*. And, you know, I was

just—I was standing about twenty yards away. Baba made some gestures, said he was happy to see *me!* That blew my wig. He was happy to see me! He said, he's happy that I was there. He said I should take a bath, have a good night's sleep and that he would see me in the morning. Eruch then turned me around and led me out.

We talked a little in my cabin and he asked me how I had heard about Baba. I told him the story. . . . I was at a strobe-light dance and stoned on acid, and there was this incredible picture they flashed, and I asked someone who that was. She said, "That's a holy man in India named Meher Baba." I said, "Far out, man, it looks like a cross between Gurdjieff and Tennessee Ernie Ford . . . then I went to see a psychologist friend of mine at Harvard and on the door to his office he had this passage from Baba:

To penetrate into the essence of all being and significance and to release the fragrance of that inner attainment for the guidance and benefit of others, by expressing, in the world of forms, truth, love, purity and beauty—this is the sole game which has any intrinsic and absolute worth. All other happenings, incidents and attainments can, in themselves, have no lasting importance.

Then when I walked into his office I saw his picture again on the wall. "Him again!" I said. Then Eruch asked me who this psychologist was. When I told him he said, "Oh, yes, I have a letter from him." He went out and came back with the letter that he had written about a year before from Milbrook when he was with Leary. Obviously he had written when he was stoned on acid. It said like Dear Baba, here I am on the Sixth Plane and like it's so far out and like where does LSD fit into the spiritual panorama?

So then Eruch asked me, "What is this thing called LSD?" I had some acid with me in my knapsack—pure,

100 per pent pharmaceutical, the best. I had stopped smoking grass and hash in the Middle East because it had at last dawned on me that none of the teachings I had gone through ever said anything about taking drugs. I figured not only couldn't it be the path, but like it must be nowhere near it. I had been smoking very heavily for several years, but like just now. I had stopped! Ten days before I got to India. But I didn't know where acid was at. So I told him what little I could tell him about acid.

So Eruch asked me, "What is an experience on this thing?" I told him my friends back in Boston called them "reality capsules" at which he just cracked up. "Only in the West," he said, "could you take a pill and swallow reality!" Then he asked, "Are many people taking this thing?" I said, "Oh, many, many, many." Well, I guess this got communicated to Baba—of course.

I had intended to take that acid and go up to Nepal and bring in the New Year colorfully and gloriously, which was not to happen. When I talked to Baba the next morning, one of the first things he said was "Go back. Because what you're looking for you won't find wandering around India or sitting in the monasteries"—which were the two exact ideas I had and which I had not mentioned to anyone. Somehow Baba knew them. "But you'll find it in society with people, like trying to be of service to them and loving them."

Baba emanated a total peace, a total acceptance of me as I am that couldn't be shaken. Whatever moods, modes, hang-ups, all the shit in me, all the goodness, everything—it was a *love* emanating from Baba that was so dynamic that— it just enclosed one, I mean you could feel it physically. It's something that I still feel. It hasn't altered whatsoever in the years that have gone by. It was a total peace, something I had never seen anything like at all, not an iota, like it reminded me of what Jesus said about the peace that passeth understanding. I mean, you just don't understand it.

Well, when he said that about society, it made such common sense that I left India two weeks later for the States. I
went back to working in a mental ward with chronic schizos.
You know, they're really crazy. I kept thinking about Baba
and his motto, you know, "Mastery in Servitude." I kept
thinking what does that really mean? I mean how can I trans-
late that into my life so that it has meaning? And I realized
that most of the obstacles that I encountered in the hospital
among people were the obstacles that I made, my own ego
was getting in the way, you know, like how to get through.
And when Baba heard that I was working in the hospital, his
face just lit up. He spent so many years working with the
mad in India—you know with the masts. Baba said that
when I got back in the States I should go back to work in the
hospital, that he would work through me with the patients.

When I had come into the room, Eruch had brought in
my knapsack, and in the knapsack was the acid—which incidentally I later threw into the ocean on the way back from
India—everything comes from the ocean, I should return it,
you know, to the mother; there must have been some very
high fish around there for a while. And so, very, very clearly,
Baba told me where LSD was at. He said that drugs, especially LSD, was a delusion within illusion, that it gave you a
glimpse into the lowest plane, only a glimpse. He said it was
nothing into nothing. He said not only was it physically dangerous, and mentally, but he said it was spiritually dangerous. And no one I had ever heard who spoke with authority
had mentioned the spiritual side effects. He said that principally what it did was that it liberated a certain amount of
energy that is used in opening the higher centers, but that it's
not something that's controlled, it's just spurts, and that taking of it could lead to madness. He was very adamant. This
was the first public statement Baba ever made on drugs.

Well, a week after I got back I got a call from R. and S.
They were planning to take a trip that night and they asked

me "What did Baba say about acid?" And I told them, man, I said, no dope, man. It blew their wigs. S. and his old lady stopped immediately, but R. said that Baba was their god on the trips and here was their god saying "no more, man"—and he didn't stop, but it gave him pause for thought. They had a very large picture of Baba in the house where they were living and they would meditate on Baba's picture when they were on acid.

. . . Without question, I can truly say that I am much higher now than I was taking drugs.

. . . It's been four years since I saw him.

. . . It transformed my life, every aspect of my being has been touched by it. It works, here and now, day to day.

Like all of the younger Baba-lovers, this man admitted to only one aim in his life: to find the God in himself by remembering Baba in everything, and attempting to love him. Everything else that Meher Baba suggested to his followers regarding such things as drugs, sex, marriage, politics, meditation and so forth, is taken as secondary to this effort to love Baba, to surrender to him and to accept what they know to be his love for them. As one young woman, a member of a Baba organization called "Sufism Reoriented," put it:

When I first came to Baba it was very hard to put what He said into practice. I felt very committed to Baba, but I still made mistakes and didn't really follow his orders very well.

This was a woman of twenty-three, an Ivy League graduate, slender, dark-haired, whose parents, she said, were "devoted atheists." Like many Baba-lovers, there was nothing ostentatious about her; she dressed quietly and spoke quietly.

Like, Baba said "no drugs." I wasn't that interested in grass, really, but there were a lot of pressures around me, like a lot of people I knew were smoking heavily. So I'd turn it down most of the time, but it was very hard.

Like Baba is very much against premarital sex. And that's one of the hardest things for young people to get into. And yet, he doesn't lay out strict things for people to do. So, I came to California and I thought it was important to get involved politically. For a long time I thought the anti-draft work was compatible with Baba! Then L. talked to me— he'd been with Baba for fourteen years. He told me how Baba wanted his lovers to stay out of politics. One day, I had like a real experience of insight. I was just sitting there twirling this little rubber ball and it had like sections of different colors. As I twirled it, my mind kind of abstracted, I suddenly noticed that while it spun the colors all blended together. I said look at that, man, it's different, it's completely different when it's spinning. And I thought how can I expect to see every aspect of this war in Vietnam; it's got a million different factors, and . . . of course there are people who can see more than I can. All I can see is what I'm conditioned to see. And it made me realize M. (one of the oldest American followers) could know a great deal more about it and have more wisdom than I had. It was just fantastic for me. And from that point, I knew I could accept her guidance, and that she knew more than I did. Because like Baba had told her, she had spiritual authority.

When I was just a Baba-lover, and not a Sufi, I wasn't so aware of my shortcomings, I thought I was pretty groovy. "I'm a Baba-lover, that's groovy man, I dig everybody." I was in this hippie thing. I mean there are some Baba-lovers today—they haven't completely made the transition, I mean like everything's beautiful and Baba's, yeah, groovy, but they don't work on themselves.

The thing is it's very hard to accept Baba's love. But you gotta confront it. You got thousands of years of bad karma you have to work through. You have to try to love, that's the thing. It's so much easier to love God, to love Baba, than to love Joe Shmoe—because Baba loves us perfectly, and no matter how limited we are, he sees us as we are and loves us—so we don't have to hide anything. Of course, we do. Around Murshida (the Baba-designated spiritual head of Sufism Reoriented) we try to act saintly and all, but she knows how we are; she loves us too. I'm not so afraid of making mistakes, my ego is not so much on guard that I'm not willing to try.

Sufism Reoriented is perhaps the only hierarchically organized group of Baba-lovers.* Otherwise, the lovers are, as they say, "on their own." They meet frequently, listen to talks by people who have seen Baba or worked directly with him, trade stories of the Master, his powers and his love, how he is aware of everything and acts, even now after his death, in precisely the right way at the right moment with supreme psychological acumen.

Many, perhaps most of the Baba-lovers, are still living the hippie way, some still take drugs against the only explicit behavioral

---

* Baba himself did, however, establish a physical center for his work in America in Myrtle Beach, South Carolina. This is the way it was described to me by one of his followers: "The main spadework for Baba's Message in this country was done by Mrs. Elizabeth Patterson and Princess Norina Matchabelli . . . One time Baba told them that he wanted to have a universal center in the United States and he gave certain requirements: it must be virgin land, having ample supply of fresh water and not be too hot for his northern followers in the summer or too cold for his northern followers in the winter. The two women got the idea that this might mean California. At any rate, they took trips by car and spent several years looking for a place and, finally, Mrs. Patterson was sitting in her home in Myrtle Beach, South Carolina, one day when it occurred to her that her father owned a good deal of ocean-front land which was probably virgin territory. She thereupon asked him if she could have it and he acquiesced. She surmounted great problems during World War II trying to get some cabins and a meeting hall erected in spite of the shortage of materials so that it would be ready whenever Baba chose to come, which finally happened in 1952. It wasn't until 1956 that Baba himself dedicated the Center and said that the public could come there. Thousands of young people rush down there for weekends or short vacations, enjoying the physical and spiritual beauties of the land. People who have never heard of Baba, if they are sensitive at all, immediately realize that there is something very different and special about the Center—a real vibration which Baba has left there. It has five hundred acres, one mile of ocean front, two fresh-water lakes and much vegetation."

stricture that Baba delivered. One is reported to have said about drugs: "I know Baba is God, but on *this* he's wrong!"

A Search for the Emotions

What this extremely heterogeneous collection of Baba-lovers has in common is not simply the professed faith in Baba. More than even most other young people, they live by their feelings. Almost every story of how they first came to Baba involves a sudden flash, a feeling, something in them that went against "common sense" of what their minds told them. I think this is very important to any understanding of Meher Baba's way. For it is quite clear to me that among the older followers of Baba, there is a strong reliance on what we might call *intuition*. And this direction toward the development of intuition is perhaps part of the discovery of something which we in the West do not even recognize: the emotions as a source of knowledge.

It is not really a question of whether or not the followers of Baba succeed in developing such intuition—I certainly cannot judge that. But the idea is ancient, that the "heart" of man is the center of real knowledge. And it would seem that a spiritual discipline based on love, which is surely Baba's way, could well begin with the fostering of trust in the feelings, even if these feelings are "confused" and "shallow" and "mixed," as they are in everyone, particularly the young. The seeming bathos and sentimentality of these young Baba-lovers may be existence on the fringe of intuition. "Love Baba" may well mean to them "revel in your feelings." Not one of them though, "revels" in his negative feelings: anger, envy or self-pity. This suggests some interesting questions as to the nature of our negative feelings, that perhaps they are not feelings at all, or that they are in some undiscovered way the result of the intrusion of the mind—that mind which so many Eastern teachings seek to control. Thus, what may appear on the surface as nothing more than a sort of saccharine mystagogy may be the be-

ginning steps toward an ancient path like that first laid down for
Western man through the "lovers" of Jesus Christ.

In any case, the sentimentality and the glow of youthful feelings fade more into the background among the older, or more
experienced followers of Baba, particularly those who worked directly with him. With them, the nature of the effort on Meher
Baba's way becomes much clearer.

Here the speaker is the leader of the organization known as
Sufism Reoriented, the woman referred to above as "Murshida,"
meaning "a teacher who has attained a certain stage on the spiritual path." The widow of an internationally known oil executive,
she now makes her home in San Francisco. Huge framed pictures
of Baba occupy the walls: not only the "happy" Baba which one
sees so often among the younger Baba-lovers, but also the "rapt"
Baba, absorbed, concentrated and, in some, suffering.

She likened certain groups of young people at the time of Jesus
to the young Baba-lovers.

> After His death, they used to send whole boatloads of
> youngsters with a ring on their finger over to Jerusalem and
> they were married to the Church or Jesus. They were called
> "Confessors of the Name." They were the ones the lions
> tore apart in the arenas because they refused to deny that
> they believed in the name of Jesus. They really became the
> progenitors of the Christian *religion*. This in one way or
> another has happened each time that the avatar has come.
> Sufism, on the other hand, goes back to the anteriority of
> time and it has always been composed of a small proportion
> of people who have reached the end of their evolution and
> reincarnation and have become what we call mystics. It is
> the avatar's job to take special care of these few. Usually, the
> avatar has given his message in what the Sufis call a veiled
> form. The parables of Jesus therefore could be intelligible to
> the masses and the religion could be kept up, but the mystic

would be the one who had the wisdom; he would know the inner meaning of the parables.

Speaking of her own organization, she said:

We do not feel we are here for everybody. This is why we have been instrumental in starting Baba groups like the Baba League in Berkeley. The members can be free to love Baba, but they mostly love Baba on their terms, whereas Sufis learn to love Baba on his terms, which is a whole lot harder. And we don't feel everybody is doing this. You really have to be sort of desperate, and *then* it's up to the Sufi Murshida and her Preceptors—I have trained four. It takes years for this training, because we have to live what we teach. We cannot go out and preach about love and come home and kick the cat, you see, we have to live it. The teacher has to be the cupid between the soul and God, and it takes a long time.

She spoke of how she had inherited the role of Murshida from her teacher and how, feeling unworthy to accept the title of teacher, she went to Meher Baba in India. "Baba was ready to re-orient any 'ism' that came to him for help and turn it into a path that would lead to him."

Baba told me that this was my destiny and that as long as I remained honest he would help me to fulfill my title of Murshida which he confirmed.

Love from the Point of Failure

Listening to her and to those she had trained as preceptors, I began to get a new perspective on the way Meher Baba worked with his disciples. "It was no bed of roses," she said, "far from it." Time and again, Baba would bring them into situations where they could not avoid seeing how they rejected his love, either through disobedience, mistrust or even betrayal. He had once said to his close followers:

> It is easier for me to come as an avatar than for you to receive my grace . . . there is no end to the conditions which restrict your ability to receive my grace. Therefore, it is difficult for my grace to flow from me to you . .
>
> The sun is now shining brilliantly outside this hall, but the sunlight does not reach you here under the root. The sun is doing its duty of giving light. You have also to do your duty in removing whatever comes between you and the sun . . .
>
> I am an ocean of grace, but I am also hard as flint when you try to draw that grace from me. The flow of my grace to you depends upon the intensity of your love, for it is love which attracts my grace to you.[11]

On the same occasion, Baba had related this story:

> About thirty years ago, before I started observing my silence . . . a visitor came to surrender to me. He could not help weeping when I told him that what he intended was very, very difficult since surrender means obedience, and obedience has but one meaning, and that is to obey. He said he knew that, and was prepared to obey me implicitly. When I inquired if he would cut his own child to pieces if I asked him to do so, he even agreed to that. But when I asked him to remove his clothes and walk around naked in the streets of Ahmednagar he began to protest and ultimately went his way. I am not going to ask you to do that . . . I never expect anyone to do the impossible.[12]

This story was told to me by a man who had spent some time in India among the mandali:

> I met a wonderful man in India named R. who is one of the outstanding Baba-lovers in his devotion. One time this man was visiting a hospital. He saw a little girl in great agony, suffering from I believe leukemia. In a fit of altruism, he wired Baba, saying, "Let me take on the suffering of this little girl." And, I was told by someone who was present at the time that when that was read out to Baba, that Baba reacted as if he had been stabbed in the back and he cried out aloud Uunh! Uunh! He sent a cable back to R. He said, "How can you give your life away when you've given it to me? How dare you consider deciding how you will give your life. You have offered your life for my work, and you tell me where to relieve suffering?"

The way of love, then, is the way of obedience, surrender. What is to be surrendered? The answer that Baba gives is: oneself. But what is that? An answer to this question, as we have already glimpsed, can only appear to the individual in the instant when he *refuses* to surrender, when he fails to love. For once the "self" is surrendered—whether it be in the form of certain desires, or thoughts, or fears—it is no longer *my* self, at least at that moment. This is the exceptional moment, the experience of grace.

For on the whole, failure is the rule. The *effort* is to love God from the point of failure. If put this way, one sees, I believe, how extraordinarily difficult for man is the way of love. Is it not true that human love, as we know it, is love from the point of *ability?* Ordinarily, "I love you" is a *promise* as well as a report. The "path of love" is nothing less than a brutal revelation to man that he cannot make this promise, that his feeling is founded on judgments of what is acceptable and what is not acceptable from another, judgments which come from the mind. Thus the mind screens man from the knowledge and experience of union by automatically setting up requirements for union. There is no *ability* here. It is the path of least resistance, following the desires. And since the desires each in their turn are only a fragment of a whole, man lives his life in pieces under the illusion, at each moment and in each fragment, that he is whole.

It is not therefore a question of whether Meher Baba is really God or just a fraud. The question is whether he acts among his followers in such a way as to help them toward the effort to love from the point of failure. As I see it, this effort means the attempt to accept for what they are the requirements that come from the mind—*in the instant that they are in force.* In this effort one might say that the *heart,* the emotions, may touch man—or, as it is sometimes put, man may enter a new state of consciousness.

For, the purification of your heart, leave your thoughts alone, but maintain a constant vigil over your actions. When you have thoughts of anger, lust or greed, do not worry about them, and do not try to check them. Let all such thoughts come and go without putting them into action . . .

But it is not child's play to remember me constantly during your moments of excitement. If, in spite of being very angry, you refrain from expressing anger, it is indeed a great achievement. It means that when your mind becomes angry your heart does not know it, just as when your heart loves me your mind need not know it. In fact, your mind does not know that your heart loves when, prepared to give up life itself, you lead a life of day-to-day obedience and duty.[13]

One can find volumes and volumes of prose and poetry about love, but there are very, very few persons who have found love and experienced it . . . Listen to love without philosophizing about it. None present here loves me as I ought to be loved. If all of you had such love, none of you would be left before me. You would all have realized God

and we would have become the One which we all are in reality and in eternity . . .

Believe me, you and I remain divided by nothing but the
veil of you, yourself. What does "you, yourself" mean?
When you feel hungry, you say "I am hungry." If unwell,
you say, "I am not well." When you say, "Baba, I slept well,"
"I am happy," "My son died," "They abused me," "I feel
miserable," "Those things are mine," it is this "I," "me,"
and "mine" which is the veil.

It is only because of the veil of the false ego lying between us that you find yourself involved in so many difficulties, troubles and worries, all of which disappear
automatically when touched by the reality of love. When
the curtain of your limited "I" is lifted—and it can only
disappear through love, and love alone—you realize unity
and find me as your real self, i.e., God. I say so because it is
only I, everywhere. There is really nothing like you.[14]

Obviously, if a man believes in and trusts only the ordinary
feelings (which, Baba says, come from the mind), he can never
come in touch with the heart and its intelligence. This is one reason why life with Baba was, as his disciples report, "chaos." He
changed plans "on a dime," he worked them "like coolies," he
"disappointed" them in countless ways, he always "perplexed"
them, and he never allowed them the security of knowing their
status with him—except that he loved them and forgave them. In
this way, it seems, their ordinary feelings were thwarted and confused, even as they continued as best they could the effort to love
Baba.

At the same time, everyone, from the newest to the oldest of
these disciples, tells of the love they felt radiating from the Master—as we have seen in the few reports we have quoted. In the
midst of difficult situations—psychological or physical distress of
various degrees, all they could hold on to was that love. The effort

to turn to that love and look for it is, I think, what defined them as serious disciples.

Love, emotion, the heart in this extraordinary sense is understood as the divine in man. To accept Baba's love means to accept the chaos of the mind and in so doing to experience the fact that the self which one has spent one's life defending and preserving is an illusion. Thus the paradox that to love oneself is to know that there is no self. Here, presumably, the center of a man's identification shifts from the requirements of the mind to that which loves and to the act of loving. Thus man experiences himself as God. "To love God is to become God."

4

Subud[*]

The Experience of Latihan

The central axis of Subud, around which everything else turns, is the remarkable spiritual exercise known as the *latihan*. Twice a week, people gather together in a large room or hall, where they remain for half an hour. During that time their effort, as individuals, is to receive and submit to the Power of God. They may stand or sit, walk around, jump, dance, sing or shout—there are no rules or requirements except the suggestion that they patiently seek a state of receptivity and freely follow whatever they may receive. There may be hundreds of people in the room or only a handful, but it is not a meeting in any ordinary sense. There is no discussion, no leader, no instruction. After this half-hour they go their separate ways and return to their lives.

In the latihan there is nothing they are supposed to feel or express. They are given no system of ideas and there is no suggestion that outside of the latihan there is something to attempt or even

[*] In my treatment of all these new teachings, my views are strictly those of an outsider who has not undergone the full sequence of experiences which they provide for their members. My presentations have been neither authorized nor officially approved by the leaders of these organizations. I wish to emphasize this especially strongly with respect to Subud.

remember. The founder of the movement, Muhammad Subuh, claims he is a quite ordinary man and seeks no publicity whatever. Married and the head of a family, he is a former local government official from the country of Java in Indonesia. He does not even claim to be a teacher, far less a Master. And although it originated in the Far East, there is nothing particularly Eastern about Subud except its name which is a contraction of three Sanskrit words: Susila, Budhi, Dharma. In Subud, Susila means "right living in accordance with the Will of God," Budhi means "the inner force residing in the nature of man himself" and Dharma is translated as "surrender and submission to the power of God." Taken together they refer to a way of life governed by something within a man which is sensitive to and expressive of the highest will in the universe.

To the outsider, Subud thus presents a surface that is un-dramatic and ordinary, even drab. Yet of all the new teachings it is the most widespread. Subud groups now exist in over sixty countries throughout the world. In the United States there are some seventy Subud Centers, and not only in such likely places as San Francisco, Berkeley, Los Angeles or New York, but also in Greenville, South Carolina; Lakemont, Georgia; Allendale, New Jersey; and Indianapolis, Indiana, to name only a few. Its many thousands of members (who are asked *not* to proselytize) come from every imaginable background: Christians, Jews, Hindus, Muslims, Buddhists; white, black and yellow; the radical young and the established middle class; hippies, lawyers, doctors, monks and nuns, professors, housewives, older teen-agers and little old ladies, actresses and bricklayers, etc., etc. "This is the world's first truly universal brotherhood," said one.

The beginner, called an applicant or a probationer, learns that the latihan is the exercise of surrendering to the Power of God. In the words of the founder:

> We do not have a teaching and there is nothing that we
> have to learn to do because all that is required of us is com-

plete surrender. . . . With his own mind and his own heart and his own desires, man will never be able to find God. Only by surrendering himself completely to God, not making use of his mind, his heart or his desire, is it possible for man to come into contact with the power of God.[1]

Beginners may not immediately participate in the latihan. They are usually required to wait about three months, during which period they may read more about Subud and ask any questions that occur to them. They may, if they wish, sit directly outside the latihan room, the latihan being held twice a week. There the "drabness" of Subud ends. For, what the applicant hears coming through the walls may be like nothing he has ever heard before all at once.

At first it may be a soft murmuring; or perhaps a single loud shout. From the women's room (latihans are segregated by sex) he may hear the beginnings of soft sirenesque moaning. Then, any or all of the following: animal sounds, groans, perhaps fierce and strident shrieks. Or a chanting and beautiful wordless singing accompanied by a deep ground bass ever louder or softer. Soon body sounds are added. Thumpings, running sounds. The din rises or in an instant subsides, only to rise again deeper and more clamorous than ever. At full blast, the latihan may sound like nothing so much as jungle animals, or maniacal, savage rites, or an eerie convocation of demons and banshees. At other times, it seems a deeply religious choir, or a joyous, raucous celebration, a Corybantic frenzy, or a madhouse. It is, in a sense, all of these, yet none of them. There may be sudden breath-taking harmonies; a sweet fragment of melody; or deep-throated sobbing.

The half-hour passes; the latihan ends. After what he has heard, the applicant does not know what to expect as the participants leave the latihan hall. Actually, there seems nothing unusual about them; they are neither flushed nor pale, neither excessively noisy nor subdued. They mill around have coffee, chat with each other and leave. They could as well be coming from a quiet lecture. In its way, this is one the most mysterious facets of the latihan and, as we shall see, points to something very important.

For the applicant, it is not so much what he hears as what he feels or senses. For some, there is an overwhelming impression of *forces* entering into them:

Well, I first heard about Subud through a friend in New York. Every time she wrote me it was Subud this, Subud that, Subud, Subud, Subud. So, finally, I get around to looking into Subud. I'm new in San Francisco and I go there and they tell me I have to prepare for three months, I have to sit in the outside room for three months. So, I have nothing better to do, so twice a week I go to this dinky building, in this dinky elevator, and sit in this waiting room and—I can't believe my ears. It's like Reichian therapy. The men on one side are a John Wayne movie, with the Indians attacking; and the women on the other side are doing their own thing, but it can be sweet sometimes. So, I'm sitting all by myself trying to get with it—why have they got me in this room? So, the emanations—suddenly, I'm beginning to get this *crap* going into me and I say to myself, "Mary, cut this out!" I don't know what was happening, but I'm taking on the room, and yet I wasn't vocalizing. I was getting upset. So, I wasn't going to do anything. I decided that during the preparation period. While I'm sitting there, I'm going to read a book, file my nails, I wasn't going to participate because it was flipping me out.

This was from a psychologist in her thirties.

Another woman, a secretary of about fifty, said of this probationary period:

As I sat in the waiting hall I had a mixture of foreboding and fear. Almost the same trepidation I had before I got married. That this was a great step and did I want this sort of step? In this step there would be changes, and did I want these changes to take place? It was a fear. I had no idea what would transpire when I went into that hall.

The idea that man is a receptacle and transmitter of many sorts of forces, both animal and divine, plays an essential role in Subud. The latihan is said to be a process of purification in which the individual gradually is freed from the dominance of these animal energies. To achieve such freedom, man need only open himself to the subtle, but potentially more powerful, higher energies, called "divine" or, simply, God, for the divine in man is constantly receiving and transmitting these higher forces. Only the noise and furor of the "lower nature" obscures this element of divinity.

After the applicant has proved his sincerity, he is ready to be *opened*. This will be his first experience of the latihan in which several of the more experienced members, called *helpers,* serve as witness to the fact that he has, even slightly, opened himself to God. The helpers—including the founder himself, Pak Subuh—are understood to be no more than the channels of higher energies. The *opening* is likened to a first *contact* with the Power of God. "The latihan cannot be taught or imitated, for it arises spontaneously from within after the contact with the Power of God has been received by transmission through a person in whom it is already established, and it is different for each individual according to his or her needs." Describing the effect of the latihan, one member put it this way:

In this life, in this dimension we live in, you have to use your intellect and your desires. But in order to transcend this dimension we have to leave all these things and "go upstairs," leaving everything downstairs. In fact, one of the weirdest things was that when I started I was told "Just think of the latihan like you do with a movie. You go to a movie and you come out of it and forget it," Now that's a strange analogy to make—with a movie, but that's the way it was put. The force is there, but the intellect will deny that force. In the opening, you may or may not feel this life force. You may or may not feel the opening. But even if you do, and I did feel the opening, for months afterward I would look at these people and think, "What are they doing?—it's psychodrama!" Until one time I doubted, and this force hit me so strong that I was flattened on the floor; I was just laid out completely. And I couldn't move. My whole body felt as if it were in a vice. And with it came such an awe, that I could understand what Moses must have felt, you know this awe, this force, because I only had a little of it. You can imagine what it must be for a *real* revelation. But this force just scared me, and I never doubted again; I never thought it was just psychodrama.

An "Ordinary" Man

The latihan is understood to be the "new dispensation" of this era: not a new teaching or system of thought, nor a prophetic message, nor the discovery by an extraordinary human individual, but a new and uniquely "easy" way for man to be "injected" with the highest energies of the universe.

Historically, this "new dispensation" first occurred in 1925 to Muhammad Subuh, now called "Bapak" (a conventional, honorific Javanese term meaning "father"). Although in Subud little emphasis is placed on the personal details of Bapak's life, we do hear of how his birth in 1901 took place at a time when there were many earth tremors and erupting volcanoes in Java. He is said to have been clairvoyant as a child and physically unable to imitate the little tricks and lies of his playmates.

His given name was "Sukarno." But when, as a small child, he became dangerously ill, an itinerant beggar wandered by and informed the parents that the baby was wrongly named and that he should be called "Muhammad." The name was changed, the illness suddenly passed and the baby grew up strong and healthy. Personal names are very important to Subud members; later we shall see why. Bapak gives new names to many who ask for them. A "Sally" may become a "Virginia," a "Bob" may become a "Hamilton," etc.

We also hear of a prophecy that he was to die at the age of twenty-four (some say thirty-two). Knowing this, he decided to search out spiritual guidance instead of pursuing a normal householder's life. He went to various teachers and gurus both within and outside of the Islamic tradition in which he was born and bred.

It is recorded that, with remarkable unanimity, all the seers, gurus and Sufi teachers to whom he went for study indicated that he was somehow different. They said that they could teach him nothing, but that whatever was to come to him would emanate direct from God.[2]

One of these was Sheikh Abdurrahman of the . . . Nakshibendi order of dervishes . . . Muhammad Subuh soon discovered that the Sheikh would not impart to the same teaching that he was giving to other pupils, and was sad to feel that he was neglected. When he asked the reason, Sheikh Abdurrahman replied, "You are not of our kin—it is not meant that I should teach you." . . . Another time, when he was only twenty years old, he visited an old woman in East Java who was famous for her wisdom and spiritual gifts, and to whom many . . . learned men came for teaching. When he entered the room, where she sat surrounded by her pupils, she astonished them all by rising, paying reverence to him, and asking him to occupy her place.[3]

Bapak, deciding that nothing would come of this search for a teacher, returned to ordinary life and family. He became a bookkeeper and a minor government official.

His biographers write that in 1925, on a dark and moonless

night, a ball of light more brilliant than the sun appeared above him while he was walking with friends. The light descended and seemed to enter him through the crown of his head, "filling him with radiant light and vibrations." This extraordinary light was observed by many others miles away.

Frequently after this, for three years, there occurred spontaneously in him the process of the latihan, "a purifying and cleansing process which . . . allowed him little sleep but nevertheless gave him the strength to carry on with his ordinary work during the day."[4] He did not understand what all this meant, nor did he welcome receiving something that was not available to everyone. "He tried to drive the experiences away by going to the cinema, but found that however he might keep his attention on the screen, the inner state would return and remind him that a quite different process was present in him also."[5]

Recently, on one of Bapak's world tours of Subud centers, someone asked him why he looked so ordinary and spent his time doing such ordinary things—going to the movies, watching television, smoking, shopping, etc. He replied that God in his omnipotence and mercy does not demand of man that he withdraw from ordinary living, that man can receive "the contact" with God and can experience within himself the working of divine power even when he is engaged in his normal occupation. Man, he said, can be open to receive this divine action within himself at every moment.

On another occasion he told one group that he himself is always in the state of latihan. He explained that this was because his own feelings and thoughts are subordinate to the rule of his inner self. Thus, he can be in society, enjoy people, music, and even watch television while in latihan. But he warned his listeners that this was not yet true of them and that therefore they must not preoccupy themselves with spiritual matters. They must go on with their ordinary, everyday concerns about their jobs, clothes, home and so forth, while letting the spiritual growth take place in them automatically. Two or three latihans each week, and no more, would ensure this.[6]

In 1928, the spontaneous latihans ceased. In the meantime Bapak had married and his children were born. Gradually, people began to see in him a man of exceptional insight and understanding of human problems. He himself realized that what was working in him, was not some new "teaching." "This raised a new question for him. He was fully aware of the importance of the transformation taking place in his own nature, but he felt that it could not be right that he alone should receive the contact."

On his thirty-second birthday, in some remarkable but unspecified way, his mission in life was "revealed" to him.

> . . . he had been chosen as a means whereby everyone who wished to do so could receive exactly the same contact and pass through the same process of transformation as he had himself . . . and herein lies the crucial and extraordinary quality of Subud that distinguishes it from any other kind of spiritual work . . . namely, that it can be transmitted integrally and without diminution from one human being to another.[7]

Thus, the members of Subud speak of this transmission simply as *contact*. One need only be in the presence of someone who has himself received the contact, for the latihan to serve its purpose. This may sound too good to be true, especially if we are familiar with the way that the passage of time seems to alter or dilute the influence of great religious leaders. But behind this claim lies a concept of transmission as the passage of a certain quality of energy. If this energy is present, all that is required is the willingness to receive it. The one way of blocking this reception is to trust the determinations and requirements of the intellect (which represents a different and "coarser" quality of energy). Thus, in Subud, as in so many of the new teachings, various traditional theological sticklers like "the problem of faith versus reason" become questions, really, of kinetics—both psychological and cosmological.

Having understood his mission, Bapak was soon approached by the pupils of a Sufi teacher in Java who had instructed them to request this contact. This was the beginning of the Subud movement. Bapak retired from his worldly work to give the contact to all who wished it. For twenty-five years the movement spread slowly in Java; then in the fifties certain Westerners became interested and in 1957 it began to penetrate Europe and the Americas.

Now it is almost everywhere. Bapak makes regular world tours visiting Subud centers. For each group he appoints several *helpers,* authorized to open anyone who wishes to become a member. Other than this, there is no hierarchy built into the organization. Theoretically, any "opened" person—since he now has the contact—can be a source for opening others.

Energies

The following is from the guidance for latihan given by one helper to a group of applicants:

> When presently we do latihan it is advisable to remove your watch, your spectacles and any hard objects in your pockets. There is no mystic reason for this. It is a purely practical measure to prevent these objects from being broken or from hurting you.
>
> When the latihan commences you should stand quite relaxed with your hands at your sides. It is a good thing to close your eyes so as to be distracted as little as possible by what goes on around you. You should not try "to think" and you should not try "not to think"; in fact, you should do nothing but relax and receive what comes to you.
>
> Now as to what may happen in the latihan. Some people

make movements of the head, the body, the arms or the legs. Some people walk, some dance, some run and some lie down. Some people make noises, some talk. Some shout, some sing, some laugh and some cry. These are only a few of the possible *outward* manifestations.

Most important of all is to remember that some people just stand and may feel nothing; some have been known to go like this for as much as six months or even longer. If this should happen to you, you should in no way be discouraged. There is no merit or non-merit in movement as such and you should on no account try to copy others. Each of you will in due course receive what is best for you.[8]

Everyone, even those who had left Subud for something else, spoke to me of the force that sometimes entered them in the latihan. One called it a sensation of "love"; another described the "incredible freedom" as he watched his limbs move on their own, "as though a great space suddenly appeared inside me." One woman in her thirties had tried Zen, encounter groups of various kinds, sensory-awareness training, as well as more conventional psychotherapy:

I felt I needed to do something to get the lid off me. I just feel that everything else I've been into, except encounter groups—which don't have the right emphasis—held me down. So it was really strange in latihan: I find nothing happening and I'm saying to myself "Come on, come on, you're supposed to be a big force," and here I am just quiet and I'm just floating around or I'm in a ball on the floor, you know, and "Speak, inner self!" I want to be in touch with who it is and, like, it's nothing. It's funny, not like what I expected at all. It was very hard. How come I'm not *leaping* around this hall! mean, isn't that the true me? Oh, God!

What I wanted for myself was that nothing from the

outside would be put on me, like no shields or anything—I do enough of that myself. My life has always been mainly in relationship. And I'm finding it so painful to rely on that as heavily as I have. And yet, Subud is a thing where you're involved in the latihan *completely* alone, and yet you're in a roomful of people. I don't quite understand what happens. But the situation is. I am alone in a room of women to whom I feel some relatedness, and yet no intimacy. Somehow it fills a need for me. And I can be any way. You know, your eyes are closed and you can be any way. But the way you are is a real discovery.

For each individual, the latihan can be tremendously various. Sometimes it is "very heavy," sometimes "light"; it is "powerful" or "nothing. " In it, people may function in entirely new ways. A singer sustains a high note far beyond her usual capacity. A dancer finds greater balance. An asthmatic breathes freely.

There are also healings, the most famous example of which involved the actress Eva Bartok. Physicians had urged immediate surgery which would have been fatal to the baby in her womb. Bapak agreed that she should receive the latihan, which was first "ministered" by his wife, and some days later by Bapak himself. A writer describes the bedroom as being "charged with energy that annihilated all personal feeling and produced a state of consciousness in which all seemed to be sharing in one and the same experience as the sick woman." Shortly after, Bapak is reported to have said, "Let her doctor give her a good sedative. It will not interfere with the latihan. Now the crisis is over, and she will not need an operation." Within three weeks, her condition had improved. Miss Bartok, fully recovered, gave birth to a healthy baby. A great many other healings are reported, some involving fatal diseases such as cancer.

But this and much else that is outwardly remarkable is understood in Subud in a special way. By opening oneself to a higher energy, the whole individual is gradually brought into a new harmony. But this new harmony cannot be understood or even clearly desired by that "lower nature" which is acted upon and brought into harmony. As in many traditions, what is called "the lower nature" embraces a great deal of what we would ordinarily value as our highest or best part. An individual has absolutely no basis for evaluating this higher force because the process and normal instruments of evaluation are themselves part of the lower nature.

The lower nature is nothing less than all of the thoughts, desires and feelings that govern our ordinary lives. The process of purification does not entail the destruction of this nature, but only its subordination to the superior energy called God. The gradualness of this process is strongly emphasized by Bapak, for the lower nature has a sense of time and timing that is often only an impatient expression of the desires:

> For this reason, Bapak advises members to resist their *desire* to engage in the latihan often as possible in the hope of accelerating the process. They are told that for a long time their feelings and thoughts will be far stronger than their soul, which has just been born, and which is as yet unable to master their ordinary outer functions. A person's age is immaterial, for that is only the age of the desires and the mind.
>
> Bapak likens this situation to a journey made with two horses. One is fully grown, while the other is but newly born and barely able to walk. The latter cannot keep up with the former, and until it has grown to maturity the journey cannot possibly proceed harmoniously. Patience is therefore necessary so that the receiving will proceed gradually, steadily and in parallel, without unnecessary disturbance.[9]

It is thus the whole of a man's nature that is supposed to receive the energy of God. Perhaps it is this element of Subud which seems so "drab and ordinary," but which might better be seen as a sort of "sanity." For, once again, one is compelled to ask: What isolated part in a man seeks the extraordinary and dramatic? What is the desire for excitement and, rapid change?

The Meaning of Submission

Against the background of such questions, we may now mention one of the most interesting aspects of the latihan: it can be turned off at will and one is fully conscious throughout. Bapak sharply differentiates it from a trance or hypnotic state. Although one has to submit completely to the action of the latihan, this submission must be absolutely voluntary.[10]

"Complete submission" must therefore be distinguished from what we might call "intense submission." The former would be submission of the complete man—the mind as well as the feelings. For the most part, human submission is never complete, only intense. That is, it involves a conflict between mind and emotions and the victory of one over the other. That is why it is exciting and dramatic, but it is also why intense submission is only partial.

Assuming there is a special quality of energy made available in the latihan, intense submission will bring that energy into contact only with the part that submits. The result may be a fractioning of the individual, rather than a new harmony. Further, it may well be that this energy, is available *only* to the whole man, and that what is received when only a part submits is something quite other than the divine energy which can feed what Bapak calls "the soul." *Intense* submission may open a man to forces that are not necessarily higher, and only to these forces.

Many men and women who have left Subud gave as their reason that they became terribly sensitive to other people's "negative vibrations."

Everyone else's shit started coming out at me; I started taking on everyone's shit, and I couldn't handle it. Even at the

office it would happen . . . somebody would be angry or
depressed and it would sink into me.

One man who had been a helper told me:

It (the latihan) opens you to all kinds of negative emotions.
A lot of people are flipped out completely by it. I know a
girl who went into a schizophrenic break that lasted longer
than any acid break ever did. Three years and she's still in
Bellevue. When she first cracked up all the doctors tested
her for acid. They couldn't figure it out.

An apparent breakdown, what is called a "crisis" or "state of
delivery," can, indeed, occur in Subud. This may range from a
single episode to a major stretch of apparent or actual psychosis. It
is an important task of the helpers to detect when someone's latihan appears to be out of his control and to help bring it to an
immediate conclusion. In short, some people do seem to "go
crazy" in Subud. The name which Bapak gives to this phenomenon is the Javanese *Zadab*, meaning, literally, "the anger of God."
The clear implication is that it is caused by the impatience of intense submission, the wish "to go faster than God," the attempted
interference by the mind or the emotions in a process which can
neither be rationally understood nor, in any ordinary sense, desired.

One well-dressed, middle-aged woman put it this way:

In a real latihan your conscious mind is always in control.
You're not a "medium." No, mediumship implies something else again, it's where you're a vehicle taken over completely by some other entity. But in a latihan it's a feeling of
freedom, completely. You know, if you're under pressure
and suddenly the pressure is lifted, this is something like
the sense of freedom you get in a latihan. Of course, when
you're throwing off negativities you can feel negativity, but

every latihan is different, and you can't know beforehand what will come forth. There is no conscious effort involved. But some people, you know, find it so "groovy" or something that they want to do it night and day. But you can't do this night and day, you have to have a sense of balance. You can't latihan more than three times a week, it's so powerful. I remember when I was just starting, this force just threw me down to the floor and so I have great respect for this force. I remember once three or four weeks after surgery I was told I could latihan alone. And I was latihaning alone and I remember this force shook me very hard, and I remember it was so strong I wondered if I was able to control it. So I stopped it right away. The intellect can turn it off. It's very difficult to know what stops the latihan. It was a fear perhaps—I was right in the center of this powerful thing and I was afraid my physical body couldn't stand it. You can't force the latihan on any part of yourself. Even if it's a mistaken fear, it'll stop the latihan. Sometimes it just stops at the moment you are reveling in it— like it's such a wonderful experience and you want it to go on and on, but it'll just stop.

It is imperative, according to Bapak, that a sharp separation be maintained between what on the one hand is called the contents of mind, heart and feelings, and what on the other hand is called the genuine feelings of the inner self. The "contents of the mind" are, for example, ordinary intelligence which makes a man feel that he really understands something—when in fact he does not understand. The contents of the heart are, as has been pointed out, the various desires, including the desire to receive God more quickly and to "progress" spiritually. Finally, the ordinary feelings lead a man to "feel" that he has already seen God face to face and has already become God's beloved. If he does not separate true inner feelings from all of this, a man may easily fall victim to imagination. For Bapak, it is this imagination produced by the ordinary self which prevents a man from returning to his original, timeless state of being—a state of being which is uninfluenced and uninfluence able by the kind of experiences which prevail in this world.[11]

The half-hour latihan may not be done more than two or three times a week. But there is another equally interesting "exercise" which plays a large part in the lives of Subud members.

This is called *testing*.

The effect of the Subud latihan is that we submit ourselves to an action in which we receive power or guidance from a source that is beyond ourselves. Testing is where we pose a question and then allow the latihan to commence in us in the hope that we may receive an answer.[12]

Testing, in short, is the search for guidance in everyday life, and it is used by various members for various problems: jobs, marriage, sex, friendship, children, etc., etc. Often this testing takes place after the regular latihan when the individual is considered to be in a state of maximum receptivity, but it may be done any time by simply posing the question and allowing the latihan to commence. Beginners usually put their questions in a form which can be answered yes or no. "Shall I marry George?" "Shall I quit my job?" As times goes on, the questions may become more complex: "How shall I get off drugs?" "Where should I live?"

The answer does not come in words, but in a sort of code, the language of the individual's own latihan, be it bodily movements, sounds, gestures, or simply a quality of perception. It is experienced as an inner feeling coming from beneath the usual inclinations and patterns of thought, and the individual must be prepared to accept whatever appears, even if nothing appears.

The mother of a teen-age boy told me her experiences in testing:

The only conscious effort you find in Subud is when you start having to make decisions. You'll find yourself not wanting to make them from the outer, from an intellectual, rational stand-point. Because the rational mind will jump here and there, it should be this, it should be that, and you'll see both sides of the thing, and you can't really come to a decision. So what you do is you start going *in* for guidance. And then you may get some weird answers, but they're *right*. I'll give you an example. When I went to work for the Park Service all my friends said, "What are you doing to your teen-ager, this could be very dangerous." And I said I'm sorry, this is what I got in a latihan. So I got this guidance: "You gotta go," despite what my child wants. And later it came out it was the finest thing for him. He said, "I really found myself." He had to think for himself for the first time. He didn't even realize he was an entity unto himself until that time. I could not have foreseen this. I wasn't that bright, I don't know anything about child psychology; all I knew was this was what I was told to do, I tested on it and it said I had to go. Now, when you test you get one answer, and you don't go right off quitting your job and dashing to the wilderness. You have to test the other check-points. If other things start opening up, it has to show, it has to open up in a rational way all down the line. And that's what happened.

To verify the results of their own testing, members may request that their question be tested by the helpers, or sometimes even by Bapak himself. As with the latihan proper, the temptation exists to use it to excess, in areas where the ordinary mind and feelings are an adequate guide. This may, according to Bapak, also lead to the "crisis," an unbalanced exposure to extraordinary inner energies.

By and large, testing replaces or supplements the rules of conduct and behavior laid down by society or by religion. Still, general principles about "external life" are given out to Subud members, though usually in terms of their instrumentality toward "inner growth." A glance at some of these ideas may raise intriguing questions about the forgotten instrumental roots of our own weather-beaten Judaeo-Christian moral code. Take, for example, sex. On various occasions Bapak has advised Subud members that before intercourse they should try to become quiet and calm—in exactly the way they try to become quiet before the latihan.[13]

Even before citing the reasons Bapak gives for this, we can already sense something here worth pondering.

The Energies of Sex

By now almost everyone in America and the West is quite certain that our religions have been double-faced and psychologically destructive on the subject of sex. We are certain that guilt is our great enemy because it inhibits our passion. We know that something like love exists, we wish to manifest it and we are sure that we need to receive it. In the rare moments that we are free of the feeling of guilt, we feel more alive, we feel life circulating through us. By rejecting the strictures of orthodox religion, our minds can now sometimes assent to this great passage of force which we call sexual passion. Perhaps it is always mixed with the requirements of the ego, and perhaps it usually begins and ends with fear—still there are moments when the sensation of sexual love conquers all, and much of our life and motivation is connected to the judgment that this is good. In any event, we recognize that it is a force of nature and we earnestly desire to submit our minds and feelings to it. If the mind refuses or strays, we despair of our minds and seek greater passion that will compel the assent of the mind. This intense submission is called by some "loss of the sense of separateness."

Much of our daily life is thus based on the awareness that there are different kinds of forces or energies in us, and on the wish to experience those energies which bring us and others sensations of pleasure to which the mind can give assent. The statement by Bapak suggests that in sex there are energies of an extraordinary sort which are available to us only when the requirements of the mind and feelings do not govern us in this way. The idea, strangely enough, seems to be that the intense submission of and to sexual excitement bars us from the highest energies of sex.

Is there a clue here to the practical basis of sexual strictures in religion? Is what we now experience as mere moral fiat and the grim repression of joy a fragment of some forgotten knowledge about the role of sex in inner transformation? Was there a time, in our own religious traditions, when men and women held back from the pleasures of sex out of an understanding rather than out of puritanical fear? And is the historical omnipresence of monastic communities with their elaborate and stern organization a sign of the superhuman help that is required for the practical psychological utilization of sexual energy?

Add now the aspect of sexual reproduction and such thought opens up some remarkable perspectives. For if the quality of human states of consciousness has to do with the nature of the energy available to the entire organism, then one may—without feeling totally insane—speculate about the influence of a couple's psychological state upon the child that is being conceived!

And we shall not find it quite so easy to scoff at Bapak when he says it is necessary to become calm before intercourse so that one may be free of lower forces which, as it were, soil and confuse the inner feeling and which thereby affect the formation of the child's character and destiny. He tells his people they must not engage in sex when they have quarreled either among themselves or with others. What is needful, he says, is to maintain a sense of quiet and a feeling of the greatness of God. He adds that this is one effort which is indeed possible between men and women who have not yet received the complete guidance of God in all of their inner life. The implication is that there is a totally new and extraordinary sexuality for the completed human being, but no one can know how many years will have to pass before that completion is reached.[14]

I was often told of "Subud children" who were said to be unusually kind and gentle. In any case, all of this forms an important part of Subud's mission in the world: the addition to the population of ever more children conceived under higher influences.

It is true of many who are drawn to the new teachings that sexual pleasure, which has been the leitmotif of the revolution in thought started by Freud, is no longer held to be of such overriding importance. "Sex is sacred" no longer means, necessarily, that sexual pleasure is sacred. Thus, from these "alien" Eastern ways, with their concepts of a universe composed of qualitatively different levels of energy, life and intelligence, come teachings about such things as sex which resonate strangely with much in our own orthodox traditions. Considering that so many who follow these teachings seem outside "the establishment," we might have expected otherwise. Perhaps these new teachings are providing an empirical, experiential basis for an entirely different way of thinking about such questions of the day as contraception, marital fidelity, homosexuality and so forth. Hopefully they are, for in the absence of experience is not certainty close to lunacy?

Bapak sets forth only a few external regulations for the latihan, but in the light of what has been said about openness to the forces and influences, they are worth noting here, particularly those involving women. The following is quoted from the "General Information Sheet for Women Members Only"*:

> Women during menstruation should not do latihan in a group or alone (unless it arises spontaneously). At the end of the period it is advisable to wash the hair and recommence latihan. Pregnant women should not attend open-

---

* It is important to note that such instructions are meant only for Subud members or for applicants who have decided to join.

ings. Pregnant women should, in general, not take part in latihans with others nor do latihan alone after the sixth month. . . .

It should be explained to women that the latihan is automatically present in a woman without need for her to do anything both before, at the time of delivery, and afterward, and that no woman should feel that either she or her child is losing anything by not doing the latihan. . . .

The significance of menstruation is the purification of the blood of woman . . . And the reason why this occurs with woman is simply that the nature of woman is to be a recipient vessel, whereas that of man is to be a channel of transmission.

For this reason, it should be clear that, during her period, a woman truly needs repose, so that the process of purification that is taking place in her should not be hindered. If the woman could but know it, she would be aware that this kind of repose is really a latihan. . . . Now, concerning clothes, since the clothes worn should provide what is needed for the female nature, their design should correspond both to the bodily form and the movements required by her feminine nature. Similarly, what is required for a man is that the clothes he wears should correspond to the male form and the movements required by his male nature. . . .

It is quite true that if a woman wears trousers she finds it easier to make movements; but since the resulting movements will be of a male character, it must not be forgotten that such facilitation of movements really offends against her feminine nature, and, if they become a habit, they will be the cause of harm to her inner self.[15]

Social Order and Self-Perfection

With this we are brought to the question: Is it possible that the details of *all* human civilized forms, from temple to toilet, were once occasions for the reception or purification of inner energies? Modern sciences of man—psychology, anthropology, archeology—might agree that traditional societies indeed believed them to be such. But suppose they actually *were;* suppose modes of life having to do with sex, clothing, food or education, actually were precise instruments and means by which men could work to perfect their psychological condition. How would this affect our concept of what traditions are and where they come from? And how would we then look upon the human enterprises—past, present and future—of reforming tradition?

As for the question of moral behavior and social concern, in Subud this is essentially the question of the sense of life outside the latihan, ordinary everyday life. It is here that the real function of thinking and emotion, which are held to be transcended in the latihan, can be understood. According to Bapak, man must use these ordinary functions to work for the welfare of human life on this planet. He cautions his people not to neglect these ordinary functions, nor let them fall into disuse. It is quite enough, he immediately adds, that a man ceases to use his thinking and emotional functions twice a week during latihan; these two half-hour periods are all a man really needs to receive the working of the Power of God within himself.[16]

What we have here is not so much a moral stance as an attitude toward the feelings and desires which are involved in social issues great and small. To a very large extent, these feelings and desires are what generate problems of morality and, in Subud, the beginning of spiritual growth has little to do with the direct effort to solve these problems of mankind.

Bapak was once asked if being in Subud meant that one should resist being drafted during wartime. He answered by saying man's life on earth requires that it be properly ordered, and that for this, man-made regulations are necessary. Such regulations, having been made by men, are binding upon men. To those who asked specifically about military service, his reply was that these are clear examples of laws which derive from men and which serve an important function in maintaining ordinary life. He added that there is no spiritual law forbidding military service; one cannot disobey laws which are one's own creations and one cannot, therefore, commit an offense against one's own country. In ordinary life, men must be consistent.[17]

This is not anti-morality, nor even amorality. The task is, rather, to separate the moral and social concerns of man, which have to do with the satisfaction of desires, from that which concerns the "soul" behind the desires, feelings and thoughts. It is only when the individual's contact with the Will of God has become deeper and more constant that right action in the largest sense becomes possible. For then it is a new man who is acting, purged, through the Grace of God, of dominance by the more selfish and egoistic side of his nature. This is the ideal. The danger along the way is to confuse satisfying functioning in the world as judged by thought and desire with the growth of "inner feeling."

And so, while reminding the members that receiving the Will of God is "above morality," Bapak still urges social action. More is required of man, he says, than merely receiving the grace of inner feeling and holding it for the inner life alone. Such receiving should be manifested in action, social action, the giving of help to others who are in need and the struggle to right what is wrong. A man must be able to bear witness to what he has received.[18]

It is the growth of a balanced relationship between the inner and the outer which is the main goal regarding action in the world. For though one must use one's thinking and emotional forces in everyday life, they are, by their nature, "always unwilling to give way" and such as to make a man feel superior, or "in the right, or more capable than other people."

It may be well to bear this last in mind. For, as these teachings become better known in the West, they are sure to be faced with the accusation that they are too "quietistic," that their followers tend to retreat into themselves, turning away from the suffering of the world while leaving the field to the forces of injustice. In response to this, and in the light of Subud, one may simply ask: What does it mean to struggle for a better social order? Is a certain level of psychological development necessary before a man can know what is good for another human being? If so, how much, how far must man develop? How far can he develop? Is help required?

Understanding Death

All the new teachings are teachings about death, and Subud is no exception. But it is not so much what they say about death, for some say very little. Generally speaking, what is offered is a set of more or less controlled conditions in the midst of which the individual seeks for himself to experience something of the truth about death.

For example, if in the latihan a man experiences something in himself that is truly independent of his thoughts, feelings and desires, it stands to reason that his relationship to death will change. At the very least, he may begin to see the fears and beliefs which had hitherto shaped his concept of what it means to die. According to Bapak, this "inner feeling," by means of which a man sees the ordinary self, is precisely that which survives the death of the self.

The point is that over the course of a Subud member's life a separation is said to take place in which the mind, heart and desires become subordinated to the increasingly mature inner feeling. They become, Bapak says, servants of the soul, servants whose only field of useful application is this life on earth. When the time of death comes and a man returns to his true origin, the servants cannot follow him and they must "remain behind" in the place where they belong. They cannot follow the soul after death.[19]

As death approaches, mind, heart and desires are said to weaken and lose their force. If by this time the inner being has not grown by the reception of higher energies, the individual falls into "darkness" and what survives is "rigid and lifeless." But if in the latihan the Power of God has truly become active, then the inner self comes alive and, according to Bapak, one gains a knowledge of what life is like after death and "before I was born." Such knowledge totally undercuts the question of what takes place after one's death, for the moment of such knowledge is already a moment in which the inner feeling is freed from the influences of mind, desire and heart.[20]

The implication here is that one will have already tasted something like the after-death state in which the soul, of necessity, separates from the mind and desires. The mind and desires which put the fearful question in the first place are not, in fact, what can survive. We might put it this way: the questioner (the "mind") will, in fact, be destroyed by death. But to discover this it is necessary for a man to experience something in himself which is independent of his ordinary functioning. The real discovery of mortality need not be negative since it can only take place by the opening of an inner feeling which is not of the mortal body.

The soul, Bapak says, is the origin of one's life, while the mind, heart and feelings appear later. Since they are in principle subordinate to the soul, these ordinary functions cannot be the force which trains the soul or helps it to grow. A man can only receive such help passively, "from above." All *thinking* about spiritual matters is thus bound to be fruitless, since thinking is just such an ordinary function. But a "place," so to say, has to be made amid these ordinary functions for the soul to grow. This means that thought, emotion and feeling must be "relaxed" or "allowed" during the latihan. Bapak likens the soul to water or air; if the space is narrow, very little water can occupy it.[21]

He goes on to say that this inner feeling remains narrow when it stays under the dominion of mind and heart, or "worldly concerns," as he also calls them. In order for the "inner feeling" to expand, the heart and mind must turn their concerns beyond their own interests, beyond man, beyond the world. Again, this turning cannot be done by mind and emotions alone; complete submission to the Power of God is necessary.

Bapak speaks of the narrow soul as *satanic*. After death, such a soul remains narrow, imprisoned and blind because it has never been allowed to grow and become open to a wider life. It is the latihan which gradually effects the expansion of the soul and which, quite literally, prepares man for death and after-death.[22]

For, Bapak says, we do not always die in conditions that are peaceful and calm. We may be killed in a violent accident or we may die of a stroke at the theater, or because of some sudden shock, such as losing our job or winning a lottery. He tells his people that while they are alive they must become accustomed to a wide variety of circumstances so that they will know how to die and be ready to die. One purpose of the latihan is to help them to experience the Power of God in the midst of many different external conditions, and to learn thereby how to die in any circumstances, tumultuous or peaceful. Men, he says, must acquire this knowledge while they are still on earth. They must not delay until they are faced with death. For then it is too late.[23]

By now, we have heard enough about the new teachings to know that their intention is always pragmatic. Yet here, suddenly, we are plunged into talk about the soul, the satanic, the hereafter, etc., concepts which not long ago we in the West may have rejected precisely because they seemed hollow, or naïve. Was this because our religion never made clear to us the practical significance of such ideas? I think we must keep this possibility in mind as we ponder the content and methods of these new teachings. I mean the possibility that all genuinely religious ideas have an empirical basis, and are embedded in a method by means of which a man may obtain the experience necessary to verify and use them.

To appreciate the spirit of the new religious searching in America, it is not so important to decide at the outset whether certain ideas are to be accepted or rejected. The more interesting question is, How are they understood to be a help, an instrument for change? The moment we put this question we become that much more alert to the *use* of ideas in any new teaching and that much less insistent that this teaching fit into familiar categories.

5

Transcendental Meditation

(Maharishi Mahesh Yogi)

Promises

We all remember the Maharishi. It was at the end of 1967 and during most of 1968. His picture seemed to be on the cover of every magazine in America. *Life, Look, Time, Newsweek, Esquire, Saturday Evening Post, The New York Times Sunday Supplement,* and many, many others from *Dance Magazine* to *Ebony,* carried major stories about him and his teaching. There were the Beatles, the Rolling Stones and Mia Farrow. There were Harvard, Madison Square Garden, the Johnny Carson show; and the same thing was happening throughout Europe in London, Holland, Germany and Scandinavia.

It was a gold mine for the reporters. Here was a "classic" guru, delivered by Central Casting: the flowing hair, the white robes, the floral cascades, the gnomelike twinkly eyes and the "Eastern serenity." At the same time this was a holy man surrounded by money, matinee idols, public-relations men, private planes and air-conditioned meditation halls. Every journalist's account was the same: charmed by the man, humorously skeptical and perplexed by the message, mildly approving of its effect on the young. For, following upon the great popularity of Timothy Leary, the Maharishi's was the first voice the alienated masses of young people would listen to that derogated drugs as a path to greater awareness. "He signaled the beginning of the post-acid generation," said one young man.

Not only the young, however, were interested. Tens of thousands from the solid middle-class were also paying their fee for instruction in the magic of transcendental meditation. We saw photographs of huge auditoriums filled with well-tailored adults, their eyes closed, and their minds—the captions told us—plunged into the deeper levels of thought.

Various authorities on Yoga and Eastern religion quickly lined up against this gentle guru with the thunderous following. They condemned what they called his idea of "instant Nirvana," his claim that discipline, concentration and long effort were all a waste of time and a misunderstanding of Eastern wisdom. All one had to do, he said, was to sit comfortably for a few minutes every day and silently repeat a special sound or phrase called a *mantra*. Other than this, nothing else was necessary, and one could lead whatever sort of life one pleased; within weeks the change would be apparent. One would begin to feel more energy and less tension; one would become more efficient, more alive, less negative, healthier, *happier*.

> Expansion of happiness is the purpose of life, and evolution is the process through which it is fulfilled. . . . The purpose of individual life is also the purpose of the life of the entire cosmos. The purpose of creation is expansion of happiness which is fulfilled through the process of cosmic evolution.[1]

Thus, according to the Maharishi, it is man's cosmic duty to be happy, for insofar as he becomes happy he best serves the purposes of creation. And transcendental meditation opened the way to happiness. For, the mind naturally seeks happiness. Its constant movement and wandering springs from its endless search for happiness among external objects that in themselves cannot satisfy the mind deeply or for long. By coming in touch with the source of thought, great bliss is experienced which far exceeds all previous happiness. Transcendental meditation was given out as the simple and direct means for the mind to come to the source of its activity. Wrote the Maharishi:

> The technique may be defined as turning the attention inwards towards the subtler levels of a thought until the mind transcends the experience of the subtlest state of the thought and arrives at the source of the thought. This expands the conscious mind and . . . brings it in contact with the creative intelligence that gives rise to every thought.[2]

Thus connected with the fundamental striving of the universe, man's life would automatically improve. On the personal level, his inner conflicts would subside and disappear, he would get along with others and make others happy, and he would function at a level far beyond his usual capacity. No problems of human life would remain if only enough people practiced transcendental meditation. War, poverty, injustice and crime would vanish, permitting humanity happily to fulfill its function in the cosmos . . . all from repeating a strange sound a few minutes in the morning and evening.

> Without our having to observe or struggle with ourselves, quite spontaneously our natural inclinations begin to come into greater harmony with the natural laws of the evolution of life. Our desires become increasingly life supporting and simultaneously increasingly fulfilled. This happens gradually. We are not angels from the first meditation, but as the sense of inner well-being grows, naturally the mind becomes well-intentioned, warm, loving and clear, and no longer irritable or fearful. . . . The wars that break out in

the world are the result of the build-up of tension generated by tense, irritable people. We may think they are the results of economic factors or of arguments between politicians but these are simply the results and the expression of existing tension. . . . [3]

Was all of this simply another form of naïve faith which merely altered the name of that kindly, but outmoded, personal God of the Western world? Were these people now expecting something called "the source of thought" to do exactly the sort of thing the world had vainly expected from its former "God"? Had this diminutive, giggling Hindu left his monastery in the Himalayas only to "bring to the West" the rosy cosmic optimism which had gasped its last in Auschwitz, Hiroshima and Vietnam?

When such questions were put to his followers, they replied, "But it works! We have a method that actually does the trick. Try it!" Hundreds of thousands tried it and found that it did work. But what did that prove? There had always been "methods" which hundreds of thousands, even millions, of people had "successfully" tried—and the result was, if anything, more war, brutality, confusion and personal misery in the world. Such methods had all come bearing similar promises.

Critics were thus not only put off by what they called the Maharishi's "commercialism" (all pupils, including, of course, such as the Beatles, had to pay a week's salary to be told their mantra). What really set their teeth on edge were the Maharishi's promises.

In all of this, many Westerners began remembering what it was about Eastern religion they never really liked in the first place. The Judaeo-Christian tradition, whatever else one might say about it, at least knew the weight of human suffering. When held against the torments of grief, loneliness, pain, disease, self-doubt and anxiety, the Maharishi's talk about "bliss-consciousness" seemed romantic, even cheap. Perhaps Western teachings had shoved man down too far into a sense of incapacity and guilt, but was it any better to waft his ego into the pink clouds of "divinity"? When the Maharishi so cheerfully brushed aside the whole idea of effort and inner struggle as a "misunderstanding," not only he but all his followers, including youngsters who had been tested in life by nothing sharper than a low grade on a term paper, were casting their understanding above that of Socrates, Augustine, St. John of the Cross, Rabbi Akiba, Maimonides, Al-Ghazzali, and countless others including, perhaps, even Jesus Christ himself!

As everyone knew from reading the magazines or watching television, the Maharishi had come with the avowed intention of changing the course of human history. If only 10 per cent or even 1 per cent of the world's population were to practice transcendental meditation, it "would be enough to neutralize the power of war for thousands of years." The Maharishi was surely leading with his chin.

Toward the end of 1968 the Maharishi announced that his ten-year period of missionary activity had come to an end and that he was returning to India. He had "turned on" vast numbers of people, but had not come anywhere near his hoped for 10 or 1 per cent. The general feeling was that even if he had, it would not have meant very much. He was reported to have acknowledged the failure of his mission. The Beatles said they were disillusioned with transcendental meditation. There were similar stories about the Rolling Stones. The Maharishi left the West, and on a national scale, little more was heard of him or his movement.

The appearance of this man and his teaching had seemed more like the run of a Broadway show than the coming of a new spiritual dispensation. There was the same quality of publicity; the opening-night crowds were enthusiastic and for a year the play was a popular success. But the reviews were uniformly cool, even though the performance of the leading man was generally well-liked. A fair show, but not even in the same league with such all-time smash hits as Zen Buddhism and Christianity.

The Attracted Mind

Who were these judges? *We* were. Here, writ large, were some of our own society's criteria and attitudes about the new in religion. Because of these criteria—concerning publicity, immodest claims, money, secrecy—it is doubtful if anyone ever discovered whether the Maharishi had brought something really new or not.

The movement he began, however, is not dead or dying, even though the Maharishi has returned to India, and even though glamorous people are no longer advertising him. His followers estimate that throughout the world some three to four hundred thousand people are practicing transcendental meditation. I was informed, moreover, that the return to India itself only signaled the end of the first stage of the Maharishi's mission.

> Maharishi is very pleased with the way the movement is going. Right now his main concern is to create as many initiators as possible. And so he's very busy in India doing just that. In the United States we need at least 20,000 initiators considering that we have a population of 200,000,000. So the plan right now is to take some initiators who have a great deal of experience and teach them how to train others to be initiators. Once that is done, then Maharishi will probably go into silence. And the whole movement will be self-sufficient.

Initiation is the procedure whereby the mantra is imparted. To receive this initiation, the aspirant need only attend two introductory lectures and be interviewed. He is requested to refrain from drugs or any spiritual practice for a period of about two weeks both before and after being given the mantra. This is so he will be clear in his own mind as to the results, or lack of results, of transcendental meditation.

Not everyone receives the same mantra, or sound. "Instructors select the mantra that fits the personality of the student." When a reporter asked him about this selection, the Maharishi replied that he had succeeded in mechanizing the whole procedure of imparting the mantra.

"Think of blood specimens," he said. "As specimens may vary, so may the proper syllable or sound for a person. It should resonate to the pulse of his thought and, as it resonates, create an increasingly soothing influence."[4]

To determine the right sound, all the teacher has to do is ask certain questions about the person's health, feelings, education, profession and marital status.

One student, who had long since grown discouraged with the method, complained about it:

> All he (the initiator) did was ask me my name and my occupation. I told him I was unemployed. Then he gave me my mantra. I guess I was kind of vague with him. So I guess he gave me the mantra for vagueness.

Yet, he immediately added:

> But I still have never told anyone my mantra. I probably won't tell you either.

Why the secrecy? On this subject everyone gave the same response, using precisely the same simile as though reciting a credo. The speaker here, one of the initiators, is a housewife in her early thirties:

> When you're instructed in the use of your mantra, you're told how to use it properly so that your mind will go to more and more subtle levels. It's like a seed that's planted. To misuse it or tell it to someone else is like pulling the seed out to see how it's growing.

Another initiator, however, added something to this:

There is no secrecy here. The whole idea is that once a
sound is given during initiation it's like you take a seed and
put it in the ground. Okay, now if you're going to reveal this
sound it's like taking out the seed, looking underneath—
you're bringing it back to the gross surface. The sound is
given on a very subtle level of the mind. You can't just take
it out, like a seed, and plant it again. When a person is given
the mantra he is taken through steps so that he gets in a
transcendental state. It's not just given. Also, if a person tells
someone else his mantra it may be the wrong one for that
other person. And he may try it and not get results and be
needlessly disappointed.

Once he has received his mantra, the student is instructed to
sit quietly and comfortably for about twenty minutes in the morning and evening before meals. He is to repeat the mantra to himself throughout that time, but without forcing the matter.
Whenever he sees his mind wandering, he merely brings his attention gently back to the repetition.

The followers of the Maharishi tirelessly emphasize how easy
the whole procedure is. Students are told they must make no attempt to control their minds or discipline their thoughts. In fact,
no effort of *any* kind is to be made. It is this total effortlessness,
they say, which distinguishes their way from all other teachings.
As one twenty-year-old girl put it. "I tried Zen, but it was just too
hard. Then I found this!"

There is an arresting psychological theory behind this stress on
the easiness of transcendental meditation. It is clearly stated in
one of the organization's brochures:

The attention of the mind has a particular characteristic. It
is like a radar beam, scanning the field of its experience for
a greater intensity of happiness than it is at the moment

experiencing. The mind wanders in search of happiness. . . . The attention is governed by the natural tendency of the mind to search for greater satisfaction, greater joy, greater fulfillment than it is at the moment experiencing. This is what holds and directs attention to whatever the mind is upon. It is the force which is responsible for all human endeavor.[5]

This is the premise of transcendental meditation and, roughly speaking, it agrees with the way the ordinary mind is seen in most Eastern and Western religious disciplines. But:

For centuries it has been assumed that it is the nature of the mind to wander and for this reason it has been understood as hard to control. Like a monkey jumping from branch to branch, it has to be disciplined and coerced against its natural inclination before it can effectively accomplish anything. This is a misunderstanding. We have mistaken the *activity* of the mind to be its essential nature.

Now, why does the mind wander? We find that it wanders; it is our experience that it is difficult to control. It is certainly very difficult indeed to hold the attention fixed upon something which is giving no satisfaction or interest. But if something is giving satisfaction and continues to do so, we can attend to it without any difficulty at all. The mind wanders because it is thirsty for a greater happiness than it is at the moment experiencing. It wanders in the changing field of experience as long as it finds nothing permanent to hold its attention by giving it the perfect satisfaction which is its only fulfillment.[6]

The moment this wandering mind is exposed to the bliss of subtler levels of thought, its attention is drawn without having to be controlled. Transcendental meditation is thus understood simply as a means of opening the wandering mind to the riches of happiness which it has wrongly been seeking in external objects and events. The Maharishi writes:

> . . . in this practice of transcendental deep meditation the conscious mind . . . finds that the way is increasingly attractive as it advances in the direction of bliss. A light becomes faint and dim as we go away from its source, and the intensity increases as we proceed toward the source. Similarly, when the mind goes in the direction of the absolute bliss of the transcendental Being, it finds increasing charm at every step of its march. The mind is charmed and is led to experience the transcendental Being.
>
> Thus we find the practice of transcendental deep meditation is a pleasant practice for every mind. Whatever the state of evolution of the aspirant, whether or not he is emotionally developed or intellectually advanced, his mind, by its very tendency to go to a field of greater happiness, finds its way to transcend the subtlest state of thinking and arrive at the bliss of absolute Being. That is why the practice of transcendental deep meditation is not only simple, but also automatic.[7]

These are richly provocative thoughts. For one thing, they seem to base the whole enterprise of inner development on the same pleasure principle that other disciplines have diagnosed as the source of human fractioning and confusion. Great saints in all traditions have, to be sure, told us that the intensest pleasures of ordinary life pale beside the joys of higher states of consciousness. But they also warn us that the pleasures of the ordinary life are so mixed with fear, self-deception and fantasy that the ascent to higher levels of happiness is impossible without at the same time struggling against the overpowering tendency of the mind not only to wander, but to take its "pleasure" by means of fears and falsehoods. They warn us, in short, against underestimating the complexity of the human psyche and the degree to which it "enjoys" the unreal. Otherwise, reliance on the *attracted* mind results, at best, in mere tranquilization, the substitution of daydreams for night mares.

Clearly, such questions cannot be settled simply by a discussion of concepts. All the new teachings agree, in one way or another, that they are practical, experiential questions—that it is up to each individual to find a way to experience directly the truth of the matter. It is precisely this practical, personal perspective that prompts one to ask: To what in a man does the idea of easy spiritual progress appeal? What sort of pleasure or "happiness" does it bring to accept the thought that no struggle or sacrifice of any sort is needed for the radical transformation of the inner life?

If the methods of science have taught us anything, is it not that the attracted mind cannot of itself be the verifier of truth? Perhaps twentieth-century science blundered by ruling out all possible human emotion as a source of knowledge. We shall raise this question later. But are we really prepared to say that our ordinary everyday feelings are not often misleading? When the issue is put this way, we can see why the psychological disciplines of the great religious traditions are ways of developing the *directed mind* as a balance against the attracted mind.

The Theory of the Mantra

The theory of the mantra dates far back in the history of religion. Sound, when understood generally as matter in a state of vibration, obviously encompasses much more than what we ordinarily hear with our ears. We can readily acknowledge that sound, even in the ordinary sense, has effects beyond bringing pleasant or unpleasant associations to mind. It can directly affect our body, just as certain sounds can break glass. Theoretically, it is thus obvious that all sound has some effect upon us, even though we may not recognize what it is. Many ancient psychological disciplines lay claim to a method of determining these effects. If such methods do exist, it stands to reason that they could be used as part of a technique of manipulating or studying the states of human consciousness.

If ours is a universe of energy, it is also a universe of vibrations. And as energy can be various, so vibrations may vary. Moreover, if we may speak of qualities of energy, then we may also speak of qualities of vibration. It is not far from this to the equation of divine energy with divine vibration or sound, and the correspondence of levels of reality with a hierarchy of sound. At any rate, it is not a fantastic idea; fantastic thinking only enters when we immediately assume we can *easily* have both the knowledge to make these distinctions in practice and the ability to make use of sound for finely controlled psychological purposes.

"Sacred language" may, from one point of view, be defined as a system of sounds based on knowledge which we, in present times, do not have. Thus, speaking very abstractly and speculatively, a sacred language is a reflection of the entire spectrum of creative energies in the universe. The use of music and chanting, the arrangement of words in a song or myth, probably have to be understood in this context. Theoretically we would have to recognize the distinction between that aspect of language which provokes certain images and ideas which in turn affect our organism, and another aspect of language which *directly* affects our organism by vibration in a carefully controlled way. Surely scripture, if it is "sacred," does both. "Secular," or ordinary, language then may be understood simply as language in which these elements are poorly recognized and uncontrolled.

It is said that Sanskrit is, or was, such a sacred language, and that the Vedic hymns—the root of all later Hindu scripture— were composed and sung as reflections of the divine play of creative energy. Many mantras are short phrases or words from the Vedas, others have different sources, but all are from the sacred language of Sanskrit. Even where Indian disciplines have spread to foreign lands—such as Tibet, China and Japan—the mantras, when they are used, tend to remain in Sanskrit because of what is understood to be the cosmic and psychological properties of the language.

Although certain mantras, such as *"Om,"* are supposed to produce the same effect for anyone who intones them in the right way, the practical use of mantras is also based on the idea that individuals vary in regard to which special sound is helpful to them. Thus one may well believe that the dispensing of mantras requires an extraordinary psychological knowledge not only of men as they are, but of men as they can become. For, obviously, repeating any mantra—or any sound whatever—over and over again for months and years will produce effects of one sort or another which, if the individual is so inclined, he may view as interesting or beneficial. But the ability to know precisely which sounds will have what effects on what types of human beings, and to know how these mantras must be given to these varying types of men in proper balance with other aspects of a general practical method, surely requires the preternatural psychological understanding of the great masters.

"It's Easy!"

The followers of the Maharishi implicitly believe he has such knowledge, though they do not believe it is extraordinarily difficult knowledge to acquire. A student may become an initiator, authorized to dispense mantras, merely by taking a three-month course at the main ashram in India.

I asked several initiators if they could tell me something about what they learned during their three-month stay in India. Their reply was invariably: "the knowledge of how to give mantras." Said one, a twenty-eight-year-old plant superintendent who had been meditating for about a year, "It's just that we have the knowledge of how to do it. It's as if you had no knowledge of chemistry and asked me how to make a cup. There would be no sense in my telling you all about the chemical composition of this cup. I would just say, well, I have the knowledge how to mix chemicals to make the cup. I just have the knowledge of how to give mantras. Knowledge is not difficult to obtain. Knowledge is very simple, the simplicity of life. Mistakes are impossible."

One student described the process of initiation in this way:

> I was told to close my eyes and make my mind blank, which I did. Then I was given the mantra and told to let my thoughts come in without making any effort. I was to bring the mantra to the thoughts and to keep that up as I kept reaching subtler and subtler levels of thought, just to keep bringing the mantra gently up to meet the thought.

In the words of another initiator, "When this is done we reach subtler and subtler levels of thought until we transcend thought itself and reach deep into the Being and come into the transcendental state."

Sometimes meditation "goes well," sometimes not. "There's a trick we're given if we're really tensed up or upset about something or someone. I make my mind like a blackboard or a screen. Then I put the person I'm upset about on the screen and I don't try to do anything to him, I just bring the mantra to this thought. And sure enough, the person usually just melts away and I'm not upset any more. The vibrations of the mantra do the job."

Once the student has been initiated, he is urged to return periodically for the procedure known as *checking*. This is to make sure he is meditating in the right way, or to help him resolve any particular difficulties he may be having. Often, it is simply that "after a while you lose the inspiration, you lose the reason behind it; it goes away, I guess. Or you just sort of forget about it. Your mind gets involved with other things and you just sort of forget about it. It's sort of to keep you doing it, basically."

An initiator told me:

The moment someone comes we know if he needs checking. There's no need for words, and we just take him through the steps of checking—unless someone feels very, very disturbed in which case we listen to him for a minute or two and then take him through the steps. There is no analysing. I know some people who drop out and get involved with drugs or something, and then they come back three or four months later and ask to be straightened out. So we take them through a checking and put them back on the correct way.

Although occasionally it involves only questions and answers, checking is for the most part very much like the initiation process where the student is instructed how to keep applying the mantra effortlessly to his thoughts. Apparently, checking need not only be done by initiators. Once, while I was waiting inside the Berkeley building—a large, airy, beautifully clean and quiet house located amid grand old fraternity buildings two blocks from the campus—a very pretty young girl who had been meditating less than a year came skipping happily down the stairs and said to another student, "I did it! It's easy!" She had just conducted her first checking session.

In addition to individual meditation and checking, there is much group activity; and now, with such great numbers of people, even checking sessions are a group affair in Los Angeles. There are regular lectures which are open to the public, and there are frequent short periods of communal meditation. There are also occasional week-long "courses" where a very advanced meditator, often from India, leads meditation, gives lectures and instructs students in simple Yoga exercises. For these courses, whole hotels or resorts may be rented. There is nothing cheap or makeshift about any of the external operations, beauty of surroundings counts for a great deal.

Practically everyone hopes some day to go to India in order to become an initiator and help spread the teaching. They also want very much to spend time in the Maharishi's presence.

> Just being in his presence, I just feel higher. He had such a goodness about him that he just radiates happiness and you can't help but feel some of it. You just feel constantly that everything is fine.

What Is a "Practical Method"?

In general, students feel that transcendental meditation gives them everything positive that drugs could give, but with none of the drawbacks. As to comparisons with psychotherapy, students who have been analyzed claim that one or two sessions of transcendental meditation did more for them than years of psychotherapy of any sort. "All that talking and no communicating! Poor shrinkers!"

> People can talk and talk about meditation, but the proof is what kind of results you have in your daily life. I'm not working for spectacular results, but what I am getting is an ability to cope with things a little better, and not let things upset me so much, and *that* is the greatest gift I could have. Because before I started meditating, I would burst into tears at the slightest thing, and everything was a great big melodrama, and now there's a part of me that really feels more secure, and not secure from anything other than myself. . . .
>
> I definitely feel a close bond between all of us who are meditating. Of course, everything's not completely peachy here, people get upset, there's arguments sometimes or, you know, people say they're going to do things and they don't, you know, it takes work to run the Center, it's all volunteer. Nothing changes immediately, it . . . it's just easier.
>
> Life can be bliss. It can be *easy*. You don't have to deprive

yourself of wanting things. You don't become free from desire by wanting to be free; that's desiring it. You just meditate twice a day and all the other things just fall into place.
You start at the root of the problem; you water the roots,
not leaves, because that's where you grow from.

We were sitting, the speaker and I, in the spacious, sun-filled
living room of the Berkeley Meditation Center. She said a great
deal about the purpose of life and about man's place in the cosmic
order; and she said it very well. But she was so young, not more
than twenty years old. She spoke, as do followers of all the new
teachings, about the need for practical methods, practical ideas.
    What does it really mean for ideas and methods to be practical?
Surely it must mean that they help us to achieve our goal. But
what is our goal? Do we know? If so, are we quite sure it is our
own goal and not some vision to which our mind is merely attracted as it has always been attracted in the past? And if not, if we
do not know our goal, what is the use of some other person's practical methods? What attracts us to them? Perhaps the whole question of practical ideas is put in a wrong way. Perhaps it is
fundamentally only the mind, and not some idea, which can be
practical—that is, directed by the intention to discover our own
nature, our own goals, *by a dispassionate study of the attracted mind*.
If so, then only in the moments that we are practical can an idea
or a method be practical.

6

A Note on Krishnamurti

Instantaneous Self-Observation

Nothing about Krishnamurti is as interesting as his work from moment to moment with the people who come to hear him speak. The problems he addresses are perennial with man: war, violence, love, fear, time. But his uniqueness lies in his effort, and in the effort he demands of his audience, then and there, to experience these problems directly as objects for impersonal, ongoing self-observation. Without this constantly renewed effort of immediate verification, one cannot well follow the procession of his thought. It becomes merely elegant, or, on the other hand, discontinuous, full of unwarranted leaps and unorthodox juxtapositions of ideas. And one thereby ends by either agreeing with him or disagreeing.

"What does it mean to agree or disagree?" Krishnamurti asks. It means that one has matched what one has heard against one's own thoughts, and found that it either conforms to these thoughts or does not. In either case, one has learned nothing new; one has either reinforced a previous opinion or rejected a new thought. When our opinions are reinforced, we call it verification, but this is very far from the verification which is demanded by Krishnamurti.

The new teachings are all, each in its way, expressions of a new intensity of searching in the mind of America. But what, Krishnamurti asks, are we searching for? If we immediately respond with an answer, it is clear that we are not searching for something new, but only for something old, something which we can recognize. This is another way of saying that we are searching for something with which we can *agree*. To agree means that the mind is attracted.

For millennia, man has relied on the attracted mind and this reliance has changed nothing for him; quite the contrary. The tragedy of man is not that he never finds what he seeks, but that he *always* finds exactly what he seeks, and no more. Men have found God, happiness, honor, wealth, fame, pleasure. But because they relied on thought, the attracted mind, to identify what they sought and found, there was no change in their lives. Conflict and sorrow continued.

When searching is based on evaluation and judgment, it is thought that is searching, and that always means the search for the known, that which can be recognized. It follows that ordinary searching is really the effort to remain where one is, no matter what the facts are about one's inner or outer life. One seeks confirmation which, in Krishnamurti's language, is psychological security. One seeks to maintain oneself, protect oneself. But what is this self that one is protecting? It is actually a thought, an opinion, or an image, a picture of oneself.

At such a point, one either makes the effort to verify these statements, or one no longer follows Krishnamurti's mind. In a word, one *looks:* am I only a thought?

How is this looking to take place? Here the mind immediately produces its thoughts: one must do such and such, one must relax, or become blank, or breathe a certain way, or free-associate, and so forth. Thus, psychologically, time enters again, for, says Krishnamurti, thought is time. But the looking, the verification which he demands of his audience, must be instantaneous, without thought, quicker than thought. Is that possible? Try it, he tells us, try it now!

If we try it, now, and only if we try it—it makes no difference what we find—it may then be said that we are communicating with Krishnamurti. Communication is possible only between people, not between thoughts or images. To communicate with another, there must be the common instantaneous movement of something that is quicker (or "higher") than thought. There is no process of communication, for process implies time, the future, which means the search for what is recognizable. Communication is out of time because outside of thought.

> Please realize, as we were saying the other day, that merely listening to a few words, or accepting a few ideas, will not solve the problem (of violence) at all. What we are trying to do together is to examine our own minds, our own hearts, the way we think, the way we feel and how we act in our daily life—to examine what we actually are, not what we should be, or have been. So, if you are listening, then you are listening to yourself, not to the speaker. You are observing the pattern of your own thinking, the way you act, think, feel, live.[1]

A New Understanding of Freedom

It is only in the act of self-observation that one learns of its possibility; thought can only conceive of it, not do it. According to Krishnamurti, this is the only way man can taste true freedom, which is freedom from thought, thought being the product of conditioning and memory. Thus he can say, again in speaking about inner and outer violence:

> Perhaps this morning we can go into this question and find out for ourselves whether it is actually possible—not as an

idea, not as a concept, but *actually find out how* to live a
daily life in which there is no disorder inwardly . . . (italics
mine).[2]

Obviously, what he is speaking about here is not the presenta-
tion of a psychological method which is only to be taken home
after the lecture and attempted. The act of instantaneous
self-observation is itself the discovery of how to live without inner
disorder. It is this which the listener must attempt if he is to follow the speaker.

It makes no difference what it is that is observed. Disorder observed is already order. Why? Because psychological disorder involves the attempt to change or deny what is the case in oneself.
But on what basis is this change desired? Again, it is thought, the
picture one has of oneself. Thought, however, cannot change anything, it can only think about it, picture it. Thus, the ordinary
attempt to change ourselves according to some picture we have
within our minds is really a total misfunctioning of our faculties.
And even if it were possible to change ourselves by action that
emanates from thought, in the time it takes to effect this change
there is disorder, action and resistance, conflict between forces.
Who is to say how long this conflict will last, or how it will be
resolved, or what we shall not do—to others or to ourselves—in
order to bring it about? And once it is done, supposing it can be
done, is that an end to the process, or does not thought again, by
means of some new conditioning, start up the whole process once
more?

Instantaneous self-observation is order because in that moment
one is free of the wish to change what is observed. One can attempt this, Krishnamurti tells us. One can attempt to see oneself
without the desire to improve what one sees. No one has ever told
us of that possibility. Indeed, our whole conditioning, our entire
society, is based on the idea of effort as the process of altering
what is. This is true as well of what we call psychological effort,
whether in the systems of Freud, Jung, encounter groups or be-

havior therapy. All of these, sometimes under the name of *seeing,* are really encouraging an effort to be different, rather than to look, instantly, at what is. The various imperatives of recent psychological systems—free-associate! remember your dreams! express your feelings!—are all efforts to change: for, at this moment I am not "free-associating," I must *do* it; I do not remember that dream, I must change that; I am afraid to be angry, I must overcome that. Why must I change this present psychological state? Why do I desire to do it? What thought is leading me, what conditioning?

One has to understand this question of desire, but not intellectually, for there is no such thing as intellectual understanding . . . Why shouldn't there be desire and what is wrong with desire? When one sees a beautiful house, a lovely stream, a cloud lit by the evening sun over the mountain, when you look at all that, there is immense sensual pleasure, the enjoyment of lovely color and so on. What is wrong with it? Why should one suppress it? And when one sees a lovely face, why shouldn't one look at that face? We know how desire arises, it is a very simple and a very obvious phenomenon that doesn't need a great deal of investigation. There is seeing, contact, sensation, and when thought interferes with that sensation desire arises. . . .

But to react is normal, healthy, sane. It would be absurd to see a marvelous light on the cloud and not enjoy it, but thought dwells upon it and makes it into a pleasurable memory, and it wants that pleasure to be repeated. This is the whole nature of sex, thought chews over the pleasure, over and over again and it wants it to be repeated. So there is thought and desire which are always in contradiction with each other. Is it clear? Look, these are only ordinary explanations and, as explanations, have no value at all. But what has value is to see how desire comes into being, how thought interferes with sensation and makes it into a memory and the desire for the pleasure of that memory is given continuity and sustained by thought, nourished by thought . . .

I see myself in a state of contradiction. I see how this contradiction has arisen, and that this contradiction is disorder and that there can be no order brought about by thought, because thought in itself is fragmentary, is limited; thought is the response of memory, and when that memory, which is fragmentary, acts upon this contradiction it breeds further contradiction. So I see the whole of this phenomenon and the very *seeing is the action within which there is no contradiction.*

Look, let's put it very simply. I see I am dull, stupid—the response to that is, I want to be more clever, intelligent, brighter. Now what has happened? I am dull, stupid, and I want to be brighter, more intelligent, in that there is contradiction already, therefore there is further conflict which is a further waste of energy. But if I could live with that stupidity, with that dullness, without the contradiction and therefore with the capacity to look at that dullness, it would be no longer dull. I don't know if you see? Or, I am envious and I don't want to change it, I don't want to become non-envious—the fact is, I am envious. Can I look at that envy without introducing its opposite, without wanting not to be envious, or to change it, or to be specific about it? Can I look at that envy, which is a form of hate and jealousy, can I look at it as it is, without introducing any other factor? The moment I introduce any other factor I bring in further contradiction. But envy in itself is a contradiction, isn't it? I am this, I want to be that, and so long as there is any form of comparative thinking there must be conflict. And this does not mean that I am satisfied with what I am, for the moment I am satisfied with what I am, I only breed further conflict. Can I look at my envy without bringing about conflict in that look?[3]

Thought and Death

Obviously such ideas are not connected by logical implications. Where has one ever heard *seeing* defined in terms of conflict and contradiction? or *desire* as the interference of thought with sensation? One must surmise that Krishnamurti's talks are the expressions of his own self-observation, and to follow him one must make the effort to share that work. Then, presumably, the material of one's own observation provides the basis for understanding the connection between his ideas.

One of the factors of life is death. We are frightened of living, of old age, disease, pain and the sorrow which we know from the moment we are born until we die, which we call living, and we are also frightened of something which we do not know, which we call death. This whole field is our life.

One can see how thought creates fear. Please go into it with me, not just following the speaker, but take the journey together, share the way of moving together. So, we are frightened of life and we are frightened of death, of the known and the unknown, and that fear is bred by thought. I have had experience, I have reached a certain status, a certain position, achieved certain knowledge, which gives me vitality, energy, drive and that whole momentum of thought sustains me and I am frightened to lose it. Anybody who threatens my achievement and success, my platform, I loathe, I hate, I am his enemy. Surely this is so obvious. Don't you know in your business, or when you are teaching, how, when anybody surpasses you, you are frightened, you are antagonistic? And you talk about God, spiritual life, and all the rest of it, but in your heart there is venom. And you are frightened to lose that, and you are frightened of something much greater which is to come, which is death. So you think about death—you think about it and by thinking about it you are creating that interval between living and that which you call death. This is simple enough. The things that you know, the pleasure, the joys, the entertainments, the knowledge, the experience, the achievements, the despairs, the conflicts, the dominations—you know, the things to which you cling, your house, your petty little family, your little nation, you hold on to those with grim death because they are all you have. By thinking about them you create an interval between what you think, as an idea, is lasting, and the actual fact.

Thought breeds, through time, not only the fear of living but the fear of death, and because death is something you don't know, thought says, "Let's postpone it, avoid it, keep it as far away as possible, don't think about it"—but you are thinking about it. When you say "I won't think about it," you have already thought about it. You have thought out how to avoid it and you can avoid it, through the many escapes, the churches, gods, saviors, the resurrection and the idea that there is a permanent, eternal self in yourself which India, Asia, has invented. That is, thought has cleverly said that there is a permanent, eternal self in yourself. . . . Thought has created the idea of an eternal self—the soul, the Atman—in order to find safety, hope, but what thought has thought about is already a secondhand thing, thought is always of the old.

One is frightened of death because one has postponed it. So the problem arises of how to go beyond this so-called living and the thing called death. Is there an actual separation between the two? You understand? To live so intensely is to die to everything of yesterday, obviously—all the pleasures, the knowledge, the opinions, the judgments, the stupid little achievements, to die to all that—to die to the family, to die to your achievements, which have only brought such chaos in the world and such conflict within yourself, to die to all that. Then to die to that brings an intensity, brings about a state of mind in which the past has ceased and the future, as death, has come to an end. So the living is the dying—you cannot live if you do not die.

But most of us are frightened because we want surety, because we want to continue the misery which we have known, the disease, the pain, the pleasure, the anxiety. Because we avoid, push away, death—thought pushes away death—there is fear of the known and fear of the unknown. When there is no interval between death and the living, then you know what it means to die, to die to everything that one has. Then the mind becomes extraordinarily fresh, eager, attentive and innocent. When one dies to the thousand yesterdays, then living is dying. *It is only in that state that time comes to an end and thought functions only where it is needed and not at any other level or at any other demand.*[4]

The Surface of Krishnamurti

For the greater part of the twentieth century, Krishnamurti has traveled through Europe, America and Asia, speaking to millions of people. Still more millions have read his books, many of which are records of his talks. One may safely say that no philosopher, teacher or poet of our time has attracted the respect of more people over such a period. Yet of all the well-known teachers, religious leaders, philosophers and writers of the twentieth century, none has spoken with such austerity of the uselessness of teachers, leaders, organizations and systems of thought or belief. None has maintained such impersonality in his thought, such rigor in his rejection of a following. And surely none has approached the fundamental problems of human life in a way that offers less consolation, less sensationalism, less cleverness, less metaphysical excitement than Krishnamurti. We shall find in his thought no God, no religion, no ethical norms, no life beyond the grave, no new theories or explanations. Nor can we comfortably side with him when he rejects society so totally: because he quickly makes it very clear that we, you and I, *are* society, and that society is brutal, barbaric and chaotic because we, you and I, are brutal, barbaric and chaotic within. This applies whether we are generals or hippies, capitalists or acid heads, whether we live in the big city or in a New Mexico commune.

> War is the spectacular and bloody projection of our everyday life, is it not? War is merely an outward expression of our inward state, an enlargement of our daily action. It is more spectacular, more bloody, more destructive, but it is the collective result of our individual activities. Therefore, you and I are responsible for war . . . [5]

There is, of course, the tremendous electricity of his personal presence. An audience of thousands of people, most of them young, sits totally quiet, with not one person moving, as he speaks. Can one really believe that most, or even very many of them are attempting to follow Krishnamurti by the constantly renewed act of self-observation? If not, then what are they hearing? The same question must surely be applied to any of the great audiences which came to him. If they are not answering his demand, then what are they hearing? Why are they so still? so enraptured?

Anyone who has seen Krishnamurti inevitably speaks of his extraordinary beauty, to which now is added the fragility of age. The Chilean author, Miguel Serrano, wrote that "No one in India, except possibly Nehru, has a more beautiful face than Krishnamurti has."

Finally, there is his fabulous past. Most of the young people who now flock to hear him know little or nothing about his earlier life, how he was "adopted" at the age of thirteen by Annie Besant and C. W. Leadbeater, the two founders of the Theosophical School at Adyar, India, and was immediately proclaimed to be the future avatar of the Age, the new World-Teacher and incarnation of the Lord Maitreya. A new society, called "The Order of the

Star in the East," founded with him as its center, existed for the sole purpose of promulgating his words. From early adolescence, Krishnamurti was thus literally worshiped by thousands of people who saw him as the new Messiah.

In 1929, he threw the whole thing over, dissolving the Order of the Star, repudiating Theosophy as just another cage for man, and disclaiming any authority, spiritual or otherwise, over people's minds. A Theosophist who was one of the women closest to the young Krishnamurti writes of her own desolation over his "abdication":

> I began to feel that Krishna's teaching was inadequate. Krishna, who had written and spoken so beautifully of the "Beloved," who had proclaimed that he and the Beloved were one, seemed to me now to be rejecting all beliefs, even in the existence of God, whom he maintained man had created out of fear, whereas for me a "Beloved," someone to worship, was a necessity . . . I . . . felt lost in what seemed to me cold abstractions, having no relation to the life we are called upon to lead here and now.[6]

Today Krishnamurti's books are proudly displayed and sold in libraries of the Theosophical Society. I asked one elderly Theosophical lady what the general feeling was about him and she merely replied that the truth was all one, and that they still felt close to Krishnamurti.

The point is that many people still think of him as the World-Teacher, even when he tells them to their faces that there is no such thing as spiritual authority, and that he is not anyone's teacher. American students, who do not know his background and reputation, often hear his talks mainly as a profound expression of their own disgust with society, its hypocrisy, its ideas of national honor, duty, race and class, its bourgeois ideals and morality. A close companion of Krishnamurti commented:

Quite naturally, yet also a little surprisingly, Krishnamurti is
suddenly the hero and friend of these students, for long before they met him, the thing he talks about had become for
them as important as eating and breathing. They love what
he says and feel for him a very familiar affection, without
fear or awe.[7]

The Existence of Psychological Help

But is it really possible to love or even to like what Krishnamurti
says? Does this mean one agrees with him? and is attracted to what
he says? He tells us to observe our thought, quickly, now, without
further thought, and hence without *further* self-deception; to do it
now, instantaneously. What possible sense does it make to like or
dislike such a demand? One either responds by making the effort
or one does not. Since this response must be immediate, without
thought as to its results, its possibility, its desirability, its efficacy,
or its dangers, then if it is not done immediately, it shall be only
thought and desire, and the thought-created ego which "makes
the effort." The result will be only more deception.

One may well speak of this as a *leap* into the unknown. Why
should I do it? Theoretically, logically, I can have no reason for
doing it, no motive, for that implies a wish for results and further
slavery to the pictures painted by old thought and desire. But the
facts, psychologically speaking, are perhaps not quite so logical.
My mind must be prepared, for my mind, wretched and full of
deceit as it may be, is all I have now, before this leap. It is all I am,
granting it is not very much. The mind must assent to this effort.
It is only a further deception to think it need not assent; it is simply another pleasant belief that I can make this effort of
self-observation. The mind, somehow, must be persuaded that
this effort is both desirable and worth trying. Otherwise, there
will be lassitude or violence, and, as Krishnamurti tells us, this effort can never be violent. Faith, in its degenerate sense, is just such
violence against the mind.

Now, in all of this we are obviously drifting out to sea. The whole issue is obscure, we do not know how to think about it or be toward it. It is an uncharted terrain and we do not know how to proceed. We are not athletes of the inner life, we have not spent twenty years in desert cells, observing the self-deception of the devil called thought.

I think this is so, and I think because it *is* so, there are some people who go to hear Krishnamurti even after he tells them there is no authority, he is no teacher, no organization can help, etc. Something in his speech, his presence, his life of thought, call it what one will, *helps* the act of self-observation. Not so much that it causes me or compels me, but that something comes to my aid in the moment I choose to try. That is really all one could say; one cannot, and perhaps one need not, be sure if it is Krishnamurti's language, the silent presence of so many others also in my situation or something else.

Often it may be only due to his charisma, his beauty, his reputation, his emphatic tones, or because some phrase or other agrees completely with my pet theory, that I go to hear him, and feel good when he talks. Perhaps most people go to him for such reasons, and perhaps almost none really make the effort he demands. But perhaps some do, those who experience the help that his presence and thought provide. Then, in this sense, one obviously cannot deny that he is a *teacher,* a channel of help for the self-initiated effort of self-observation.

If there are certain conditions, and a certain individual, all of which, when taken together, provide help in the personal struggle for inward freedom, are we not then speaking of a certain form of organization? If so, the question naturally arises as to whether these conditions can be extended to cover more of my life and whether this individual, or the influence he transmits, can be made more accessible. That is can this *help,* whatever it is, be increased, extended, or deepened? An approach like Krishnamurti's may thus open an entirely new idea of what it means for people to be organized for the sake of psychological freedom. For it may well be that all organizations we know are useless, and even an obstacle, if the aim is this freedom.

Each summer at Saanen, Switzerland, a series of talks is organized which extend over a period of some two weeks. Added to this is one week devoted solely to a daily dialogue between Krishnamurti and his audience:

> When we talk about revolution we are concerned with the *psychological* structure of society in which we are caught and of which we are part. And apparently we are not very serious about the psychological structure or the psychological nature of our being which has brought about a society which is so corrupt and which really has very little meaning. We don't take very seriously the question of how to be free from that society. At least there must be a few, a group of people, not organized round a particular form of dogma, belief, or leader, but rather a group of individuals who are seriously and with complete intent, aware of the nature of their psyche and of society and of the necessity of inwardly bringing about a total revolution—that is, no longer living in violence, in hatred, in antagonism, in merely pursuing every form of entertainment and pleasure . . .
>
> What we are concerned about, in this tent, during these talks and discussions, is to see if as individuals we can bring about in ourselves that quality of seriousness which in itself, through awareness of one's own nature, brings about a revolution: to bring this about, not through propaganda, not because we are here every other day for the next three weeks, not because we conform to a particular ideological pattern, but rather as human beings gathered together to understand the very complex problem of living—not belonging to any group, any society, any nationality, to any particular dogma, religion, church, and all that immature nonsense. . . . Also we are concerned with action, not ideological action, not

action according to a particular principle, or action according to Communism, Socialism, Capitalism, or action according to a particular dogma or sanction, but the action of
a mind which, because it has freed itself from the sociological and psychological structure of society, has become a religious mind.

By "religious mind" we mean a mind that is aware not
only of the outward circumstances of life and of how society is built, of the complex problems of outward relationships, but also of its own mechanism, of the way it thinks, it
feels, it acts.[8]

There is not much to be gained by simply labeling Krishnamurti's talks or the three weeks at Saanen an *organization*. It is
much more interesting to put it that there exist certain conditions, and a certain man, and a group of people—all of which,
taken together, offer help in the process of dispassionate, individ-
ually initiated self-study. With this as its aim, such an "organization" can change its outward form totally, from top to bottom,
without a moment's notice. *Who* would change it? Krishnamurti,
of course. But who is *he?*

Relationship: An Example

Very clear examples of Krishnamurti's every-changing way can be
found in the records of his dialogues and discussions at Saanen.
The following is a fragment of one of these dialogues.

The discussion has been on the subject of what it means to
know oneself. Krishnamurti has asked why the mind is always
building up images (of such things as pleasure, pain, resentment,
etc.) which screen one's relationship with another.

Krishnamurti: Say, I am married to you and I have built an
image about you—sexual pleasure, or the insulting things

you have said to me, the nagging, the flattery, the hurts—all that has gone to build up an image about you. Who has done this? Thought, thinking about the sexual pleasure, thought thinking about the insult, thought thinking about the flattery: you say, "How nice you look today, I like your looks!" I adore you when you say that!—so I have collected all that and I have created an image about you. The I is the thought. Right, sir? Wait. So thought has done this and thought is an abstraction, whereas you are real. The image is an abstraction, not real, but you are very real. So I run away from you in abstraction. And then I get hurt because you look at someone else. So now I say to myself, "Why am I doing all this?" Why is thought doing all this?—creating the image, adding to the image, taking things away from the image, and asking the question, "Why is it doing it?"—and who is going to answer it? Is thought going to answer it?

Questioner: Thought cannot give the answer. We must see this.

Krishnamurti: If you understand it, what takes place.

Questioner: Then there's silence.

Krishnamurti: Don't use that word "silence." Just look at what takes place—which means that you have no image. That's what is taking place. When thought says, I have built it and I am going to find out why I have built it, and sees the absurdity of such a question, then *all image-making ceases!* Right? Are you doing it? Then I can look at you—my wife or husband—without an image. Follow this. Go into it a little more deeply. What takes place when there is no more image?

Questioner: There's no observer then.

Krishnamurti: No, sir, go into it; don't reduce it. Go slowly, sir.

Questioner: There is real relationship.

Krishnamurti: I don't know what that means! So far, sir, I've discovered only one thing; that thought has created the image and thought, seeking to find an answer why, will create another image in which it will be caught. It's a vicious circle as long as thought is operating. Right? I have discovered that. Therefore, thought is no longer creating an image, So what is my relationship—please follow this—what is my relationship to things, to people.

Questioner (1): Direct awareness, sir.

Questioner (2): When thought ceases, the real me, the self, becomes in a way more apparent.

Krishnamurti: Is there a real me without the thought? Sir, don't get caught in your own words, be careful.

Questioner: I see you as you are.

Krishnamurti: No, no, I'm not concerned about you. What takes place, what is that relationship when I have no image about you?

Questioner: The dead person becomes a living thing . . .

Krishnamurti: Sir, I wish you would do this, actually: put away the images you have about me, or about your wife, or about somebody else and *look*. Then find out what that relationship is.

Questioner: If I am in relationship, then I can follow the moods and thoughts of that person.

Krishnamurti: That's not what I'm asking, if you don't mind. We are asking: "If I have no image about money, about property, about you—my wife or husband or friend—what is that relationship?"

Questioner: To ask this question is to be back in thought.

Krishnamurti: No, no, madame, just look at it. I have no image about you—and that's a tremendous thing I've discovered. Then I say to myself, "What is my relationship, what is this relationship then, if I have no image?"

Questioner (1): This relationship ceases to be.

Questioner (2): Sir, it's an extremely difficult question to go into, because when we try to find out, put it into words, then thought springs into action.

Krishnamurti: Look, sir, let's make it very simple. You're my friend, I have an image about you. Now, I have no image about you. (Don't answer me, sir.) I have no image about you. What has taken place in me? Not in my relationship with you, what has actually taken place in me? I want to know, what has actually taken place in me?

Questioner: Every second is new.

Krishnamurti: Oh, no. Please, madame, you're all guessing. This isn't a guessing game.

Questioner: You're a fact, you're no longer an idea.

Krishnamurti: Oh, no. You're not going into it. What has taken place in me when I'm not creating an image about everything? You don't even have time to examine and you are ready to answer! Please, look at yourself. Find out what happens if you have done this, if you're no longer an image-making entity, what has taken place? . . . When thought is completely quiet and not building an image about anything, what has taken place? . . . Make it simple. Thought has been chasing its tail, over and over again. And thought says, "What a silly thing I'm. doing," and stops. Right? Then what takes place?

Questioner: I cannot stop it, sir.

Krishnamurti: Then go on, chase the tail.

Questioner: Sir, then thought comes to an end, that's all we know now.

Krishnamurti: I'm showing you, sir; if you do it yourself, it's very simple. Thought has been chasing its own tail. Right? Now thought realizes how silly it is, therefore it stops! What takes place then? Please do it.

Questioner: At the moment when there is no image of you, there is no image of myself.

Krishnamurti: No, sir, That is not the question I'm asking. When thought stops chasing its tail what takes place at that moment, at that second?

Questioner: We don't know.

Krishnamurti: If you don't know, you haven't stopped chasing the tail.

Questioner: The thinker disappears.

Krishnamurti: You see, you're all so eager to answer. You haven't really looked at yourself at all. You haven't spent a single minute looking at yourself. If you had, you would have inevitably come to this point, which is that thought is chasing its own tail all the time. Then thought itself realizes how absurd this is and therefore it stops. Now, when it stops, what takes place?

Questioner: We would be very still.

Krishnamurti: How quick we are to answer, aren't we! Do we give up the game? That's what you're making it into, a guessing game. Look, sir! Listen to this. When thought stops chewing its own tail endlessly, when it stops, what takes place?

Questioner: You are open to . . .

Krishnamurti: I am asking something which you are refusing to face. It is very simple; the moment thought stops chewing its own tail, you're full of energy—aren't you? Because in that chasing, your energy has been dissipated Right? Then you become very intense. No? What happens to a mind that is very intense, not under strain, but intense? What takes place? Have you ever been intense, about anything, have you? If you have what happens?

Questioner: Then you are not, as far as . . .

Krishnamurti: Wait, wait. Sir, you say something and dissipate it. When you are intense, what takes place? There's no problem, and therefore *you* are *not. You are* only when there is conflict.

Questioner: Then you're out of the door.

Krishnamurti: You see, you're verbalizing. Don't do that, sir, please, we have gone into something very deep. It you would only go into it. In that intensity there is neither the observer nor the observed. Sir, only go into it. In that intensity there is neither the observer nor the observed. Sir, when you love—go into it when you love, is there an observer? There is an observer only when love is desire and pleasure. When desire and pleasure are not associated with love, then love is intense—isn't it? It is something new every day because thought has not touched it.[9]

Right Education

In the most recent phase of his work, Krishnamurti has established a school not far from London known as The Educational Center at Brockwood Park. It is meant for a small number of boys and girls in their later teens who, according to the announcement, will study their academic subjects while living "in a fine old house set in magnificent grounds . . . and in a community held together by Krishnamurti's teaching . . "

What is right education? Krishnamurti's singular perspective on the problems of human life is nowhere more sharply apparent than in his views on this subject. Indeed, taken in the widest sense, education is the major theme of all his work.

> Though there *is* a higher and wider significance to life, of what value is our education if we never discover it? We may be highly educated, but if we are without deep integration of thought and feeling, our lives are incomplete, contradictory and torn with many fears . . . .[10]

Like many contemporary critics, Krishnamurti deplores the tendency of modern educational systems to emphasize the acquisition of mere technical skill and factual information. The reasons he gives, however, are uniquely his. We strive for efficiency, he says, because we do not understand the total process of life, which must be experienced anew from moment to moment. We "are afraid of the unknown, and so we establish for ourselves psychological zones of safety in the form of systems, techniques and beliefs."[11] The modern ideal of capacity and ability thus reinforces fear and the endless pursuit of psychological security.

Krishnamurti cannot, however, be placed among those who wish to introduce more of "the affective domain" into contemporary education. Such theorists seek to bring the methods of sensitivity training and psychotherapeutic interaction into our schools in order to make education more emotional. But, Krishnamurti warns, how can we presume to educate the emotions of our children when our own emotions are nothing more than fragmented reactions? Modern psychological methods, moreover, are based on a theory of man which, as we have suggested, radically underestimates human possibility. In Krishnamurti's language, modern psychology, whether of the humanist or psychoanalytic persuasion, fails to distinguish between the personal and the individual. "The personal is the accidental; and by the accidental I mean the circumstances of birth, the environment in which we happen to have been brought up . . . The personal or accidental is but momentary, though that moment may last a lifetime . . . "[12] In short, the new wave of educational reform seeks to develop the personality which, according to Krishnamurti, is merely the product of conditioning and is the cause of so much human suffering. The purpose of education is, rather, to help the child "to be free from the ways of the self."

The crisis in modern education is a mirror of the crisis in religion. The same issues, the same words, arise in both spheres: traditionalism as against relevance, intellect as against the feelings; the question of authority, reward and punishment, discipline and love. The revolution may be more outwardly violent in education, but the general context is almost identical to the revolution in religion. In our society, religion ceased to be a form of education;

and education ceased to be religious in the sense we have been exploring in this book. For Krishnamurti, the meaning of both real religion and education is the search for a quality of stillness in which the mind is free of its conditioning.

Changing or refurbishing ideals, whether of the establishment or of the revolutionaries in our society, and whether they are the ideals of political systems, psychology, or organized religion is, Krishnamurti tells us, merely to substitute one form of conditioning for another. What, then, is left as the main work of education? Nothing less than the work of self-observation! Truth, says Krishnamurti, is far beyond thought or emotional demands. "Parents and teachers who recognize the psychological processes which build up fear and sorrow should be able to help the young to observe and understand their own conflicts and fears."[13]

There is something extraordinarily interesting about this objective—surely nothing quite like it has been promulgated by anyone else: the central purpose of education is to help children toward the act of instantaneous self-observation. What does it tell us about children to learn that they are quite as capable of self-observation as adults? Even more important, what does it tell us about the effort of self-observation? One may hear it said again and again that self-observation, or consciousness of self, is independent of thought, quicker and higher than thought. But nothing brings home the direct and *simple* quality of self-observation more clearly than to realize it is a work for children.

But what sort of educators can help children toward this effort?—*that* is the question.

> The child is the result of both the past and the present and is therefore already conditioned. If we transmit our background to the child, we perpetuate both his and our own conditioning. There is radical transformation only when we understand our own conditioning and are free of it. To discuss what should be the right kind of education while we ourselves are conditioned is utterly futile.[14]

Therefore:

the teacher himself must first begin to see. He must be constantly alert, intensely aware of his own thoughts and feelings, aware of the ways in which he is conditioned, aware of
his activities and his responses . . .[15]

We can now glimpse the dimensions of Krishnamurti's experi-
ment at Brockwood Park and the significance of its being described as a community "held together by Krishnamurti's
teaching." In the light of all we have said, such a community can
only be one held together by the search for self-knowledge, a
search shared by teachers and students alike—indeed, by all who
are connected with Brockwood Park, including of course Krishnamurti himself. Can such a community exist in which the central
aim of all is simply to learn—about oneself, one's relationship
with others, and about the world in which one moves?—to learn,
and not accumulate knowledge, technique or personal gratification? Can a community exist founded on the *unknown* in this way?—
without the support of authority, ritual or ideals? If communication
is possible only between people engaged in the instantaneous pursuit of self-awareness, can an organic society be founded upon
that pursuit?

As we shall see, very much depends upon the way we seek to
answer these questions: not only our understanding of the nature
of civilization, but even, perhaps, the survival of civilization.

Tibet in America

The Appearance of Tibet

Gradually, Tibet is coming into view. Instead of a romantic land haunted by a primitive or perverse mystical spirituality, we see the outlines of something breath-taking: an entire nation defined and ruled by the search for inwardness. Not since the great theocracies of ancient Egypt and Sumeria has there been such a nation.

But its brilliance is reaching us in the moment of its destruction. Twenty years ago the Chinese began their work of invasion and murder. They burned down the great temples and monasteries, slaughtering or imprisoning thousands of monks and lamas. They destroyed the sacred texts, the monuments and the incredible works of art. A land which had stood for a thousand years as the only living link with the organization of ancient wisdom was, in the blinking of an eye, submerged by the floods of the barbarian.

Refugees streamed through the dangerous mountain paths that led to India. Many died or were captured by the Chinese, but many others succeeded and established large colonies along the northern borders of India and Nepal.

Thubten Jigme Norbu, the elder brother of the present Dalai Lama, writes:

(The) total eradication . . . of Tibetan religion and tradition . . . was and still is a major goal of the Chinese, for
until they have succeeded in this they will not have con-
quered Tibet. To this end there has been an unbelievably
tragic attack not only on our ancient shrines and monasteries, but also upon the monks whose homes they
were. . . . The persecution of the monks, their murder, tor-
ture and degradation is a story that has already been told.
Perhaps it is precisely because the story is one of such horror
that the world at large seems to have chosen to ignore
it. . . . There is no point in going over the disaster that has
befallen our country. What is known to have happened is
bad enough, and there is a great deal more that is unknown . . . And in a way, it does not matter that much. It
might have mattered if the outside world had been able to
help. But it is done. All that matters now is that we preserve
the one thing we have left, our faith.[1]

The preservation of Tibet is being visibly pursued in two major
ways. One is by maintaining the tradition and discipline among
the refugee lamas, monks and laymen in India. But in addition to
this, a movement out of India has slowly begun and with it has
begun the effort to seed the teaching among Europeans and
Americans.

Will this be possible?—even the briefest glance at the structure
of Tibetan Buddhism reveals some of the dimensions in this question. For the entire country of Tibet—almost half a million square
miles, and with some four million inhabitants—was, in its way, a
monastery. The Himalayas, both symbolically and actually, held it
apart from the world, from the full play of forces that have carved
the destinies of all other nations in our millennium. To be sure,
Tibet has known its wars and conflicts through the centuries, but
they seem in the long run to have served principally as occasions
for reawakening the psychological and spiritual goals of Tibet's
religious tradition.

The Compassion of Reality

Tibetan Buddhism is centered in the idea of compassion, and its hierarchical structure and ritual cannot really be approached apart from that idea. This compassion may for the moment be defined as: the precise transmission of a supremely benevolent force to each plateau or station of sentient reality according to its capacity for responding to it. The structure of Tibetan society, from the authority of the high incarnate lamas to the peasants in the fields, is an expression of this chain of compassion. It is in this sense that Tibet was a "monastery," an organization or channel of psycho-spiritual help. In a similar sense, the planet Earth itself, indeed the whole universe, is a "monastery"—but of this later.

The country was ruled—and in its dispersal still is ruled—by the Dalai Lama. The "Dalai Lama," however, is not primarily the name of a person, nor even the designation of a political and religious office. It would be truer to think of him mainly as a high metaphysical station or node of force through which the energies of compassion are made present and available to the people. This will help us to find a more interesting place in our minds for the concept of reincarnation which is associated not only with the Dalai Lama, but with the entire spiritual hierarchy of Tibet.

It may sound queer to speak of a religion as a hierarchy of stations of energy, for it seems so abstract, as though we were speaking of an organization without people. But then the question is: what are "people"? No one can approach the religion of Tibet, composed as it is of so many *extraordinary people* without in some way running into that rather odd-sounding question. It is not only the Dalai Lama who is understood as the incarnation of a high spiritual influence—called, in this case, Avalokitesvara, the principle of compassion. All of the spiritually advanced people of Tibet are such incarnations, or vehicles of metaphysically primary energies. In general, such manifestations are called *tulkus,* Just as Tibet as a whole is under the authority of the Dalai Lama, so each of the many monasteries, great and small, are governed by tulkus.

What of those people who are not such incarnations—"ordinary" monks and laymen, including, let us say, you and me? The idea here is that such people, all people, are incarnations, manifestations of energies and forces. But of course there are forces and there are forces. As one of these tulkus, now in Scotland, writes:

To understand the doctrine of *"tulkus"* in Tibet it is necessary first of all to understand the Buddhist attitude to "rebirth." It is true that the Buddha spoke of an undergoing of countless existences by each one of us, and almost all Asian people envisage life in this sense: naturally, one has always to distinguish between popularized versions of this doctrine and its proper understanding by those who do not confuse the issue through overvaluing their individual selves. In fact the Buddha's message was not that these countless lives possess an intrinsic reality, but that there is for all of us the possibility of release from their illusion. He saw that a stream of suffering pervades the lives of men and other beings and that their desire to perpetuate their own individuality is one of the stongest forces keeping them wedded to suffering. He taught that to abandon the sense of "I" leads to release from all those tendencies that bring about successive birth and death.

While we remain more or less enmeshed in a selfhood regarded as our own, past and future lives are continually being produced by those forces which still bind us to worldly existence. In the case of a tulku, however, the forces which produce his existence are of a different order. Something, or someone, that has no "individuality" or *ego* in the ordinary sense decides to work on earth for the sake of all beings. He (or "it") therefore takes birth over a certain period of time, in a series of human individuals, and it is these who are named "tulkus."[2]

Thus, the hierarchy of man corresponds to the hierarchy of forces in the universe. What differentiates an "ordinary man" from a tulku is not the matter of individuality, but the quality of energies which shape his life. The impulses of fear, greed, resentment, vanity, self-satisfaction, etc., which rule the lives of ordinary men represent a lower or coarser quality of energy than that which is readily available in the life-station of a tulku. But, and here is the crucial point, all men have within them the entire range of universal energies. What they need is help to reverse the relationship which obtains in their lives between these levels of energy. The stations of tulkus exist for the purpose of bringing about that shift in all human beings.

A teacher, or guru, is that being in whom higher energies take a form which makes them more able to resonate in the lives of relatively ordinary men. Thus, even a tulku needs a teacher to bring his own ordinary side into conformity with these supreme forces. But, unlike an ordinary man, a tulku carries out his life in a social station which itself is a bearer of these forces. The salvational structure of Tibetan society depends on the education of these tulkus who may be said to embody not only the ratio of energies which are present in all men, but also these same energies as they exist in the order and scale of Tibet—and hence the universe—as such.

Our mind staggers between perplexity and disbelief when we stand before the phenomenon of Tibet: a nation and society which mirrors the scale of cosmic creation and evolution; which, moreover, is ruled by human beings in whom this same scale is also mirrored; and which exists in order to realize this scale in all individual human beings. Is it any wonder that there are those who derogate the usefulness of organizations and groups as we know them? For, if Tibet is an example of the structure and source of life that an organization must embody if it is to be a channel of psychological help (compassion), how shall we place the organizations which now and always exist all about us?

Why Are They Here?

It is clear that the migration to the West of these Tibetan holy men is not a very simple thing. For, the physical and social background of Tibet is not mere background. On the other hand, the teaching and the energies connected with it can only exist and be transmitted through men, not by monuments alone, nor books, nor temples. Moreover, if Tibet was a vehicle of the higher, creative energies of the universe, why was it destroyed? It is interesting to ask this question, though it is probably wrong to believe we can answer it. If it is true of great spiritual teachers that "the spirit bloweth, where it listeth," how much more must this be true of a land like Tibet which perhaps stands to the whole world like such a teacher stands to ordinary men. And how much more absurd would it be to imagine we can easily grasp the laws that govern the destiny of such a land.

In any event, the diaspora has begun. It now touches the European continent in Paris, Switzerland and Great Britain. In Scotland, hundreds of British and Americans receive instruction from Chögyam Trungpa, a young tulku of the Kagyu school who, at the age of twenty, led a band of Tibetans in a perilous escape through the Himalayas to India. He describes that escape, and the inward use of its hardships and dangers, in a remarkable book, *Born in Tibet*—surely the clearest and deepest lens that has yet been held up to Tibet for the Western world. Also described as never before is the incredible early training of a high incarnate lama. So intense—physically, intellectually and spiritually—is the education these tulkus receive, that, as the Communist shadow approaches, one of Chögyam's teachers puts the future to him this way.

He said I must understand that a tulku like myself who has received such deep spiritual instruction has a duty to pass it on to others, so that I might have to consider escaping, not to save my own life, but to save the spiritual teaching of which I had become the repository.[3]

Yet another of his teachers told him.

You must look after and guide yourself, as in the future there will be no further teachers. A new era has begun in which the pure doctrine of the Lord Buddha lies in the hands of individuals; each one is separately responsible for I do not think we can carry on in the way we have done up till now. We can no longer rely on groups and communities . . . [4]

The paradox is clearly in front of us. Extraordinary men whose lives have been embedded in an unimaginably vast and subtle spiritual hierarchy are now in the world more or less "on their own." May we speculate—without for now worrying about being naïve—that the energies which have created and sustained Tibet are now more directly required in the life our whole planet? If we do think along those lines, the chilling question is: Why, why *now?* What is the real crisis of our epoch?

He (the Bodhisattva) does not act on "religious" or "charitable" grounds at all. He just acts according to the true, present moment, through which he develops a kind of warmth. And there is a great warmth in this awareness, also great creativity. His actions are not limited by anything and all sorts of creative impulses just arise in him and are somehow exactly right for that particular moment. Things just happen and he simply sails through them, so there is a continual, tremendous creativity in him. That is the real act of

Karuna—a Sanskrit word which means "Noble Heart" or
"Compassionate Heart." So in this case, compassion does
not refer to kindness alone, but to fundamental compassion, selfless compassion. He is not really aware of *himself,*
so compassion has greater scope to expand and develop, because here there is no radiator but only radiation. And when
this radiation exists, without a radiator, it could go on and
on, and the energy would never be used up. It is always
transformed and as it expands further and further it changes
always into something else, into a new creative activity, so it
goes continuously on and on.[5]

If we follow this thought of Chögyam Trungpa (the above and
what follows are from a recent series of his lectures), the question
of why these Tibetans are here is bound to be broadened to include ourselves as individuals searching for a way to be open to
these compassionate energies:

The whole thing boils down to this overlapping of thoughts
which goes on all the time in our minds. We never allow
anything to really happen or take place in our mind. One
thought comes and almost before we finish that another
one comes in and overlaps it and then another. So we never
allow any gap which would permit us to be free and really
digest things . . . And that is why one has to develop this
generosity of really opening oneself.[6]

Thus, in one move, the immensity of Tibet and the weight of
its destiny are hung in the fine tangles of my own mind. One begins to see why Tibet has been too big to understand, too "magical" to be taken seriously: because, like Scripture, itself, a sacred
organization cannot be understood externally, that is, apart from
the effort to understand oneself. In this context, of course, what
that involves is the task of coming in touch with energies within
oneself which are constantly screened out by our "overlapping

thoughts." In short, if Tibet is to "pass on" its Teachings, it will be to individuals and not to some abstraction called "the West." "Compassion" and "generosity" in even their most metaphysical meanings thus obviously concern transmission, which, in turn, involves the establishment of conditions in which individuals may turn to receive the transmission of their own inner and higher energies. Perhaps these are the terms in which we can begin to understand something of the role of Tibet as a teacher.

The next stage is perhaps a deeper form of generosity. That is to say, being prepared to share one's experience with others. Now that is a rather tricky thing because there is also a danger that you will be trying to teach somebody else what you have learned. It is a rather delicate matter . . . Nevertheless, putting it into words—whatever you have achieved—and giving it to someone else, is the only way to develop yourself. This particularly applies to teachers. And for advanced teachers, in fact for any teachers, it is necessary not just to learn things and keep them, but to use them and put them into effect by giving them out, though not with the idea of any reward. That is what is known as the Dana of Dharma, where you give out all the time . . . on the whole, one has to give out if one wants to receive anything in. A continual process of transformation takes place. There is a tradition in Tibet that if you want to receive any teaching or instruction, you generally give some present to the guru . . . (The) concept behind this is that when you want something— "I would like to receive Teaching. I want to know something"—then you have to give out something as well . . . and one of the most important things of all, of course, is giving out Ego, which is one of our most precious and valuable possessions. We have to give that out. And there are certain practices, such as prostrations, in the Tibetan tradition, where before one can practice any of the further stages of meditation one has to do a hundred thousand prostrations—this is in connection with the practice of Buddhist Yoga. And the idea of prostration is giving out, surrendering, opening—a kind of emptying out process, or preparation of the vessel or container, in order to receive. You have to open and empty out an already sound cup. That is what you have to offer, and then you can receive everything intact with complete value, with complete quality,[7]

Tarthang Tulku

Early in 1969 the Incarnate Lama Tarthang Tulku, a husky, cat-like man in his middle thirties, arrived in the San Francisco Bay area, bringing with him his expectant wife, a collection of rare Tibetan sacred texts, and little else in the way of possessions or money. His first American pupil, a twenty-six-year-old Berkeley graduate, had met him on a trip through India and the Orient:

Near the end of my trip I got to Benares—a fantastic place, everything in the world goes on there, it's really the seat of very, very many holy happenings. So, I went out to the Benares Hindu University, and I was just walking around the dormitory and started knocking on one door after an-other to see what I would come up with. So, I met this one really nice student, and we started talking and I said Do you know any Tibetans? He said he knew one teaching at San-skrit University, who turned out to be Tarthang Tulku. So I went out and met him. Just one day, four hours is all I spent with him. So, we were rapping, and he didn't teach me any-thing, or touch me, or turn me on or anything. As a matter of fact, I forgot all about him after that, and I went on trav-eling and then came back here to California. About, two years ago I got a letter from one Tarthang Tulku which said "Dear Joel. I don't know if you remember me. I don't remember you. But if we met, I probably liked you very much. My wife and I are trying to come to America now. Can you help us and send us some money?"

Really a straight, beautiful letter. So I wrote him back, sent him a little money and I said if you ever get to California and if there's anything I can do—you know. You know, I thought he could always sleep on the couch—at that time I was doing more dope than anything else. After that, he just kept writing to me. I liked him, his letters were really wonderful, warm and open, so we just kept writing; I never thought he'd get here—it's so hard for them to get here, they have no money, visa problems and all that. One day I got a letter: "Hello Joel, I'm in Paris! Very nice here! I'm coming soon!" So I said to myself, "Keep coming baby, I'm waiting for you!"

So, a couple months after that: "Hi; Joel, I'm in London! I'm coming!" Couple months later: "Hi, Joel! I'm here in New York! I'm going to come to California!" And by this time I started to believe it. And then one day . . . there he is.

Rinpoche, as he is called (a term meaning "precious master"), soon rented a house in Berkeley and, with the help of a handfull of young men and women, began the work of establishing The Tibetan Nyingmapa Meditation Center. The following is quoted from their brochure, written by a young Tibetan scholar who is now also one of Rinpoche's disciples.

At the present time, there are four sects or schools of Tibetan Buddhism: the Nyingmapa, the Kargyudpa, the Sakyapa, and the Gelugpa. Of these four the Nyingmapa is the oldest and original one. Founded in the eighth century A.D. by Guru Padmasambhava and Shantirakshita, it is the source and fountainhead of all later developments and traditions. In the Tibetan language the name Nyingmapa means the Old Ones or Ancient Ones . . .

Nyingmapa literature is divided into Kama and Terma. The Kama are teachings handed down both orally and in writing from master to disciple from the time of the Lord Buddha Himself. This includes the Sutras and the Tantras. The Sutras are primarily philosophical in content, while the Tantras deal with more esoteric doctrines and the actual practices of meditation and sadhana (practical methods) . . . The Termas are secret books which were concealed in various wild and out of the way places by Guru Padmasambhava before he withdrew from Tibet. They were recovered in later times by various learned Lamas or Terma-Masters. *The Tibetan Book of the Dead* is such a Terma.

The Nyingmapa school embraces all other forms of Buddhism because it alone uniquely possesses all nine Yanas or vehicles to Enlightenment. The first two vehicles comprise the Hinayana; the third is the Mahayana. The six higher vehicles embody the Vajrayana teachings found in the Tantras. The Kriya Tantra, Carya Tantra, and Yoga Tantra are possessed in common by all schools of Tibetan Buddhism. But the highest Tantric teachings of Mahayoga, Anuyoga, and Atiyoga are preserved by the Nyingmapa alone, and are not found elsewhere, because they were transmitted directly by Padmasambhava and Vimalamitra to their disciples.[8]

The Vajrayana

It is such rare texts which Rinpoche has brought with him, many of them being the only copies in existence. But, in addition to preserving and publishing these singular books, the Rinpoche's central task is the transmission of the Vajrayana—known as the "highest" or most advanced system of Buddhist thought and discipline. As is stated above, the Vajrayana makes use of the methods found in the Tantric texts. But the moment one hears the

word "Tantrism," various wild and lurid associations spring forth
in the Western mind which add up to a *pastiche* of psychospiritual
science fiction and sexual acrobatics that would put to shame even
the most imaginative of our contemporary pornographers and
quite eclipse the achievements of our hardiest erotic warriors. If it
is difficult for us to approach even the simplest *asanas* of hatha-
Yoga without immediately subverting them to the service of bodily
vanity, or the fear of illness, or simply the desire to "feel good,"
then how much more bedazzled are we by the mixture of complex
breathing exercises, telepathic and psychokinetic phenomena,
magic syllables, and dream manipulation—all within the rubric of
heightening and prolonging the ecstasy of sexual intercourse—
which we have been told make up the discipline of Tantric Yoga!*

But what makes Vajrayana "high" or "advanced" is the degree
of *understanding* sought by the practitioner. The idea here is that
the various "ways" or yanas are geared to different degrees of understanding. What does it mean to have a small understanding? It
means that one has relatively little experience of the place of
thought, feeling and sensation in the total functioning of the organism. There is thus relatively little ability or power to search for
the use of these functions and the energies they work with for any
purpose other than their satisfaction.

Moreover, since such satisfaction is sought not only for its own
sake, but to confirm and support the sense of self, it is always in
the service of fear and egotism. The "lesser" yanas are directed to

* A recent book (Omar V. Garrison, *Tantra: the Yoga of Sex,* Julian Press, Inc., New York, 1964,
for example), provides an elaborate set of instructions for Westerners on how to place the body
and sex organs, how to breathe during the sex act, how to retain the semen, contract various
sphincters, and open various vital centers—all while contemplating an assortment of holy
scriptures and profound Sanskrit phrases. At the other extreme, an esteemed scholar sums up
his discussion of Tantrism by writing: "(The tantrik adept's) 'worship' takes the form of sexual
activity of tremendous proportions and the whole purpose of it all is to achieve supernatural
powers. In spite of these cosmic feats, the tantrik adept rarely reaps a greater reward on the
earthly plane than siddhis (powers) as the ability to live on snowy mountain summits without
clothes, or draw up water through the anus" (Benjamin Walker, *Hindu World,* Allen and
Unwin Ltd., London, 1968, vol II, p 486)

men who are not yet able to search for freedom from all satisfaction, and who are therefore not yet able to use all of the organism's functions as means for the transformation of energy. The lesser yanas still allow that certain energies will be *spent,* rather than transformed by means of contact with the higher energies of compassion which produce and sustain the universe at its most original level.

Men differ in the sorts of energies that their organism is designed to *spend* rather than use for knowledge; that is, men differ in the satisfactions they crave by their very nature. The fact that there are many yanas is thus also understood as an expression of the compassion of Lord Buddha—the precision by means of which transmission of the truth is offered. To one type of man this yana; to another that yana. The "ways" are as different as the types of human nature and also as different as the degrees of subtlety by which various men are disillusioned with satisfaction.

Balanced Disillusionment

Disillusionment with satisfaction requires, as was said, the experience of the place of all the functions in the organism. Satisfaction is the spending or loss of energy; thus a *balanced disillusionment* is really the search for a method of transforming all energy in the organism. Obviously, such a balanced disillusionment is very rare among men; perhaps no one is born with it. Tantrism is said to be just such a method for transforming all the energies of the organism in their great variety of kind and quality. It is called *the short path* because it presupposes some degree of balanced disillusionment, whereas the other yanas presuppose only one or another sort of partial disillusionment. Men on the "lesser" or "longer" paths therefore deal with one thing at a time, one function at a time, whereas the short path is a method of dealing simultaneously with all functions and energies in the organism.

When he speaks, Tarthang Tulku's words explode like fireworks or penetrate one's chest like high-velocity missiles. Sitting straight on an overstuffed floor pillow, and amid high humor, he seems to use every muscle in his body to communicate directly through a screen of bad pronunciation and non-existent English grammar. One quickly forgets that the man is practically shouting and strains to catch the extraordinarily interesting sense of what he is saying.

"Vajrayana easy path!"

Since my reply to this was nothing more than a slight squinting of the eyes, he laughed and immediately added:

"Easy for man with understanding!"

Then he went on:

Different people have different levels. Why that happens? Because everybody has action, like karma. Some of them has less than bad karma, you know, like good karma, like more pure, not too much deeply hidden in coverings. Everybody has coverings, but possibly Vajrayana coverings looser, not so much difficulty become clear. Hinayana, Mahayana slower work. Not straight. Gradual. Vajrayana straight. Also is dangerous. Why? Because: go to hell Man on Vajrayana can go straight to hell. Directly to hell. Really happens! Absolutely! Because Nirvana also the same: if you have teaching is very high you can go directly up—these things Westerners cannot understand. It has great power, you can't argue with power. It have good ways, bad ways, both ways happen, everything works actions. Example: Vajarayana say you kill everybody so maybe man understand he can kill; Vajrayana say maybe you can sex, so man understand that wrong too and goes to sex Vajrayana perfectly internal, no killing, no sex. You cannot force this thing on your own habits, you maybe have doubt, you can't force this thing on your wisdom, you can't this thing do! Emotions nothing, very small thing, not high, emotion is feeling, feeling is part of the mind. Internal means experience.

Like you have plant, and somebody say it is poison, you

have to cut it throughout and also put on like petrol on bad
root, then completely destroy it. This is like Hinayana view.
Old desire, old emotion, old samsara things you complete
destroy. Otherway no getting out of samsara, therefore you
needed to destroy it. You become a monk, you do this one
and that one, you kill it: Hinayana, example! And, later on,
somebody says not necessary to kill it, we can maybe something like useful, like medicines, because some medicines
also poisonous. Not necessary to throw out, can be useful if
you know that medicine. This is like Mahayana: even all
your samsara doesn't matter, you can make yourself clari-
fied, reach to higher states. Then another man, he says: Oh,
if you change plant the right way, it is *nectar!* The nectar is
made by poison. Like peacock, example. Peacock is poison,
all beauty, wings and color most beautiful if they can eat
posion. They love poison, and they get so beautiful.

Samsaric things like habits. Actually, if someone doesn't
teach us samsaric things like habits, what do you think? Desire is habit, habit not existing, is taught to us from outside.
Okay? Research yourself, suffering habit! Where is bad feeling? Where is your bad feeling? You need to research yourself: where is it? You have to think. Not necessary yet
meditation, think!—how did these habits come? Think!
You stop, you want something. Who want it? Think! Keep
questioning: who is questioning? This not yet Vajrayana,
but foundation for Vajrayana. This is beginning start, otherwise you cannot understand for later stages, the meditation, what the yanas mean, what is the teaching. Not only
questioning do, but thinking!

Think very slowly, We do not yet reach the Buddha nature, we are not yet to there, we are with emotions, problems, suffering, that kind of thing. Think slowly, very very
slowly, for five minutes. Fast thinking not produced by very
useful emotions. Thinking is like subject and the object is
too big to be known, researched. If you s-l-o-w-l-y think it

automatically give toward answer. If you think and talk
veryveryfast, thisandthat, useful sensations and feelings
doesn't come, Slowly thinking, research example: what really mind means.

Not necessary to cut out any desires or anything, that
Hinayana. Begin by research!"

Thus, Vajrayana is said to be the internal path because no function, no manifestation in man is spared exposure to awareness.
The teacher and the teaching is necessary because ordinary man
has no conception of how many and varied these functions are.
The tendency is to stop with some unusual function, perhaps even
to label it awareness. Only the teacher and the accumulation of
experience which is called tradition contain the knowledge that
this, too, can be exposed to awareness, and is therefore not the
highest possibility for a man. In his admonition to think, think
about everything, the Rinpoche is perhaps suggesting that a certain quality and persistence of thought is already the beginning of
this internal path. But to think, think, slowly and persistently, requires that one not stop with answers, which represent satisfactions. And in general, one doesn't think in this way about
satisfactions, one does not question them—especially not such intense satisfactions as sex, praise, etc. Obviously, such a quality of
thought will be possible only to the degree that exists in one a balanced disillusionment with all satisfaction.

The Path to the Path

Like salt sea water that turns
Sweet when drunk up by the clouds
So a firm mind that works for others turns
The poison of sense-objects into nectar
. . . .
Once in the realm that's full of joy
The seeing mind becomes enriched

And thereby for this and that most useful even when it
    runs.
After objects it is not alienated from itself.

The buds of joy and pleasure
And the leaves of Glory grow
If nothing flows out anywhere
The bliss unspeakable will fruit.

                                    from *The Royal Song of Saraha*[9]

When . . . you see the hysteria of the world as the antics of
a drunkard tumbling into an abyss, and when without being attached to this life, the thought of what will become of
you in a future life has been firmly established in your mind
day and night, then the mental level of an inferior human
being has been reached.

    Through thinking again and again about the general
plight of the world you must acquire a feeling of disgust
with it, for if you do not feel disgusted with the world in
general, no interest in deliverance from it can grow . . .

    . . . by serving in a proper way by thought and deed
spiritual friends who are the undisputed source of all im-
provements, and by accomplishing what they tell you to do,
you will prepare the ground for all achievements . . .

    If you cannot stand a little heat and cold now, what will
you do when you are boiled in molten lead or frozen in a
fierce blizzard?

    from *The Gold Refinery; Bringing Out the Very Essence of the
                                        Sutra and Tantra Paths*[10]

Thus, in order to reach the citadel of Vajradhara, the goal
unity, a study of this unity must precede its realization; and
in order to reach this goal, the experience of the real radiant
light must be had earlier. Before this there must be the realization of apparitional existence, before this the semblance

light or the union of bliss with no-thing-ness by immersing
ourselves in our existentiality, before this the practice of the
coarse and subtle forms of the Developing Stage, before this
the initiatory empowerments and the proper observation of
all commitments and restraints, before this the purification
of ourselves by traversing the common path, and before this
the service of spiritual friends as the source of the acquisition of all that is positive.

from *The Instruction in the Essence of the Vajrayana Path or
the Short-cut to the Palace of Unity*[11]

Though it has only just begun, the work of Tarthang Tulku in
California, or Chögyam Trungpa in Great Britain, has given the
West a glimpse of the avenues which lead to the Vajrayana path.
But the path itself, which begins from a much higher plateau
than we can yet see, remains hidden from us. We have heard the
idea that a special quality of thought or attention, by being
brought to bear on all our human problems and manifestations,
can begin to transmute the energy in these problems. Presumably,
such an approach, immeasurably deepened and refined by study
and experience, can at some point touch even those of our functions which now inevitably overwhelm us by their pleasures and
pains, and their attendant forms of imagination. Perhaps somewhere on that path there is a place where the forces of sex and
physical death can be directly used for the purpose of liberation,
and where one's disillusionment with satisfaction may be so subtle and complete that even the manifestation of "supernormal"
functions such as telepathy and bodily transmutation can work
not as a distraction, but as a tool of compassion. But, meanwhile,
as we in the West cannot even discern the beginning of that path,
we are fools to believe we can read Tantric texts with any degree
of comprehension.

The Rinpoche says that for people like us, we can't profit
spiritually from things like sex—not for a long, long, long

time. I mean, they use sexual energy for this and that but
it's pretty much for those who are very far along the Tantric
path where sexuality can be turned into true spirituality For
most people it remains a physical and emotional act. So, he
prefers just to say No to any questions about whether Tantra involves sex. Sometimes he'll just say No, it doesn't—
and for these people, it's true, it doesn't.

Here the speaker was a young man who previously had been
deeply involved with political activism on the Berkeley campus.

In the summer of sixty-four, the "long hot summer," I went
down South, working with Quakers in North Carolina.
Right in the Black Belt, plantation country, very tightly
racially segregated, pretty uptight community. But our attempt was not just to register voters, but to do things with
the people, try to establish some rapport . . . we did a lot of
teaching, all of us were middle-class white kids stuck right
in the middle of the black community working out our
own personal karma—it was really kind of weird—trying to
understand our own selves, our own nature, with this outward action. You could say we were all sincerely dedicated,
so there was some compassion involved, but we were sort of
blind, too . . . So it began and ended; like a thought, it
arose and lasted for two months and passed away.

Then I came back and the next year was the Free Speech
Movement here, and I was doing some things in that, but I
think that was what really broke the back of my political
doings. Oh, I worked in it, you know. But again it was like
a thought, it arose, became, and passed away, and nothing
really seemed to happen. The whole transiency of the thing
got to me . . . the mobness, the massification of people,
drawing lines between friend and foe, the good guys and
the bad guys. I enjoyed how exciting it was, being able to

run around cutting classes, the campus was all in turmoil, and I can dig anarchy and chaos . . :

But then, after FSM (Free Speech Movement) I met a guy who was a big politico and he was writing a book, you know, sitting around interviewing people who had worked in the South. And there was another guy there, who had done the same thing and, then, this second guy started talking about Krishnamurti and the nature of the mind, and how things are not really what they seem, and he went on like this for quite a long time, and just being in the same room with him and listening to him somehow re-awoke in me all the feelings that I had had when I was younger—when I was about fifteen until I was eighteen, when I started to be really intellectual, and socially aware and left sort of all my religious feelings behind. It all suddenly came back, everything I had put down all these years. It all came back. In a moment! And I just walked out of that meeting—shaking; I couldn't do anything for a couple of weeks. I didn't know what to do with it, at all. All my friends Were all political, social types. I didn't know where to turn; so I sort of just wandered around and was like cut loose . . .

The "Accumulation of Merit"

As a pupil of Tarthang Tulku, this young man now works at what is called *Bhum-nda,* a series of five exercises done a hundred thousand times each.

As one pupil described it:

Suppose you come here as a new student and want to study. There are these five *Bhum,* which means 100,000 in Tibetan. The first one is the prostration. And that's what we do at the beginning of the *puja* (a communal ritual, led by the Rinpoche).

With that, he placed his palms close together, but not touching, and lifted his hands above his head. Then, keeping palms in position, he brought his hands down to his throat and then to his chest.

The hands are held together like this, with a space in between the palms, because you're offering a precious jewel to the Buddha, the Dharma, and the Sangha. Then, when it's at the top of your head like this, it's the salutation to the Buddha, before your throat it's a saluation to the Dharma, the teaching, and before the heart, it's salutation to the Sangha, the community. And then you go down onto the ground, and your body has to touch the earth in five places, the two knees, the palms of the hands, and the forehead. At the same time, with each gesture, there is a complex visualization, and also a mantra. And you must keep in mind all the time that you are taking refuge in the Three Jewels, the Buddha, the Dharma and the Sangha, and that it is being done not just for yourself, but for all sentient beings. Doing a hundred thousand of these not only shows you are sincere, but it builds it into your whole psychic structure. Mind, speech and body must be totally involved. If you just do it mechanically, or if you're daydreaming, then you're not doing this practice.

At this point, the Rinpoche interjected: "This take three month. Tibetan Buddhist take one month time," I quickly calculated that to accomplish the first Bhum would take three months only if one were able to perform some one thousand such prostrations every day. I had tried a few of these prostrations myself during the puja ritual to which I had been invited, and after about ten of them my back and legs were already aching. For myself, it would have been an enormous effort to have continued at all, not to mention adding the visualization and the recitation. I immediately felt a new respect for the sincerity of these young people who surrounded the Rinpoche. It occurred to me then and there that for most Americans, sincerity begins with the body.

The Rinpoche seemed to be reading my thoughts, and added: "Even you take only hundred prostrations a day. That is only maybe thirty minutes takes time. And a hundred prostrations a day you collect, and maybe in one year you finished. Much better than yoga exercises this way to take refuge."

After this, the student undertakes the second Bhum, which consists of one hundred thousand complex visualizations. These are given when and as the Rinpoche deems it appropriate. The third Bhum is the recitation of what is called the One Hundred Syllable Mantra, together with certain meditation practices.

"These *Bhumi*," said the student, "are only the foundation. First you have the foundation, and only then do you have the path. The fourth Bhum is the offering of the mandala, a visualization of the universe in miniature. This all involves what we call 'accumulation of merit' which has to do with the doctrine of karma: all actions in this life have effects in the future, both the immediate future and the distant future. The actions produce effects which are advantageous from the spiritual point of view, and this is what we mean by 'merit.' Some actions are the opposite of advantageous, what modern businessmen might call 'counterproductive.'

"The fifth Bhum is *The Meditation on the Guru*." He then showed me this recitation, two pages of Tibetan, romanized for Westerners.

"After this," said the Rinpoche, "they have meditation practice for three years, three months, three days. Then complete and become lama, according to Nyingmapa tradition." He then described how in Tibet he had spent these three years, three months and three days without any communication with the outside world, save for food that was brought to him by other monks.

"Do you really intend to demand that of Americans?"

"This country," answered the Rinpoche, "you can work before you go to mountains. You can collect much money and friends can bring you food."

His student eagerly added: "Or, if we set up a monastery, like Zen Center did, then it could be done, then you'd have the facilities."

"Three years of sitting!" said I. "In one position?"

The Rinpoche laughed. "Lie down. Walk around. Sleep, two, three hours sleep. See guru.

"Better than Yoga ways. Yoga way bring samadhi, but not always wisdom. Vajrayana wisdom way. Yoga ways nothing very high. Control breathing and can still be samsara; become very calm, still be samsara. Wisdom and mind is separate. Mind not permanent. Wisdom is like permanent. Many levels to samsara mind, may seem high, but not wisdom."

Following a schedule based on the reckoning of the Tibetan lunar calendar, the Rinpoche conducts a puja for a gathering of his pupils some four or five times each month. Space does not permit a description of this complex ritual which involves much in the way of chanting, meditation, prostrations and formalized eating and drinking. Nor is it possible here to discuss the idea of *merit*, which occupies a central place in the puja; we may simply note that it has little in common with what that term suggests to us. In such esoteric traditions, a ritual is, among other things, a form of action patterned upon the way cosmic energies descend and rise in the play of creation. To the degree a man participates, inwardly as well as outwardly, in this form of action he becomes a channel through which the energies of compassion flow to the world at large. The "acquisition of merit" has much to do with the extent to which a man becomes such a channel and, so to say, resists attachment to those fragmentary patterns of action which he ignorantly claims to be his "self." The liturgical text itself states:

The purpose of the puja is to acquire merit through the activity of one's body, speech and mind. This merit, however, is not for oneself alone, for it is dedicated to the welfare of all sentient beings. A puja is an offering ritual whereby one's present finite consciousness, through ritual and meditation, is brought into contact with a higher spiritual sphere and with the blessings and power which radiate down from it. To enter the puja is to enter the mandala, a sacred consecrated space beyond worldly activity and profane time.[12]

The Weight of Tibet

If we could imagine the entire tradition of Christianity, the rituals in all their manifold forms, the sacred literature, the philosophical texts, the various ways of Christian life; and if we could add to that all of Christianity of which we know so little, the mystical thinking, the monastic disciplines and the psychological knowledge upon which they are based, the meditational techniques, the psychospiritual reasoning that led to the construction of the Gothic cathedrals and the composition of the original liturgies—if we could bring all this together in our mind, we might have some picture of the immensity of what is now just barely touching the West with the arrival of these Tibetans and Vajrayana Buddhism. For while it would be absurd for us to try to compare the value of Vajrayana and Zen, one might say that the former is complete Buddhism and the latter essential Buddhism. The genius of Vajrayana, if we may use so mundane a word, seems to be that of inclusion, while the genius of Zen surely is one of exclusion. All the forms of Buddhism that have ever had real life seem to have their instrumental place in the Vajrayana tradition. Yet, like Zen, the far goal is the same; the realization of what is called emptiness *(sunyata)*, the full relativity or non-self-existence of all entities and their components. That far goal, which sounds so cold to us, is nothing less than the "transfiguration of suffering" of the entire system of creation with its immeasurable dependent cascade of energies that constitute the "groaning and travail" of the world.

In the words of Chögyam Trungpa:

> . . . in order to express space, one might have first to create a vase, and then one has to break it, and then one sees that the emptiness in the vase is the same as the emptiness outside. That is the whole meaning of technique.[13]

Perhaps, in the end, that is also the whole meaning of Tibet, of Buddhism and of all the great religious traditions of mankind. But meanwhile, as we are so very far from comprehending that end, the fact of Tibet and the effort toward its rebirth, here before our eyes, commands our present attention as an ongoing lesson concerning the nature of compassion as organization.

8

The Hunger for Ideas

A More Fundamental World

What is the nature of that more fundamental world which the followers of the new teachings seek to penetrate? Does it actually exist?—not above the clouds or beyond the grave, but here and now in the midst of our own familiar world? If it does exist, what is the nature of its power or its call?

Such questions must be brought if we wish to think about the significance of these teachings and about the impact of the whole "spiritual explosion." Otherwise, we may naïvely turn to the sociologists, the psychologists, the theologians, or even to our poets and belle-lettrists for ways of understanding this phenomenon. And we will then find our judgment tied to forms of thought in which the question of a more fundamental world either does not arise or does not arise as a question.

The teachings we have just described are but part of a phenomenon which in a wider view seems almost apocalyptic. The number of Americans engaged in some sort of spiritual discipline is impressive enough. When we add to that number those who now seek to guide their lives simply by ideas which are associated with these traditions, we cannot avoid the picture of a "spiritual explosion."

For a moment let us take this wider view before attempting to assess the individual and collective significance of the various teachings.

On the level of ideas, a whole new set of categories has taken root which expresses the search for new ways of relating to other people and to the events of one's life. Where before one heard talk of anxiety, guilt, anal and oral personalities, superego, and so forth, one now hears of "working out one's karma," "past incarnations," "rising signs" and "sun signs." Where dreams were once taken as an index of suppressed desires, they are now scanned for prophetic messages and extrasensory communications. The language of existentialism with its concepts of "the absurd," "dread" and "radical freedom" is also giving way to the language of astrology, psychism and mysticism. Even Marx and Chairman Mao now have to compete with the I Ching and the Tarot cards. Suddenly, the ideal of pleasure or momentary fulfillment is no longer the sexual orgasm, but the spiritual insight, the "flash" of "cosmic meaning."

I am speaking now not only of the radical or alienated young in or out of the drug scene, but of great millions of people throughout the country. Of course, much of the interest in such things as astrology remains on the level of a fad. And even a more serious study of such ideas is very far from the commitment to a spiritual discipline or teacher. And yet, since the ideas which attract the mind are expressions of our relationship to the world and to ourselves, the new ideas represent the beginnings of a searching which eventually leads many people to the new teachings themselves. Their prevalence is a clear sign of the great shift in the consciousness of the West.

Astrology

THE IDEA OF INFLUENCES

Concerning astrology, it is as easy and justifiable to scorn its popular side as it is difficult to deny the sense of its cosmological basis: the idea that all elements in the universe, from atoms to galaxies, are interrelated. Everyone agrees that the sun, moon and planets, and even the stars, exert an influence on the earth. What separates modern science from the ancient systems of astrology is the question of the nature and extent of that influence. In the modern scientific world-view, the idea of levels of reality is meaningless. This is because science has found it pragmatically useful to exclude purpose and intention from its conception of reality. Now, the idea that something is on a higher level than something else only makes sense if the "lower" serves the purposes and intentions of the "higher." The intentions of the higher act, very strictly, as an influence upon the lower. Thus, if there is a higher or more fundamental world than our own, it is because our world serves its purposes.

In this sense our organism, for example, is "higher" than various organs of the body, which in turn are higher than the tissues, and so forth down to the cells and their components. If the idea of intention and purpose is excluded from our conception of the organism—as it is in the scientific view—then it becomes just as true to say that the organism serves the liver as it is true to say that the liver serves the organism. And the very idea of influence dissolves into mere cause and effect which in turn is relative to our conception of time and our subjective opinions about the nature and composition of the entities we are observing. To be influenced by something, however, means to participate in its intention, to serve its purpose.

Pursuing this analogy, the cells in our body would be "astrologers" to the extent that they studied the intentions and purposes of the tissues and organs which their lives served. Self-knowledge, the observation of the forces that influence one's life, is thus the basis of astrology. And from this point of view, mere astronomy, without the study of the purposes served by the mind and the senses, and without the study of the interlocking influences and intentions that make up the organic universe, can lead nowhere. A non-hierarchical and non-psychological study of the universe reveals only patterns, but not meaning.

This is only one aspect of the idea of astrology as it existed in those systems of knowledge which originated in ancient Egypt, Greece, India, Tibet and elsewhere. It was never an isolated science in these cultures, but part of a system of teachings that were integrated by the symbolic forms which we know as myths. These symbolic forms are the language of a purified emotional perception that had as its object the great unitary intentions of the cosmos itself. They thus embrace a knowledge not only of the stars and planets, but of human psychology and physiology, plants and animals, physics and chemistry—all placed within the context of man's divine mission of self-perfection through the service of God. If we have lost the key to these ancient systems and myths, it is not because there are insufficient archeological findings, but because we have lost the means of verifying even the findings we have. That verification begins with the purification of the emotional life and the uncovering of real, not imaginary, intuition. Thus, even the largest aspects of those systems which embraced astrology were tied to existential goals similar to those we have found in the new teachings.

What we are witnessing in this country is therefore a renewal of the interest in astrology, but hardly a renewal of astrology itself. As long as we are quite clear about this; the turning to astrology is significant in its own right. The symbols of astrology, however subjectively they are understood, provide a potentially far richer framework than our contemporary psychology for approaching people and human relationships—richer, that is, in questions and hence in openness. There is the ram, the bull, the scorpion, the archer. There are the planets and the associations they call forth—

Jupiter, the symbol of magnificence, Saturn, the principle of resistance and instruction; Uranus, the force of transformation. There are the *houses* of the horoscope in which the pattern of celestial signs is applied to every sphere of an individual's life from the trivial to the momentous. There are the elements of fire, air, water and earth whereby character traits are linked to an idea of various forms of energy in the universe. There are the *aspects* of the solar bodies with their sense of a constantly shifting relationship of forces generating everything from whole destinies to momentary life-events. And there is much, much more.

How pale psychoanalytic concepts seem next to all this, not only in nuance, but in the sense of alienation from the whole of nature and the universe. The general interest in astrology represents, at the very least, a rebellion against the idea of an un-alive cosmos which modern science has given us, a cosmos in which man is at best a lonely anomaly. If I think of you as, say, a Scorpio rather than as an "extrovert" or "oral type," I have room in my mind to see you in relationship to the great cosmic forces of destruction and regeneration, symbolized by the sign of the scorpion. I could not thereby say that I understand you any better than if I labeled you an extrovert—obviously not, since I cannot say I understand anything at all about such great forces. But for that very reason, I may be more able to resist passing judgment on you; to do so would be like passing judgment on the universe itself. When taken like this, astrology can open relationships, rather than close them.

In terms of the "spiritual explosion" it is this sense of greater forces at work which makes the interest in astrology significant and which is congruent with the emotion of wonder. One cannot say that present-day astrology is knowledge, much less a spiritual path. But it can be the expression of an intimation that it is contemporary man, rather than the universe, which is blind and purposeless. That is surely why so many followers of the new teachings maintain a fascination with such things as astrology, the Tarot and the I Ching.

The open-minded or skeptical astrologer is, of course, the exception. The intricate mathematical computations that go into the erection of a horoscope and into the reading of what is called "the progressed chart" can lull one into: equating arithmetical precision with real knowledge. And the exciting symbolism of astrology can close the mind as easily as it can open it—for exciting labels are still only labels. Moreover, one can come from a session with an ardent astrologer absolutely stuffed with a phantastic sense of one's own cosmic importance. These are no doubt some of the reasons why the Judaeo-Christian tradition, as we know it, has always scorned astrology. But things are different now, and the present interest in astrology can be as much a sign of the incipient spiritual search as was, for example, St. Augustine's turning away from astrology in his day.

Reincarnation

The idea of reincarnation, which is now so popular, can be approached along similar lines. Even more than astrology, it has pervaded all the great religious traditions of the world, and whatever its distant origins, it is hardly an idea that is peculiar to Eastern thought alone. It was taught by many of the greatest minds of early Christianity, by Plato and the whole Neoplatonic tradition, by the Essenes, the Kabbalists and the Hasidim, and by many so-called "Gnostic sects" throughout Western history. It is only the Judaeo-Christian tradition *as we know it* which rejects the idea of reincarnation. The present surge of interest in this idea is one of the aspects of "spiritual explosion" most directly relevant to the sense of our own established traditions. The turning to the religions of the East has been accompanied by a turning to the "esoteric" side of Judaism and Christianity.

IDEAS AS TOOLS

The subject of Western esotericism is extremely important for our study of the new religious consciousness in America. For now, we may briefly characterize an esoteric idea as one whose meaning and usefulness are so controlled as to depend solely on the psychological developments of the student. Obviously, the meaning of any idea whatever deepens as a man becomes spiritually more mature, and in this very loose sense all ideas are "esoteric." But if we wish to speak more precisely about esotericism, we must recognize that esoteric ideas are those ideas which are part of a psychospiritual discipline. They therefore exist under the control of the masters of the discipline, the teachers. As part of a discipline or path, esoteric ideas are thus presented to the pupil in a way that can be most useful to him in his struggle for psychological freedom and at his particular stage of growth. Furthermore, esoteric ideas are presented not only in the light of their use to individuals as individuals, but also insofar as individuals are members, of a culture and a period of history. Naturally, such control requires an extremely precise knowledge of both individual and collective human nature, but who can doubt that teachers like the Buddha, Moses and Jesus possessed such knowledge?

When such esoteric or controlled ideas enter the lives of men who are not on the path, they immediately become "exoteric," or "popular." As we have suggested, this does not mean that they cease to be spiritually useful—for they may serve to bring a man to the gates of the path, It is just that they are no longer *controlled*—simply because the minds that are attracted to them do not yet wish for the total discipline of a spiritual path. They thus tend to fall into the service of the desires and fears, whereby they are misunderstood and may even become a force which obscures the way to the discipline in which they originated.

We do not know where the idea of reincarnation originated. Some say in ancient Egypt, others say India. Of course, it need not have originated in any one place. It probably formed a part of very many spiritual disciplines. In any event, when we speak of reincarnation we are really speaking about a cluster of formulations. In one tradition it refers to the. idea of a soul moving from one human body to another until it perfects itself. Certain traditions speak of the soul taking forms other than human. Still other traditions, such as the Buddhist, use the idea of rebirth to combat the belief that there exists such a thing as the soul. Or, we may encounter the idea of recurrence; the eternal return of the same. In this formulation the same life is repeated endlessly in all of its detail until consciousness or remembrance is attained and freedom genuinely desired. Some teachings speak of spiritual progress through various incarnations, while others take the very fact of incarnation as a sign that significant progress has not yet been made. Almost everywhere, however, the idea of karma is connected With the idea of reincarnation. At its clearest, the idea of karma is essentially an extension of the law of cause and effect, somewhat like Newton's Third Law of Motion applied to all of reality including the psychological and moral sphere.

Compounding the whole problem is the fact that esoteric ideas are often expressed symbolically and mythically. Such forms of expression are extremely precise from the point of view of a spiritual discipline, for in these forms both the intellect and the emotions of the pupils can receive the idea under psychological conditions in which emotions can be a source of knowledge. But when esoteric ideas become popular or exoteric they tend to be taken either literally or poetically. This happens because, outside of the path, men in a state of psychological imbalance cannot help but receive such ideas with either insufficient feeling or insufficient thought.

Fortunately, we do not have to know the truth about an esoteric idea such as reincarnation in order to examine the new religious mind of America. As with astrology, it is the interest in reincarnation which is important and not so much the probability that the idea has been taken wrongly. At the present time, this interest is being expressed in several ways. Throughout the country hundreds of groups meet together regularly in order to delve into their "past incarnations." Many of these groups take their inspiration from the readings of the remarkable Edgar Cayce.

The Hunger for Ideas

Others use hypnosis in one form or another, and still others simply speculate about their "previous lives."

The idea of reincarnation is not just a matter for group exploration. It has become category of thought for millions. As such, it functions not so much as a consolation in the face of death, but as an antidote to the apparent arbitrariness of life. Like the idea of astrology, it expresses a sense of the enormous forces that have brought one to his present life-situation, forces which in intelligence and consciousness are not less than oneself. In this way, one's life can be seen as a task. The scientific world-view, on the other hand, has made it difficult, if not impossible, to face one's life-situation as a task, since the forces recognized by science are blind and unalive.

The wish to see life as a task is surely the wish to be in communication with reality, to be part of created nature and not to be a metaphysical freak in the scheme of things. If the forces which brought me here to this place, with these people, in this station of life are less sentient than I, how can I ever respond to them? The belief in a blind universe is an invitation to the psychopathy of pure monologue, or the despair of a life spent in pursuit of satisfaction.

Christianity and Judaism rejected the exoteric idea of reincarnation because it often worked as a distraction from the task of one's present life. The thought of numberless future lives numbed men to the need for efforts in this life. But, as with astrology, things are different now, and the contemporary interest in reincarnation is not at all oriented to the future. On the contrary, it is now a sign of the general wish to understand the meaning of spiritual effort in this life.

The Sacred in Nature

A *hanhepi wi* (night sun, or moon) should be cut from rawhide in the shape of a crescent, for the moon represents a person and, also, all things, for everything created waxes and wanes, lives and dies. You should also understand that the night represents ignorance, but it is the moon and the stars which bring the Light of *Wakan-Tanka* into this darkness. As you know the moon comes and goes, but anpetu wi, the sun, lives on forever; it is the source of light, and because of this it is like Wakan-Tanka.

A round rawhide circle should be made to represent the sun. The light of this sun enlightens the entire universe; and as the flames of the sun come to us in the morning, so comes the grace of Wakan-Tanka, by which all creatures are enlightened. It is because of this that the four-leggeds and the wingeds always rejoice at the coming of the light. We can all see in the day, and this seeing is sacred, for it represents the sight of that real world which we may have through the eye of the heart.

—from Black Elk's instructions for the Sun Dance[1]

If the universe is a greater scale of force and intelligence than our science has led us to think, then we ourselves as a reflection of it have within us a corresponding scale of energies and cognition. This is surely a fundamental reason why we seek out nature: to come in touch with something in ourselves that can respond to these more fundamental forces.

Given this response, which most of us have felt, we then fall into confusion. We turn to scientific explanation and eventually find ourselves sunk in the disorder of the ordinary, isolated mind. Or, we turn to poetry and art, seeking only the intensification of ordinary feelings which obscures that extraordinary response.

THE AMERICAN INDIAN

Is it any wonder, then, that the younger generation has fallen in love with the American Indian? Here was a tradition of direct and total response to nature, in which natural forms were a sacred text. We all wish to be taught by nature, but because our concept of nature is either sentimental or arrogant, we learn from nature only what we put into it—a state of affairs which was actually sanctified by the German philosopher Immanuel Kant and which has more or less defined the Western approach to nature ever since Kant. Kant "proved" that man had no quality of mind which would enable him intellectually to intuit the order of nature as it is in itself. Since that time, the tools of scientific knowledge, known as pragmatism and positivism, have been taken for knowledge itself, and man has turned to nature more for confirmation than instruction. Separated from the intellect, the emotional reaction to nature became merely romantic and sentimental. Separated from the emotions, the intellectual reaction to nature became autistic and arrogant. In this schizophrenia, Western man turns to nature as to a prostitute.

The contemporary search for a more organic relationship to nature is expressed in many ways, great and small. There is the interest in natural foods and organic farming; there are the scores of youth communes in mountains and forests and especially amid the mesas of the Southwest, where the Hopi, the Navajo and the Zuni still seem to preserve something of their Way; there is the resurgence of interest in practicing crafts such as weaving, pottery and carpentry.

As with nature, so with the human body. The rebirth of interest in homeopathic and herbal medicine is part of the new spiritual consciousness. Modern technological medicine in its tendency toward radical intervention by means of surgery, synthetic chemicals and microatomic radiation is surely an expression of the Western stance toward nature. As such, it is distrusted particularly by the younger generation who, it must be added, still have the forces of youth working for them, and can therefore "afford" preferences in medical philosophy. Nevertheless, we are speaking in this chapter about ideas and not about the long work of living one's ideas. On that level, the distrust of modern medicine is one with the rejection of an inorganic, non-purposeful universe. From this point of view, homeopathic medicine seems to embody a philosophy that more clearly acknowledges an integrative intelligence of the body both in itself and in relationship to organic nature.

In all of this, the American Indian stands as a paradigm. His was a *way* in nature. For that very reason we must beware of reading our own feelings and associations about nature into what we know of his behavior. If his was a *way* in nature, it means that he had the knowledge and the ableness to allow nature to be his teacher. This means, further, that he asked of nature far, far more than we ask of it. It is as though I were to compare my understanding of, let us say, The New Testament—an understanding which was based on one of our well-known university courses which go by such names as "The Bible as Literature" or "The Historical and Archaeological Background of the Message of Jesus"—it is as though I were to compare such an understanding with that of a Hesychast in Mount Athos who for sixty years, day and night, inwardly recited the Prayer of the Heart and who sought by every psychological and physical effort he could find, constantly to rediscover the full sense of the teachings of Jesus in the merciless self-exposure of his own human nature. We may say, therefore, that the Indian lived in *esoteric nature,* while we live in exoteric nature.

THE SILENCE OF NATURE

We ask of nature only that it satisfy our desires. The Indian, on the other hand, asks nature for help in the transformation of his desires. His traditions, insofar as they are esoteric, are a form of knowledge by means of which such help can be received. We tend to think of our desires as apart from nature, or else—if we ally ourselves with modern psychology—we think of them as part of blind nature. To the Indian, perceived nature, nature as it presents itself to the untransformed desires, is but a shadow of real nature. To read the shadows as shadows, as expressions of a more fundamental world, he submits to the long traditions for the task in nature that will call forth, both from it and from him, the power that is necessary for the transformation of man. That power, or energy, and it alone, can read the book of nature. The search for that power and the task of obeying it when it appears in oneself are what set the whole pattern of Indian life.

It is therefore not too far-fetched to say that, unlike the Indian, we take nature too literally, just as we tend to take Scripture too literally. Or, what comes to the same thing, we may take nature and Scripture symbolically, which is simply a process of first taking them literally and then applying the associations of the isolated, discursive intellect. As we have seen in several of the new teachings, and as we sense in the core of our own traditions, Scripture can help to serve as a tool for the awakening of a power of total response which alone can understand a divine communication. If it is difficult or impossible for us to approach Scripture in this way, which at least is written in words, how much more removed from us is the key to understanding nature as a communication. For surely, nature's "silence" is more complete even than that of a Zen master or a Socrates. Nature is *all* indirect communication, which means the communication of conditions by means of which one has the opportunity to experience the truth for oneself. But who has the ableness or the wish to learn from such a teacher? Perhaps the truly great masters do, but obviously most of mankind needs the invented silence of traditional forms which can meaningfully speak simultaneously both to the part of man that wishes to be whole and to the part that is ignorant of wholeness.

Thus, it is hard for us to understand the Indian not only because his is a way in esoteric nature, but because even his failing, when he fails, is certain to be very different from our own. We fail largely from the interference of our minds, but we do not even know how the Indian fails. Therefore we do not understand the dual nature, the invented silence of his own traditional forms, his rituals, his language and scripture, his medicine, his agriculture. That is, it is doubtful if we can even clearly understand the exoteric sense of the Indian traditions.

What we *are* receiving from the Indian, however, is the revitalization of an idea which lies at the heart of our own traditions; the idea of an organic universe which continually speaks to us, if we would but seek for a way to listen to it.

Western Esotericism

When the boughs . . . are withered, they shall be broken off;
The women shall come and set them on fire;
For it is a people of no understanding;
Therefore He that made them will not have compassion upon them.
And He that formed them will not be gracious unto them.
—Isaiah 27:11

Jesus said:
If you bring forth that within yourselves
that which you have will save you,
If you do not have that within yourselves,
that which you do not have within will kill you.
—The Gospel According to Thomas[2] Log. 70

Jesus said:
I took my stand in the midst of the cosmos.
— The Gospel Accoding to Thomas[3]
Log. 28

CIVILIZATION IN THE MIDST OF THE COSMOS

In the larger view, of course, all ways are ways in nature, since nature contains us all. All civilizations exist in nature, are sustained by nature and destroyed by nature. If the American Indian searched for his relationship to divine energies in the midst of his response to the winds, forests and sky, then no less did the ancient Egyptian find his way under influences of the sun and the stars, amid the life- and death-giving rhythms of the river Nile; no less than Tibetan in the high reaches of the Himalayas, or the Semitic nomad wandering in the desert.

Because we in the modern world, tend to think of nature only on the scale of our own planet and because our science does not recognize levels of influences we may well be stunned by the idea that *all* human civilization is fundamentally a process of intersection between cosmic nature and nature on the scale of our planet, and that each separate civilization comes into being and continues to exist only as a way or channel of exchange between these two levels of nature.

One often comes across the idea that man is such an intersection or channel—"both demon and God" or "halfway between the angels and the beasts." The idea is that man has two natures, one of which corresponds to cosmic or divine nature, and the other of which corresponds to "earthly" nature; much as a common electrical transformer contains both an element that can receive a certain energy and an element that can distribute it in a less intense form. Similarly, man is said to have an inner aspect which can accept or submit to the more fundamental energies of the universe, and an outer or lower aspect that communicates these energies to his environment, the planet Earth.

The idea we are presenting here, however, applies this formulation more to mankind than to individual man: it is civilizations which are such "transformers." Individual men may well have the potential for directly receiving the influences of cosmic nature, but in fact it is necessary only that some men actualize this potential. Men are thus divided into two fundamental types, a division immediately apparent in the fact that most men do not seek to become sufficiently independent of their earthly nature, the ordinary desires and fears, so as to receive higher influences directly.

We thus come to the idea that all civilizations are "religious" in function, that their outer, visible aspects are like the distributive elements of a transformer. These outer forms—institutions, morals, popular religions, philosophies and the like—while they exist on the level of earthly nature and its influences, must at the same time serve as an adaptor of the finer energies which are channeled through esoteric teachings. The esoteric is thus the heart of human civilization. And should the outward forms of a civilization become totally unable to contain and adapt the energies of great spiritual teachings, then that civilization has ceased to serve its function in the universe.

If we now add the obvious fact that separate civilizations no longer exist side by side as they once did, and that we are all really becoming one civilization, then our speculations bring us to a chilling question. Are the forms of contemporary civilization still sensitive to the more fundamental energies of the universe? Or have we become the leaves of a branch that cannot share in the exchange of energies which the tree requires? For though the leaves may grow and the buds shoot forth for a time, they are actually all but dead. Is our civilization only the reflex of genuine civilization?

Obviously, it was the teachings of Moses, Jesus and Muhammad which bred the nucleus around which our present Western civilization was formed. It is therefore significant that among the many elements which make up the current "spiritual explosion," we find widespread renewed interest in the idea of an esoteric Judaism, an esoteric Christianity, and an esoteric Islam, Not only have ideas been pouring in upon us from Eastern sources, but also from Kabbalistic and Hasidic texts, from the apocryphal books of the Bible, from the teachings of the "Gnostics," that vast, ill-understood cluster of disciplines which flourished in late antiquity, from the early Christians, the desert Fathers, and the great sages of Eastern Orthodoxy. The desert itself has yielded forth the scrolls of Qumran and Upper Egypt.

In addition, there are all those sources, which have always been known, but which only now are attracting the same quality and degree of attention as Eastern ideas. There are the great mystical writings of the Middle Ages: Meister Eckhardt, The Cloud of Unknowing, Walter Hilton, the alchemists, the Sufis Al-Ghazzali,

Ibn-Arabi and Avicenna, whose influence upon Christian doctrinal formulations was immeasurable. There is the towering Medieval Jew Maimonides with his doctrine of an inner and outward Judaism. There were the Neoplatonists, a cornerstone of Western religious thought and one which itself rests on the esoteric sense of Plato and Pythagoras—Pythagoras who is said to have drawn his knowledge and teaching from the Wisdom schools of ancient Egypt.

The list is very, *very* long. Mention of even a tiny fraction of the number is enough to convince us that our own civilization, no less than those of the Orient, has been held together and vivified in all its aspects by spiritual disciplines and teachings. To point as well to two thousand years, violence and human suffering is only to say that our civilization, again like all others, has existed amid the forces of earthly nature as well as cosmic nature, that all the supreme Masters took their stand "in the midst of the cosmos."

Thus, all the great ideas which we think of as characteristically "Western" may have had their beginning as controlled ideas in an esoteric teaching. Released to the world at large—"preached upon the housetops," as Matthew has it—they would have then worked as a renewed call, to men submerged in the influences of the Earth. As that call weakened and those ideas, now uncontrolled, gradually became exoteric, was not the stage then set for a new call from the same source, for "new ideas" serving the old and ancient function?

We can, perhaps, put this question by means of a few examples. Was the forgiveness which Jesus spoke of a matter of releasing men from external blame or was it closer to the rigor of the Zen Buddhist's instantaneous self-acceptance? Was His commandment to love a demand for psychological self-conquest or was it closer to the inward movement of accepting love at the point of failure, which Meher Baba taught? Was the Judaic covenant fundamentally a supreme business contract or was it closer to the dispensation of Subud: that while vigorously acting in the midst of life man may simultaneously receive higher life by complete and invisible submission to the intentions of God? Was the contrite and broken heart of the Psalmist, or the despair of the Christian, closer to the tears of ordinary human disappointment or to the balanced disillusionment of Vajrayana? And is the truth which can "set you free" a matter of propositions about man and the world, or was it closer to the freedom from thought, memory and conditioning of which Krishnamurti speaks?

Obviously, no one can answer such questions from the mind alone. It is of the nature of esoteric ideas that they can penetrate through the mind into the heart. Until the mind has been reached and awakened by the intelligence of the heart, its attractions and repulsions remain the very chains that bind it. Thus, all esoteric ideas must be *new* (or "scandalous") to the mind, even as their action is old and ancient, and ever toward the same goal. So while the prevalent interest in "esoteric" ideas is surely a hopeful sign of the times, we must remember the possibility that our minds are, by their very nature, *exoteric,* which means in the service of our desires and fears. As such, they shall ever prefer the security of old formulations, however mystical and grand, to the personal earth-quake which the intelligence of the heart can set in motion.

But once a man is struck by this earthquake, interest may become hunger, the hunger for the food of real ideas that can penetrate again and again through the gratifications of the mind. Where can we find that precise understanding of our psyche and the psyche of our threatened civilization which such "feeding" demands? If we find that, shall we not have found again the source of energy which for all time has been calling man in the controlled language of real idea? Does that precise understanding of our psyche, here and now in this place and this time, exist among the new teachings?

9

A Note about the Ideas
of Gurdjieff

George Ivanovitch Gurdjieff, born about 1866 near the Persian border of Caucasian Russia, appeared in Moscow in 1912 bearing a teaching of extraordinary power. Amid the chaos of the Russian Revolution he gathered a remarkable nucleus of men and women who chose to follow him over strife-torn Russia, through Eastern Europe and eventually to France, where he based his work until his death in 1949.

After his death, his followers together carried on his work, and have in the past twenty years established various centres of practical study throughout the Western world, notably in France, England, the United States and South America. During this time, his name has become widely known, due mainly to the numerous statements of their experience with him which have been published by his pupils.[1] Yet he remains one of the great enigmas of our time. What sources did he draw on for his ideas, his music and sacred dances, his method of life? His own writings,[2] even where they are autobiographical, communicate the sense of another reality far more than they satisfy curiosity about his early journeys to centers in Central Asia and the East.

Here, we shall only attempt to consider the exceptional light which Gurdjieff's teaching throws on the function of ideas in the work of transforming human nature. For on this score the problem for modern man is quite clear: very few of us understand which ideas are important for such a work, and which are not. The new religions which we have been discussing bring with them methods such as meditation, chanting and physical exercises, all of which have the power to produce new experiences. But we have not yet asked: what preparation is necessary for such experiences to be food for psychological growth? On what soil do these seeds of experience fall? Western man, the experiencer: What is his nature? What does he bring to these experiences?

He brings thought. And, as I understand the teaching of Gurdjieff, what is deadly about this is that our sense of self is produced in these thoughts which come into us by association we know not how or from where, and which over the course of out lives play themselves out almost entirely disconnected from the rest of our human organism. Our "I" is absorbed in these thoughts. By means of a mechanism which we have never directly witnessed, we are turned like the hanged man of the Tarot into believing that they and the shadows of feeling that accompany them make up a genuine self.

What, then, is necessary for a sense of individuality to be present in the whole of ourselves? If our experiences of the world and of ourselves are immediately captured by thought, what struggle is required for the energy in these experiences to be distributed in a natural manner to the whole of us? Having forgotten the need for this struggle, modern man has become alienated from the life of the surrounding universe.

For some time now, Western man has believed he could break through the state of alienation by a shift of concepts or through a call for action. Yet how can the call for action help a man who is unaware that he is moved into life from a very small part of himself? And how can new concepts change our condition if we allow them the power to divert the whole force of our attention? This perspective gives fresh meaning to the oft-repeated charge that

Western man has lost himself in the desire for action. He has lost himself, according to Gurdjieff, because he is unable to act from the vital center of himself.

The first impact of Gurdjieff's system of ideas is to put in question everything upon which men base their lives. To a person seriously searching for the meaning of his own existence, this impact is neither a goad to action nor to self-improvement. On the contrary.

A system of serious ideas helps a man to become still. How it does this is a mystery, but faced with such ideas, one may be free for an instant from the automatic attractions even of one's thoughts. In that instant I see that I am and that I really do not know what I am.

It is true that sometimes chance circumstances bring a man to this moment—a tragic shock, a brush with death, a deep disappointment. For an instant one is serious about one's place in the order of reality. But if that impression is immediately captured by thought associations, we are once again at the mercy of accident to change our attitude toward ourselves.

And so it seems to me that to be serious about ideas means that we wish for a more constant way to come into contact with reality. We wish to secure access to a more conscious state that can withstand and contain the pulls of habitual feeling and thought.

Of all things, this is what is most difficult for us "men of ideas" to understand. We are sure we know how to think about great ideas with a critical mind that is not easily taken in by the pretensions of the past. True, modern science has painted a picture of the universe that is humbling to the human ego. But while destroying astronomical geocentrism, it has assumed what might be called a psychological geocentrism. What are the limitations of knowledge that man's ordinary state of consciousness places upon him? This seems never to be a question for the modern temper.

And yet the modern temper is more than ever ready to acknowledge that the truth must be lived, and not merely entertained in the mind. What is hard to recognize is that the ability to live according to true ideas is possible only in a state of less partial consciousness, where these ideas are acting on all sides of a man, not just on his thought.

From Gurdjieff one learns that a man's whole life is inevitably an expression of his level of consciousness. If our lives are in disorder, ruled by violence and self-deception, we do not relish enough the moments of insight and more complete experience. We need not only a surer access to the energy that such moments bring, but a clearer understanding of the way this energy is drawn away into ordinary thoughts and feelings, and degraded.

Lacking this understanding, we turn naïvely to great experiences or ideas which give us new energy, but which of themselves cannot alter our habitual manner of squandering that energy. Perhaps this is why in the history of civilization great ideas and extraordinary experiences often become destructive rather than liberating influences. Self-knowledge, meaning the direct observation of the energies which animate us, is therefore not only the first aim brought to light by exposure to great ideas but also the principal result which can make the study of ideas a labor of transformation for individual man and for the collective destiny of human civilization.

10

In Search of a
Central Question

Let us therefore put some questions to these new religions. Having seen something of what they teach, we can try to respond to them from our own problems as individuals and as a civilization. If we question them without expecting easy answers, our own religious mind may gradually stir in its slumber, and we may discover a basis for weighing their strengths and weaknesses without gullibility or presumptuousness.

Other Groups and Teachings

Certainly, some such basis is necessary. For if we are hard put to discriminate among the teachings we have already discussed, what shall we do in the face of the myriad other teachings and groups which make up this whole phenomenon? Zen Center, for example, is only one of the organizations in America which is trying to bring Zen Buddhism to the Western mind. Zen study centers, in various stages of development, exist in Los Angeles, San Diego, New York City, Rochester, Philadelphia, Boston and in many other cities. Some, like Zen Center in San Francisco, practice the Soto way, but others follow the Rinzai with its somewhat more heroic sense of psychological effort. And not all of these groups work around the presence of a Zen master, or even wish to!

As for the Hindu tradition in America, the Maharishi is, of course, only one of countless Indian gurus and swamis who have established a following here. Who has walked the streets of any of our biggest cities without encountering the young followers of the Krishna Consciousness movement? Robed in yellow and tendering their begging bowls like denizens of Benares of Calcutta, they sway and chant melodic mantras like "Hare Krishna, Hare Rama." Their faces and bodies may be striped with white, and the men will have shaven heads or an isolated pigtail curled into a bun. And there they remain—for hours—singing and moving to the drumbeat of their mantra, their eyes lowered and their lips curled in "ecstasy."

Then there is Yoga: who knows how many hundreds of groups? And for what variety of motives: cosmetic, health, social, psychotherapeutic, as well as spiritual. Are any of these Yoga societies, with their exotic physical postures and strange breathing exercises, really connected to that vast body of esoteric knowledge which lies at the heart of Indian civilization? If not, what dangers lurk there?—are they any less than the dangers of drugs?

Finally, when considering the Indian influence in America, a special place must be reserved for the Vedanta Societies throughout the country. Historically, Vedanta Society was the first Eastern religious tradition that took root on our soil, having been brought here late in the nineteenth century by Swami Vivekenanda, the chief disciple of the great Indian master Sri Ramakrishna, Intellectually, the influence of this form of Vedanta has been enormous. It was because of the American Vedantists—numbering some of the best minds of our time—that the East was first taken seriously here. And though, when compared to more recent movements, it now seems sedate, its activities constitute a very wide and solidly based spiritual discipline.

The Sufis, too, are among us—not only in some of the ideas and methods of Meher Baba and Subud. In England a man named

Idries Shah lays claim to being the foremost Sufi teacher in the Western World and his influence is now being felt in America as well. At the same time, the message of the Indian Sufi, Hazrat Inayat Kahn is still alive in various American cities where groups of people come together to meditate and draw inspiration from a teaching uniquely based on music and the theory of sound·vibration. There are also dozens of other groups which take the name of Sufi.

Unique amid all this interest in Sufism are the studies emanating at present from England bearing the names of Frithjof Schuon, Titus Burckhardt, Seyyed Hossein Nasr and others. The vivifying quality of thought in these books*—which deal with all the great religious traditions of mankind—is a stunning reminder that the intellect of man can be a liberating force when rooted in genuine orthodoxy. Such thought obviously is the product of a rigorous spiritual order and, for various reasons, one may surmise that it is a Sufi order. What their organization is like and whether it will also take root, here in America one cannot say, but these extraordinary books alone must be reckoned as an important balancing weight for our own spiritual renaissance with all its innovation.

Krishnamurti, of course, stands alone, but that does not prevent numerous groups forming to discuss his books and put them into "practice." And surely the school he has founded outside London is bound to be imitated and to have its effect on educational thinking in America.

The psychical has gained a more or less religious aspect in recent years. The phenomenal Edgar Cayce not only delivered astonishing medical and "karmic" readings while in a self-induced trance, he also interpreted the Western Bible in fresh psychologi-

---

* Some of these books are: *Understanding Islam* (Allen & Unwin, 1963), *Gnosis: Divine Wisdom* (Murray, 1959), *The Transcendent Unity of Religions* (Faber, 1953), by Frithjof Schuon; *Alchemy* (Stuart and Watkins, 1967), *Sacred Art in East and West* (Perennial Books, 1967), by Titus Burckhardt; *Ideals and Realities of Islam* (Praeger, 1967), *Three Muslim Sages* (Harvard, 1964), by Seyyed Hossein Nasr; and *The Way and the Mountain* (Peter Owen, 1954), by Marco Pallis. Shorter writings by these authors and others are periodically printed in *Studies in Comparative Religion,* a journal of exceptional quality published in England.

cal and metaphysical terms, and established the basis for group work and meditation. Some eight hundred such groups now exist in America attempting to bring Cayce's insights and methods to the search for God in everyday living.

One could go long into the night listing all the groups and movements whose existence or rebirth is part of the spiritual explosion. But the point is clear: we need basis for discrimination. This means we have to find our central questions as a human society. Otherwise, we shall simply judge these teachings on the basis of our individual likes and dislikes and from the universal human lust for self-confirmation.

Drugs and the Problem of Work

But is it not obvious what these central questions are? I think not. Take, for example, the problem of drugs. Our innate sense of the economy of the universe tells us we cannot get something for nothing and that there must be a payment, somewhere and somehow, for the drug experience. Whether or not it is scientifically proved that the mind-expanding drugs cause bodily damage, we can be rather sure that some price is being exacted from all of the young people who rely on these drugs. The question, then, is not so much how to free them from drugs, but what do we wish for them? They seek in drugs the intensification of experience; do we have anything to offer them greater than that?

We may be quick to reply: growth. But how can we believe in growth, which means the ability to understand the place both of satisfaction and of work, unless our whole being is magnetized by the idea of meaning in the universe? We are properly nauseated by the thought that suffering is good, that every difficulty in our life has been "sent to us" for our own edification by a god who shows his hand only after we have rattled our blind way to death. But, on the other hand, we are starved for an intelligent way to take life as a task—not just external life with its people and events, but also the internal life composed of our thoughts, pleasures, desires and disappointments. We tend to emphasize one of these aspects of life at the expense of the other, and the results are—if we are interested in growth—disastrous. How are we to think about out place in the universe so that the possibility is not lost of finding a connection between the inner life and the outer life?

The problem of drugs is therefore more peripheral than it may seem. Closer to the center is the question of work. We are born whole and with the capacity for intensity of experience. As we leave childhood, the world demands that we act as well as merely experience in a passive way. To act, to decide, to meet external demands—all this *requires* only a portion of ourselves at any given time. If we look at the demands of our present life-situation, we see very clearly that to meet these demands it is not necessary for the whole of ourselves to be engaged; the world—or earthly nature, if you will—does not seem to need such total engagement. This, at any rate, is true of our present civilization. The problem of psychological growth is the problem of discriminating between what is required of us to live on Earth and what is possible for us as bearers of a higher energy.

The agony of Western technology is the result of a naïve fantasy that man can live on Earth without satisfying the needs of Earth, that he need not spend his energy for purposes that are alien to his wish for wholeness and intensity of experience. The allure of drugs is only one more chapter of that fantasy, and that agony. It is quite the same thing, really, to search for wholeness without work as it is to work without searching for wholeness. Both are metaphysical errors based on a naïve picture of man's situation in the cosmic order. The earth will claim its energy from us in one way or another, with our co-operation or without it. But man being two-natured, it is not necessary that the earth claim all his energy. As we have seen, it is one of the principle messages of Western esotericism that it must not if man is to survive on this planet.

Will the new teachings from the East be able to take into account that Western man no longer senses the claims upon him that are made by his planet? This, obviously, was never the problem of

Asian civilization. Closer to nature and its demands, Asian civilization brought forth the rich techniques of inwardness and the doctrines of human divinity in a milieu where the claims of Earth and the need for work were inescapably felt. We know almost as little of how the Asiatic failed, when he failed, as we do of the failure of the American Indian. But we can surmise that, by and large, pride—in the sense of the illusion of power—was probably not his error. Perhaps his was the opposite error, who can know?

Enthusiasm

One senses this problem rather clearly among the young followers of Meher Baba. Without the presence of the Master, one wonders if they will ever be brought to the point of failure from which alone the effort to receive love can change man's life. Gentle and kind to one another, they set their own tasks under the ambience of forgiveness and, it seems to me, rarely experience the taste of resistance that is the beginning and not the end of work.

They are enthusiastic, but what is that? There are surely many ways in which the earth claims its energy, and anger or hatred may not be the only ways. The Baba-lovers are active, but they seem disengaged at the same time. They live, as do all of us, by their likes and dislikes—but without work and therefore without potential reminders of the human condition. How will they grow older? How will they be toward the shocks and disasters which await all men and which tend to drain men of life?

Baba, they say, is everywhere; he has not really died. This is an extraordinary sort of knowledge for a human being to possess. And, as they seem to neglect *ordinary* knowledge, the outsider is bound to wonder if it is only the feeling of belief, surely another way the earth claims its energy by passionately tying men together in a "cause." In distrusting the isolated intellect, have they only turned to a trust in isolated feelings?

Having asked that, we can ask the same thing of the drug-taker. What does he trust? When we speak to people who advocate drugs, there is such a sense of helplessness about it. Over and above anything that might be said, we feel that something in their lives, in their very faces, has become blurred. We recognize that we do not know the answers or even the proper questions to put to life; and that our own existence tends to be dull and meaningless. But there is something in the advocate of drugs—with all his enthusiasm and certainty—that we know is of less worth, even, than our own unfulfilled lives.

He tells us that since we haven't tried it, we have no basis for rejecting it. But, somehow, we know that is not true. In a strange way, we have been where he is, though we do not recognize his names for it. We have been there in the great enthusiasms of our life, in our thunderous insights, and in our ecstasies of experience. Mainly, we have been there in our missionary zeal to persuade others of the value of our experience. We recall, perhaps, the taste of that zeal, its ambiguity and the deep uncertainty and doubt that generated it. We remember how desperately we sought confirmation of our experience, and how vainly.

Thus we see that neither of us has come to an experience which has touched the whole of ourselves. The end of any experience is, basically, the appearance of another part of ourselves. *Enthusiasm,* therefore, is mainly an effort to persuade one part of ourselves of the value of a past experience—much as the advocate of drugs seeks to persuade us of the value of his experience. In the demands of ordinary work this becomes particularly clear. Work calls forth parts of ourselves which know nothing and care nothing for a past intense experience. Memory pleads and cajoles those parts of ourselves to acknowledge its value—in vain. Hence we may see our lives as dull and meaningless *because we trust in the memory of a past experience.*

Spiritual Effortlessness

The problem of drugs and its relationship to work comes, then, to this: where shall we find an approach to man and to ourselves which is wide enough to include all parts of ourselves? Since the one thing which the drug experience does not provide is a taste of discipline, one cannot really say that it provides an "advance view" of spiritual work, which is the continual effort to live in the present. At the same time, in our society the demands of everyday, ordinary work engage such a small part of ourselves that by and large the rest of us languishes and is forgotten. Perhaps the search for an inner life, whether with drugs or without them, is totally misguided without the simultaneous search for a more complete outer life.

As I see it, the problem of work also haunts the followers of Subud. There is a sublime purity about the theory of the latihan and the idea of total submission to the Will of God, Indeed, the history of Western religion is starred by men who have periodically revitalized our religious traditions by exposing the futility of attempting to earn the grace of God. There is, however, an extremely fine line between laxity and relaxation, and we are often told by the great saints and mystics that the energy of God touches man only with the exhaustion of human energy. The idea of struggle and holy warfare is one of the central themes of all religious teachings.

The question I am raising here about Subud, Meher Baba and some of the other new teachings is not whether they are valid teachings or genuine paths, but whether they are valid and effective for us in America. We are no longer a nation of pioneers or Puritans attempting to take both the Kingdom of Heaven and the Kingdom of Earth by storm. Our problem is not so much that we are excessively engaged by external demands, but that we are preoccupied with our feelings and desires. It is true that we are a very busy people, but this busyness is a reaction to the fact that so little is clearly demanded of us from the external world. It is as true to say of us that we are a people in search of our desires as it is true that we are in constant pursuit of their satisfaction.

It seems, therefore, that the great power in the idea of spiritual effortlessness, taken by itself, is blunted on us. Among the followers of Subud, I have been struck by the enormous discrepancy between the grandeur of the teaching and the complacency of the of the following. It is one thing to ask of the aspirant that he let his life remain as it is in order to come in touch with an energy which transcends that life. But what if conditions are such—as I believe they are—that the aspirant does not know the nature of the life he is to leave untouched? Surely some precise knowledge of what my life really is like is necessary before I can even allow it to proceed uninterruptedly.

This is why such teachings as Subud and Meher Baba, which strongly emphasize surrender and passivity, may miss the mark for us. In a strange way, they start too high, though at first blush it may seem otherwise. It may seem that by emphasizing the complete necessity for the grace of God, their estimation of man's ability could not be lower. But they do not provide us with a precise method for verifying the powerlessness of man. They do not engage the aspirant in a way that would enable him to see for himself the nature of the human condition. Without such a method, the sacred idea that man cannot compel divine energies by his own ordinary efforts becomes merely an article of belief, and we are once more at the mercy of the attracted mind.

Logically, it might seem that if our despair as a society is one of relentlessly getting what we want, then it would lead us to the trust in our own powers. In fact, that is not the case because what we really lack is the experience of the weight of resistance, either in defeat or in accomplishment. For an idea such as effortless spirituality to be esoteric, that is, precisely controlled, it must be accompanied by a method that would expose us to resistance. In short, our situation is such that we do not *know* whether we have power or not. To know our present limits is already to have reached a relatively high degree of self-knowledge. This, I think, we do not have and tacitly to assume we do, or to ignore the whole issue, is a mark of spiritual imprecision.

Perhaps this is why many of the new teachings will function in our society as religions, however much they may disclaim the title.

They are grounded in belief and in the attracted mind. Perhaps in other societies or in other times their nature as disciplines involving spiritual work would be able to flower. But Western science, technology, and the contemporary psychological cult of guiltlessness, among other causes, have greatly dimmed our minds to the demands of our cosmic situation and to the strength of the forces that resist the awakening of consciousness.

The New Religions

In seeking to approach the new teachings from our central questions as a civilization, are we forcing them into the mold of "relevance"? After all we have heard, are we still demanding that they improve the external conditions of our lives, rather than turn us inward?

Not at all. What we are trying to discover is whether they speak to our condition not only as Man, but as Western Man. The moment we put the issue in this way, we see that we do not know our condition. It is true that, unlike our popular established religions, the new teachings bring with them methods and techniques which may be directly applied to our bodies, minds and feelings; and it is true that this is one of the most significant things about them. But unless we have a way to determine our actual condition, even as we attempt to apply these methods, we shall adopt them or reject them on the basis of belief. Because of this even the most practically oriented of the new teachings— even Zen—may tend to take the place in our society which has been occupied by popular religion.

Note that we are speaking of belief, not of faith. Faith is based on a moment of certainty that there is nothing in my ordinary mind or feelings which can be trusted to bring truth. But belief is precisely such a trust in the ordinary mind. Faith is a state of being which is produced by a moment of self-knowledge, a total apprehension of my confusion. Belief is the effort to deny this confusion.

When Zen, in its profundity and simplicity, tells us, "The ordinary mind, that is the way," it is counseling us at this moment, here and now, to experience ourselves in our present situation whatever it may be. But what happens when such counsel falls upon the ordinary mind itself, which may know no such thing as the effort to awaken experience? and which has never tasted to the root its own tendency to self-deception?

The great Buddhist scholars tell us that Zen functions in Far Eastern civilizations as an essential counterweight to metaphysical speculation, religious system building or naïve otherworldliness. In China it first took root against the background of a highly intellectualized adoption of Indian Mahayana Buddhism with its vast cosmological and mythological framework. Against any or all such tendencies, Zen strikes like lightning.

But is the central spiritual problem of our present-day civilization either an overdevelopment of metaphysical speculation, or a naïve religiosity? *Centrally*, is our problem that we are drawn upward without being drawn inward? I think not. Certainly there is occultism all around us and the spiritual revolution itself often takes the form of just such an unbalanced movement "upward." But this is a reaction to our central problem, not the problem itself. Behind the visible struggle between the buriers and the exhumers of God, there is pure confusion about the idea of a more fundamental intelligence in the universe. A squinting extrapolation from the "success" of scientific method has suffocated our sense of wonder. And a bloated technology has screened out awareness of the claims of earth which past societies discovered in the demands of work. Cut off from the "upward," we are not even drawn "outward." We drift within ourselves, idolizing any chance outward pull which makes us feel "alive," and we have thereby come to mistake intense experience for "inwardness."

In all of this I think even Krishnamurti's approach may be wide of the mark for us. With unequaled clarity and coherence, he tells us that our outer lives are merely a reflection of our inner condition. He invites us, in a way that absolutely no one else does, to follow him in the effort of instantaneous self-observation, and to verify for ourselves that it is the endlessly busy, interpreting mind which generates our life and its disorder. But what are we to do when we return home and discover not that we cannot make this effort in his absence—which would at least be truth—but that we are sure we are able to do it any time we wish (though not right now)? I wonder if we shall not simply end by *believing in self-observation*.

Based upon my experience among the members of Zen Center in San Francisco, it seems that something very much like this is a major pitfall of Zen Buddhism for Americans. Much of their lives seem dominated by a *belief in zazen*. I wondered how so many young men and women in our society could be so apparently certain of their way, so strong, so seemingly free from doubt. Had they already transformed the human condition in themselves by two or three short years at Zen Center, or had they turned away from it by belief?

I realize I am treading on thin ice here, and I do not presume that this represents anything other than the observations of one outsider. But I saw in myself the tremendous attraction of zazen— even with all its discomfort and boredom. The straight back, the superb posture, the controlled breathing, the bursts of alertness, the fine weight of the master's presence, the marvelous gong and bells, the spare beauty and freshness of the zendo, and much else. Surely, all of this together can lead a man to practice more and more, but at the same time it can lead one only to believe in practice—*even as one is sitting*.

The problem of our lives, if I may put it this way, is that they are lived *between* periods of zazen, in forgetfulness and confusion, in fear, anxiety and blind enthusiasm. Theoretically, zazen is possible even in such confusion. But how can I ever *understand* the value of zazen until I know this confusion and helplessness in all its force? I saw in these young people the use of zazen to improve their lives, a goal which seems totally unobjectionable only if one forgets that many of them had not as yet even experienced their lives. Zen Center had become their home, their refuge. But a refuge from what? I am not sure many of them know.

It is just this serious and remarkable attempt to bring real Zen Buddhism to America which can bring us closer to our central question. Not only for the young members of Zen Center, but for all of us it is true that our lives are lived between experiences. It is this "space" between experiences that is our main difficulty. And it is on this level that the problem of integrating our lives must be seen.

Why is it that our popular established religions are so shaken in the face of the visible problems of our civilization: drugs, war, crime, social injustice, the breakdown of the family, the sexual revolution? Is it not because somewhere along the line belief took the place of faith for the majority of Jews and Christians? Faith cannot be shaken, it is the result of being shaken. And we can see in the writings of the early Fathers that the primary function of the monastic discipline was to shake man's belief in his own powers and understanding. This was not done simply by visiting upon men situations they could not handle or which caused them pain. Such experiences by themselves are useless, and even dementing, unless they are met by an intention to profit from them in the coin of self-knowledge. Mere belief that one has already found the way and the truth is the exact opposite of such an intention and was recognized by the early Fathers as a weapon of the devil.

The problem of drugs in our country is ample evidence that we lack the ability to live "in-between" experiences. Something in us is so totally unprepared for those moments when our ordinary patterns of thought and feeling are broken through. No doubt this is a general problem of all men. But here in the West it is heightened because of the very "scarcity" of experience due in part to the evaporation of the idea of work.

It is because we lack the knowledge of how to live in-between experiences that we are unprepared for the sort of experience provided by zazen. The point is that we do not *know* we are in-between experiences, we do not know how to wait for experience, how to think about it. As a result, moments of great clarity or joy tend to "leak" into the interstices and agitate our minds with the illusion of clarity and the aftertaste of joy. Not knowing we are in-between experiences, we become lost in the belief that we are more than we are, that we know the way.

The metaphysics of natural science and humanism gives us absolutely no reason to suspect that we, as human beings, are so prone to self-deception. Within that metaphysical framework, it seems like an arbitrary, even pathological idea. For this reason, it is of no great value to us that certain aspects of the metaphysics of Buddhism seem to support the scientific world-view. Nor is it really helpful that Buddhism, particularly Zen, shifts our emphasis in the West from what ought to be to what is. Unless we have a sure way to know what is, such support only deepens our illusions instead of dispelling them.

Moreover, if one looks at the totality of Buddhist metaphysics—for example, in the Tibetan tradition—it bears absolutely no resemblance to the Western scientific view of reality, as we have already pointed out. The single idea of a higher intelligence or of a more compassionate energy is in itself enough to make us question our own intelligence. Buddhist metaphysics begins to resemble the scientific only as long as we omit the idea of levels of energy and purpose. But when we omit that idea, we have left out the heart of all religious thought, Eastern as well as Western.

We cannot begin to question our own powers nor seek to discover our unfathomable possibilities without thinking about the cosmos and our place in it. Only by such thought can our intention be formed at all. As we have suggested, the thunderbolt of the Buddha's practicality struck at minds already engaged—perhaps to the point of exhaustion—in metaphysical contemplation. In that sense, the Buddha doubtless spoke to a people whose minds were very much better prepared for experience than our own. It is possible that for certain societies and people, a discipline can be *too* practical in that it provides experiences without the means to understand or value them. To accuse a discipline of such a thing is only to say that it is as yet incomplete, if not imprecise, for us.

Conclusion

We come to the end of our study in front of our obvious incapacity to evaluate the arrival of these new religions. For one thing, they have only just begun, and it is safe to say that few, if any, of their American followers have assimilated any one of them. If it now seems that for many their methods are merely the objects of belief, like the gods our society has just buried, that may well be due to their newness.

During one of my conversations with Suzuki Roshi at Zen Center, he waved his hand at all the Oriental appurtenances in the meditation hall and said he wished he did not have to bring these things, but that they were probably necessary for Zen to begin in America. He was referring not only to the objects one could see, but to the forms of Japanese Zen practice which he had brought here. "With these," he said, "Americans will discover what is of value for themselves."

In short, the seed has taken root, but since the soil and the environmental forces are entirely new, we cannot as yet know what the tree will be like. From where we stand, there is still the possibility that nothing at all will grow, or that what does grow will be twisted and barren. No one can be. sure, probably not even the master himself. We can no more estimate the nature of American Zen now than another culture could detect the sense of

Christianity on the basis of the early years of its first converts. The same thing holds true of other new teachings, besides Zen.

In a general and indirect way, this very fact speaks for their authenticity. We know very little of the *order* by means of which a great instrumental religion grows and flowers in the heart of a man or a society. In biblical literature we find the image of a branch grafted to another plant: at the beginning, certain props and supports are necessary but eventually they must fall away or be removed. Also one must beware of taking the props for anything more than they are. I think many historians of religion tend to make that error. They speak of a religion being changed or influenced by a society to which it has been spread, mistaking the visible order of external developments for the evolution of the religion itself. What they are really witnessing is often the falling away of the props as the spirit of the religion matures in the inner life of its followers. Such historians speak of the religion as changing its direction, when in fact it has actually found its direction.

Inevitably, the question most of us wish to ask is: how will these new religions influence our society? If we can remember how little we actually know about the laws governing the growth of highly instrumental teachings, it can greatly widen the horizons of this question. To take only one example: ordinarily, we tend to think of the growth of a movement in terms of numbers of adherents. But are we capable of judging between those who merely adopt the terminology of a new teaching without its changing anything essential in their inner lives, and those who are sincerely struggling to live by the teaching? Is there any essential difference between a million people lulled by the fantasy that they are "on the way to Nirvana" and a million other people similarly lulled by the mirage of a life beyond the grave? Or between a million people believing they are Brahman (God) and a million others who in like fashion believe in the power of almighty humane reason?

Thus, if someone were to predict that in ten or fifty years, twenty million Americans would be Buddhists, it would by itself mean nothing. If twenty million Americans became real Buddhists, that of course would be extraordinary. But it would certainly be no less extraordinary a transformation of society if twenty million Americans became real Christians or real Jews. But what does it mean to be a *real* Buddhist, or a *real* Christian? To know this already presupposes a high degree of psychological development. For the same reason, it would be naïve of us to think we shall easily judge the influence of these teachings. Christianity has spread throughout the world, but what sort of Christianity?

Here a rather important point may be made if only very briefly. We have spoken throughout the latter chapters of the distinction between esoteric and exoteric religion. It is, I think, true to say that the esoteric is "higher" than the exoteric in the sense that it is religion in its most intensely instrumental form and represents the direct human relationship to cosmic nature. But, as we have suggested, it is the whole of religion—both esoteric and exoteric—that is necessary if civilization is to serve its function as an intersection between levels of reality. What I am trying to say is that there is still an infinite gap between exoteric religion and false religion, between obeying the external precepts of a teaching and inventing or altering the precepts on the basis of subjective likes and dislikes. In all of the great religious traditions, merely external conformance to precepts is condemned; but on the other hand, only a minority are called to the rigors of the path.

Thus one unexpected way that the new religions may influence Western thought is to bring back the sense of gradations of religious life. The all-or-nothing principle which says that one is either religious or not, one either has faith or one does not, certainly communicates the urgency of religion and functions to bring man again and again to the present moment. But the equally important principle of universal compassion (in Buddhism) and catholicity (in Christianity) recognizes that there are great forces of resistance at every given moment acting upon every man that draw him away from the search for wholeness. And the greatest help a man may receive over the period of his life may be the precepts and forms of behavior that can to some extent blunt these forces of resistance and prepare him to understand and make full use of those moments when a real inward turning is possible. Perhaps for some men such a moment comes only once in their lives, perhaps only at the moment of death, who can say?

The all-or-nothing principle is particularly attractive to younger minds, but the new religions teach them as well that a certain quality of everyday life is necessary if the awakening of direct religious experience is not to plunge one into further illusion. Drawn largely by the wish for intensity of experience, the followers of the new religions discover a motive for accepting the need for a better quality of everyday life. There is then a *reason* for morality instead of the authoritarian commands of popular religious forms—a reason which relates to the deepest wishes of the individual for himself.

I expect, therefore, that if the new religions are to influence our society in a serious way, they will do so by reviving the idea of the psychospiritual instrumentality of moral behavior. Everything depends on whether the adherents of the new religions maintain clarity about what they wish for themselves.

We mentioned in the Introduction that the Eastern esoteric or practical teachings always existed in the milieu of a popular ideal of human morality, and we raised the question as to whether the practical methods of the new teachings could meaningfully take root in a society in which the whole question of external moral behavior was at issue. We see now that the answer may be both *yes* and *no*. The new religions may succeed in bringing both the experiential and the moral aspects of religion into our society in a much more organic way than we could have anticipated. One need only observe the outer lives of some of these young people to sense this. No threats of hell fire or damnation, no austere and external, *Thou Shalt* could have helped so many of them hold to their own inborn respect for other human beings and to the possibility of living in accordance with that respect in a society that has lost its way.

We are not speaking here of inner transformation, self-perfection or the psychological liberation that is the final goal of esoteric religion, nor even, to be precise, of the *Way* that leads to it. We are speaking only of a human base, a more or less tolerably ordered society in which the inevitable chaos, violence and barbarism does not obliterate the ways to the *Way*.

One of the most serious obstacles to discovering the sense of genuine religion is the belief that its function is to create a "heaven on earth," an external paradise composed of angelic beings formerly known as men. Perhaps the new religions, where their cosmology presents a universe of multileveled intentions, can disabuse the Western mind of that belief. If so, then perhaps some of us will face what we call evil in a new way, questioning our own judgments at least as much as we question the offending world. It is not a matter of approving what we formerly hated—that could surely be grotesque when what is hated is, for example, the suffering of innocents. It is a matter of searching for a new relationship to our hatred, realizing that perhaps it exists at the same level as what we hate and is part of the constellation of forces which have produced what is hated.

The cosmology of an organic universe compels men to ask: at what level do *I* exist? The psychology of microcosmic man brings the remainder of this question: at what level *may* I exist? Surely, Western society can profit from the injection of a more complex conception of human nature, complex in the sense of qualitative levels and the possibilities of being which they signify. Otherwise, shall we not go on blindly believing in the supreme reality of everything we do, think or feel at the moment, both as a society and as individuals? Or, what is more terrifying, shall we not go through our lives blindly believing we are *in* the present moment? The danger of belief in gods, men or methods pales in comparison, as all dangers pale next to the danger of dying without having lived.

We are obviously going to need all the help we can get if we wish to come to a balanced sense of our place in the universe. It will not be done simply by adopting new and intriguing theories;

we have been doing that for centuries. Nor can it be demanded of us that we plunge into something against all the admonitions of our intellect and experience, meager though they be. The one merely keeps us at the mercy of the isolated intellect, while the other leads us to that particular sort of violence known as enthusiasm.

The main problem—and this is fundamentally what makes it so hard for us to evaluate the new religions—is that we really do not accept that our own lives are at stake. It is because of this that we are the slaves of belief, defending the ideas which willy-nilly occupy our minds and claim one allegiance. If we were locked in a prison, under sentence of death, and if various people were coming to us offering plans of escape, I daresay that most of us would find in ourselves a much colder quality of attention and a much keener power of judgment than we now seem to have. We would be amazed at those of our fellow prisoners who did not even listen to these proposals, and we would pity the ones who rushed into any extravagant plan that came their way. We would certainly see very clearly the heavy price men pay for their beliefs and their conceptions of the human situation.

This prison, or narrow chamber, has been given many names throughout history. Plato called it a cave and spoke of "opinion" as one of our chains, the "double lie" which causes men to love their slavery. The Torah speaks of a condition of servitude under the Egyptians and how the people, being led forth by Moses, and being provided the "heavenly food" symbolized by manna, nevertheless cried out:

> Who shall give us flesh to eat? We remember the fish, which we did eat in Egypt freely; the cucumbers and the melons, and the leeks, and the onions, and the garlick; But now our soul is dried away: there is nothing at all, beside this manna, before our eyes.
>
> (Numbers 11:4-6)

The early Christians and the Gnostics likened the human condition to a brawling roadside tavern where men drunkenly forget their journey and their destination. Speaking directly and explicitly, the Buddhists understand this prison to be the belief in the reality of one's self, and Krishnamurti quite simply identifies the prison as thought.

But the main point for us, here and now, is that we do not very often or very deeply feel that sense of urgency which makes a man still in the face of real personal danger; which makes him watch and wait, and not budge from his spot until he is sure; and which then enables him to act instantly and with sufficient force.

References

1. INTRODUCTION

1. Seyyed Hossein Nasr, *Ideals and Realities of Islam* (New York: Praeger, 1967), pp. 121–4.

2. ZEN CENTER

1. From *The Wind Bell* vol. vi, nos. 2–4, all, 1967.
2. Ibid.
3. Ibid.
4. From *The Wind Bell*, vol. vii, nos. 3–4, Fall, 1968.
5. Ibid.
6. Ibid.
7. From *The Wind Bell* vol. v, no. 3, Summer. 1966.
8. Ibid.
9. Ibid.
10. Ibid.
11. From *The Wind Bell*, vol. vi, nos. 2–4, Fall, 1967. From *The Wind Bell*, vol. vi, nos. 2–4, Fall, 1967.
12. Ibid.

13. Ibid.
14. Ibid.
15. From *The Wind Bell*, vol. v, no. 2, March–April, 1966.

3. MEHER BABA

1. Phrases in this quotation gathered from: Meher Baba, *Listen Humanity* (New York: Dodd, Mead & Co., 1967) and a pamphlet entitled Meher Baba's Universal Message.
2. *Listen Humanity*, p. 73.
3. Ibid., p. 245.
4. Ibid., p. 247.
5. Ibid., p. 248.
6. Ibid., p. 249.
7. Ibid., p. 249.
8. Ibid., p. 250.
9. Ibid., p. 254.
10. From Meher Baba's Universal Message.
11. *Listen Humanity*, pp. 50–51.
12. Ibid., pp. 21–2.
13. Ibid., pp. 44–5 and p. 17.
14. Ibid., pp. 17–18.

4. SUBUD

1. From the pamphlet *Bapak Speaks to Probationers*.
2. Edward Van Hien, *What Is Subud?* (First published in 1963 by Rider & Co.; second revised edition published by the author in 1968), p. 29.
3. J. G. Bennett, *Concerning Subud* (London: Hodder & Stoughton, 1958), p. 52.
4. Van Hien, op. cit., p. 30.
5. J. G. Bennett, op. cit., p. 53.
6. *Subud in the World* (Ten talks given by Bapak Muhammad Subuh at the Second World Congress of the Subud Brother-

hood, held at Briarcliff College, Briarcliff Manor, New York, in July 1963. Published by The Subud Brotherhood, 1965), p. 72.

7. J. G. Bennett, op. cit., p. 55.
8. Van Hien, op. cit., pp. 46–7.
9. Ibid., p. 67.
10. Ibid., p. 62.
11. Ibid., p. 143.
12. Ibid., pp. 163–4.
13. *Subud in the World,* p. 61.
14. Ibid., pp. 61–2.
15. From the pamphlet *General Information Sheet for Women Members Only.*
16. Van Hien, op. cit., p. 122.
17. *Subud in the World,* pp. 62–3.
18. Ibid., p. 38.
19. Van Hien, op. cit., p. 144.
20. Ibid., p. 145.
21. *Subud in the World,* p. 106.
22. Ibid., pp. 107–8.
23. Van Hien, op. cit., pp. 136–8.

5. TRANSCENDENTAL MEDITATION
(Maharishi Mahesh Yogi)

1. Maharishi Mahesh Yogi, *The Science of Being and the Art of Living* (New York: Signet Books, 1963), p. 64.
2. Maharishi Mahesh Yogi, *On The Bhagavad-Gita (Penguin Books,* 1969), p. 470.
3. From the brochure *Transcendental Meditation; an Introductory Lecture.*
4. *Life* magazine, 10 November, 1967, p. 26.
5. From the brochure *Transcendental Meditation; an Introductory Lecture.*
6. Ibid.

7. Maharishi Mahesh Yogi, *The Science of Being and the Art of Living*, pp. 49–50.

6. A NOTE ON KRISHNAMURTI

1. J. Krishnamurti, *Talks and Dialogues, Saanen* 1967 (Netherlands: Servire, 1969), p. 35.
2. Ibid., p. 36.
3. Ibid., pp. 39–41
4. Ibid., pp. 96–8.
5. J. Krishnamurti, *The First and Last Freedom* (New York: Harper & Row, 1954), p. 182.
6. Lady Emily Lutyens, *Candles in the Sun* (Rupert Hart-Davis, 1957), p. 185.
7. From the Krishnamurti Foundation *Bulletin* No. 2, Spring, 1969, p. 9.
8. J. Krishnamurti, *Talks and Dialogues, Saanen* 1967, pp. 45–7.
9. Ibid., pp. 205–11.
10. J. Krishnamurti, *Education and the Significance of Life* (New York: Harper & Brothers, 1953), p. 11.
11. Ibid., p. 20.
12. Ibid., p. 12.
13. Ibid., p. 39.
14. Ibid., p. 27.
15. Ibid., pp. 102–3.

7. TIBET IN AMERICA

1. Thubten Jigme Norbu and Colin M. Turnbull, *Tibet* (New York: Simon & Schuster, 1968), pp. 336–7.
2. Chögyam Trungpa, *Born in Tibet* (Allen & Unwin, 1966), p. 254.
3. Ibid., p. 140.
4. Ibid., p. 97.

5. Chögyam Trungpa, *Meditation in Action* (Berkeley: Shambala, 1969), pp. 36–7.
6. Ibid., p. 40.
7. Ibid., pp. 40–42.
8. From a brochure published by the Tibetan Nyingmapa Meditation Center, Berkeley, California.
9. *The Royal Song of Saraba,* translated and annotated by Herbert V. Guenther (Seattle: University of Washington Press, 1969), verses nos. 11, 37, and 38.
10. Herbert V. Guenther, *Tibetan Buddhism Without Mystification* (Netherlands: E. J. Brill, 1966), pp. 80–83.
11. Ibid., p. 146.
12. From the Guru Padmasambhava Pūjā, translated and privately issued by the Tibetan Nyingmapa Meditation Center, Berkeley, California.
13. Chögyam Trungpa, *Meditation in Action,* pp. 56–7.

8. THE HUNGER FOR IDEAS

1. Joseph Epes Brown, *The Sacred Pipe,* 'Black Elk's Account of the Seven Rites of the Oglala Sioux' (Norman: University of Oklahoma Press, 1953), pp. 71–2.
2. *The Gospel According to Thomas,* Coptic Text established and translated by A. Guillaumont, H.- Ch. Puech, G. Quispel, W. Till and Yassah 'Abd Al Masih (New York: Harper & Row, 1959).
3. Ibid.

9. A NOTE ABOUT THE IDEAS OF GURDJIEFF

1. P. D. Ouspensky, *In Search of the Miraculous* (New York: Harcourt, Brace & World).
Thomas de Hartmann, *Our Life With Mr. Gurdjieff* (New York: Cooper Square Publishers, Inc.); also Penguin Books.

Katherine Hulme, Undiscovered Country (Boston: Little Brown & Co.).

2. *All and Everything; Beelzebub's Tales to His Grandson* (New York: E. P. Dutton & Co.). *Meetings with Remarkable Men* (New York: E. P. Dutton & Co.).

Suggestions for Further Reading

An overwhelming number of publications are now available dealing with the phenomenon of the "new religions," as well as with many of the ideas and questions discussed in this book. I have found the following to be among the most helpful for the general reader:

THE HINDU TRADITION

Zimmer, Heinrich. *Philosophies of India* (Bollingen Series 26). Princeton: Princeton University Press, 1969.

Encyclopedic, yet pervaded by personal warmth and humane wisdom. For a Westerner probably the best general introduction to this vast tradition.

Prem, Sri Krishna. *The Yoga of the Bhagavad Gita*. Sandpoint, Idaho: Morning Light Press, 2008.

The Bhagavad Gita is perhaps the most widely revered scriptural text of India and one of the great religious classics of the world, containing countless keys, some visible and some hidden, to both the theory and practice leading toward Self-realization. Sri Krishna Prem presents an extraordinarily lucid and penetrating introduction to this central sacred book of India.

THE BUDDHIST TRADITION

Ross, Nancy Wilson. *Buddhism: A Way of Life and Thought.* New York: Alfred A. Knopf, 1980.

A graceful and balanced introduction to what has become the most influential Asian tradition now taking root in the West.

ZEN BUDDHISM

Suzuki, D.T. *Zen Buddhism.* Ed. William Barrett. New York: Doubleday/Anchor Press, 1956, edited by William Barrett.

The writings of D. T. Suzuki effectively introduced Zen Buddhism to the West and they are still unsurpassed for their blending of scholarship, philosophical clarity and spiritual insight.

Suzuki, Shunryu. *Zen Mind, Beginner's Mind.* New York: Weatherhill, 1970.

Talks by a contemporary Zen master who in San Francisco created the American Zen community (Zen Center) that was the first of its kind and that continues to radiate a strong influence in the lives of many Americans.

TIBETAN BUDDHISM

The Life of Milarepa; Trans. Lobsang P. Lhalungpa. New York: Penguin/ Compass, 1992.

An astonishing, unforgettable story, full of "laughter and tears," demonstrating the work of spiritual transmission in all its rigor and compassion. Required reading.

Trungpa, Chögyam. *Born in Tibet.* Baltimore, MD: Penguin Books, 1971.

———. *Cutting Through Spiritual Materialism.* Berkeley, CA: Shambhala, 1973.

Together, these two books offer a superb picture of the tradition and the effort to reconstitute it within the conditions of modern life.

THE ISLAMIC TRADITION AND SUFISM

The Essential Rumi. Trans. Coleman Barks with John Moyne. San Francisco: HarperSanFrancisco, 1995.

Translated and/or adapted by Coleman Barks, the Sufi poetry of Jelaluddin Rumi has touched the heart of thousands of Americans, sparking numerous other translations and leading to a wave of popularity outdistancing for a time any other poetry in America.

Schuon, Frithjof. *Understanding Islam.* Bloomington, IN: World Wisdom Books, 1998.

No other Western writer deals with the whole of Islam from the perspective of so vast a scale of ideas. A demanding, but immensely rewarding book.

MEHER BABA

Baba, Meher. *Discourses.* (3 volumes). Walnut Creek, CA: Sufism Reoriented, 1967.

Reflects the fluidity and freedom of Baba's approach to life.

———. *Listen Humanity.* New York: Harper & Row, 1973.

SUBUD

Van Hien, Edward. *What Is Subud?* London: Rider and Company, 1968.

Vittachi, Tarzie. *A Reporter in Subud.* New York: Dharma Book Company, 1963.

Both books are honest, personal accounts.

TRANSCENDENTAL MEDITATION

Mahesh Yogi, Maharishi. *The Science of Being and the Art of Living.* New York: Penguin, 2001.

An interesting record of Maharishi's attempt to express his understanding of what is needed in the West.

KRISHNAMURTI

The Awakening of Intelligence, New York: Harper & Row, 1973.

   The power of Krishnamurti lies in his ability to express one central truth over and over with constantly refreshing intelligence. Any of his many books—which are records of his talks—will serve the reader well. I suggest:

The Flight of the Eagle. Sandpoint, ID: Morning Light Press, 2004.

GURDJIEFF

   The force and universality of Gurdjieff's teachings are reflected in his major work: *Beelzebub's Tales to His Grandson*, New York: Dutton, 1973, Tarcher/Penguin, 2006.

——. *Meetings with Remarkable Men,* New York: Dutton, 1973.

The best account of his teaching by a pupil is *In Search of the Miraculous* by P. D. Ouspensky. New York: Harcourt Brace and World, 1949.

Index

About the Author

Jacob Needleman is the bestselling author of books, including *What Is God?*, *Why Can't We Be Good?*, *The American Soul*, *Lost Christianity*, *The Heart of Philosophy*, *Money and the Meaning of Life*, *Time and the Soul*, *A Sense of the Cosmos*, and, with John P. Piazza, *The Essential Marcus Aurelius*. Needleman is professor of philosophy at San Francisco State University and former director of the Center for the Study of New Religions at the Graduate Theological Union, Berkeley. He was educated at Harvard, Yale, and the University of Freiburg, Germany. He has also served as a research associate at the Rockefeller Institute for Medical Research and was a research fellow at Union Theological Seminary. In addition to his teaching and writing, he serves as a consultant in the fields of psychology, education, medical ethics, philanthropy and business. He has also been featured on Bill Moyers's PBS television series, *A World of Ideas*. Needleman lives in Oakland, CA.

TARCHER
PENGUIN

FIND YOURSELF IN TARCHER
CORNERSTONE EDITIONS . . .

*a powerful new line of keepsake trade paperbacks that highlight the
foundational works of ancient and modern spiritual literature.*

Tao Te Ching

The New Translation from *Tao Te Ching: The Definitive Edition*
Lao Tzu, translated by Jonathan Star

*"It would be hard to find a fresh approach to a
text that ranks only behind the Bible as the most
widely translated book in the world, but Star
achieves that goal."*

—NAPRA REVIEW

ISBN 978-1-58542-618-8

The Essential Marcus Aurelius

Newly translated and introduced by Jacob Needleman and John P. Piazza

*A stunningly relevant and reliable translation of
the thoughts and aphorisms of the Stoic philosopher and Roman emperor Marcus Aurelius.*

ISBN 978-1-58542-617-1

www.penguin.com

Accept This Gift
Selections from *A Course in Miracles*
Edited by Frances Vaughan, Ph.D., and Roger Walsh, M.D., Ph.D.
Foreword by Marianne Williamson

"An invaluable collection from one of the great sources of the perennial wisdom—a gold mine of psychological and spiritual insights."
—KEN WILBER

ISBN 978-1-58542-619-5

The Kybalion
Three Initiates

Who wrote this mysterious guide to the principles of esoteric psychology and worldly success? History has kept readers guessing. . . . Experience for yourself the intriguing ideas of an underground classic.

ISBN 978-1-58542-643-0

The Spiritual Emerson
Essential Works by Ralph Waldo Emerson, introduction by Jacob Needleman

This concise volume collects the core writings that have made Ralph Waldo Emerson a key source of insight for spiritual seekers of every faith—with an introduction by the bestselling philosopher Jacob Needleman.

ISBN 978-1-58542-642-3

The Four Gospels
The Contemporary English Version
Foreword by Phyllis Tickle

Discover and understand the beauty and richness of the Gospels of Matthew, Mark, Luke, and John as never before. Here are the life and teachings of Jesus, as found in the four Gospels of the New Testament—now available in this important new collection from the Contemporary English Version translation with a foreword by bestselling author Phyllis Tickle.

ISBN 978-1-58542-677-5

The Hermetica: The Lost Wisdom of the Pharaohs
Timothy Freke and Peter Gandy

The singularly accessible collection of late-antique esoteric writings historically attributed to the legendary Hermes Trismegistus, venerated as a great and mythical sage in the Greco-Egyptian world and rediscovered during the Renaissance.

ISBN 978-1-58542-692-8

Rumi: In the Arms of the Beloved
Translations by Jonathan Star

A remarkable new sounding of the poetry of Rumi and "an experience of the Divine that you will treasure for a lifetime."

—JOAN BORYSENKO, PH.D.

ISBN 978-1-58542-693-5

The Aquarian Gospel of Jesus the Christ
Levi H. Dowling

A hugely influential interpretation of the "lost years" of Jesus Christ, in which the Son of Man is seen to travel through the religious cultures of the East, learning and preaching the unifying spiritual ethic behind all religions.

ISBN 978-1-58542-724-6

The Aquarian Conspiracy
Marilyn Ferguson

"A bible of the New Age Movement."
— WILLIAM GRIMES, *The New York Times*

A thorough, detailed document of the one of the most powerful cultural movements of our era.

ISBN 978-1-58542-742-0

Seven Years in Tibet
Heinrich Harrer

"[O]ne of the grandest and most incredible adventure stories I have ever read."
—SANTHA RAMA RAU,
New York Times Book Review

The vivid, millions-selling memoir of one of the first Europeans ever to enter Tibet.

ISBN 978-1-58542-743-7

The New Religions
Jacob Needleman

"Of all books published to date on today's 'spiritual revolution, The New Religions *is clearly superior, a brilliant, probing analysis . . . of enduring worth."*

—ROBERT GALBREATH,
The Journal of Popular Culture

ISBN 978-1-58542-744-4